The Later Career of
Tobias Smollett

BY

LOUIS L. MARTZ

ARCHON BOOKS
1967

[*Yale Studies in English, Vol. 97*]

Library of Congress Catalog Card Number: 67-19508
Printed in the United States of America

TO

MY MOTHER AND FATHER

PREFACE

THE present study is not a biography; nor does it represent a complete examination of everything which Smollett wrote after 1753, the date which I have chosen to mark the beginning of Smollett's "Later Career." Most of this study is limited to what appears to be the most important and the most neglected aspect of Smollett's later career—an aspect linked with a dominant intellectual trend of the eighteenth century.

It has long been noted that Smollett's later creative works, *Travels through France and Italy, Adventures of an Atom,* and *Humphry Clinker,* are radically different from his earlier creative works, *Roderick Random, Peregrine Pickle,* and *Ferdinand Count Fathom.* It has also been noted, much less frequently, that his prose style underwent a considerable change in the later works. But the causes and the exact nature of these changes have barely been suggested. Between 1753 and 1766 Smollett published no creative work except *Sir Launcelot Greaves,* some small pieces of verse, and the short farce, *The Reprisal;* and it has long been known that these years of his life were chiefly occupied by manifold literary drudgery: compiling, editing, translating, reviewing, pamphleteering. But the nature and the extent of these labors have never been adequately investigated.

These gaps in our knowledge of Smollett are intimately related. A study of Smollett's literary drudgery reveals the fundamental causes and helps to ascertain the nature of the changes found in Smollett's later creative works. A study of Smollett's compilations, in particular, helps to connect the later creative works with the contemporary trend toward the accumulation and synthesis of facts, historical, topographical, and scientific. In the gradual movement toward a classification and synthesis of knowledge, Smollett's work as editor and compiler proves to be of prime significance. This trend appears also to have a strong connection with the peculiar prose style known as "Johnsonian."

To elucidate all these points, the present study has been arranged according to the following plan. The Introduction presents a brief description of this intellectual trend of the century, and a brief survey of Smollett's career, which emphasizes his connection with this trend and the effect of his hack work upon his later creative period. Part I consists of a detailed investigation into Smollett's

Compendium of Voyages, an investigation designed to discover his methods as compiler and editor, and to illustrate the effect of the above-mentioned trend upon such compilations. Chapter IV of this part considers the effect of this trend upon prose style, as exemplified in Smollett's *Compendium.*

Part II is primarily concerned with Smollett's later creative works, especially with the qualities which distinguish them from his three novels of the earlier period. Chapter I considers the form and sources of the *Travels,* together with its relation to the trend of the day and to Smollett's preceding years of compilation. The next chapter deals with the Oriental framework of the *Adventures of an Atom,* with particular emphasis upon the relation of this work to the *Universal History,* which Smollett helped to compile. The next five chapters deal chiefly with Smollett's compilation, *The Present State of All Nations,* and its effect upon *Humphry Clinker.* The final chapter discusses the change in prose style which marks the later creative works of Smollett.

The whole study, I hope, will produce these results: (a) an understanding of the effect of Smollett's hack work upon his later creative period, and hence (b) considerable revision in critical opinion of Smollett's later creative works; (c) recognition of Smollett's importance as a compiler and an editor of compilations; (d) some indication of the importance of the movement toward accumulation and synthesis of facts, in relation to the literature of the eighteenth century.

This study was begun as a dissertation at Yale University, in partial fulfillment of the requirements for the degree of Doctor of Philosophy. I am greatly indebted to Professor Chauncey Brewster Tinker, both for his guidance of the original dissertation, and for other suggestions incorporated in this revised and expanded result. I wish also to express my appreciation to Professors Stanley T. Williams, Edward S. Noyes, and Richard B. Sewall, who have read all or a great part of this study, and have offered valuable suggestions. To Professor Benjamin C. Nangle, Editor of the Yale Studies in English, I am indebted for his careful reading of the whole manuscript and his constant advice and assistance in preparing the book for press. I wish to thank Professor Lewis M. Knapp, who read my original dissertation, and offered the assistance of his Yale doctoral dissertation, "The Final Period of Tobias Smollett"; I am indebted to him for numerous suggestions and some manuscript materials. I have also had the privilege of consulting the Harvard doctoral dissertation by Professor George M. Kahrl,

"Travel and the Prose-Fiction of Tobias Smollett, M.D.," as well as two other Yale doctoral dissertations: one by Professor Luella F. Norwood, "A Descriptive Bibliography of the Creative Works of Tobias Smollett"; the other by Professor Rufus D. S. Putney, "Lesage and Smollett." For assistance of various kinds I wish to thank Professor Frederick A. Pottle, Professor Frederick W. Hilles, Allen T. Hazen, William K. Wimsatt, Jr., Robert W. Daniel, Margaret Van Houten, and Stuart A. Johnson. Finally, I wish to thank Edwine Martz for numerous suggestions and for great assistance in preparation of the index, proof-reading, and verification.

Louis L. Martz

Saybrook College, Yale University,
  February 11, 1942.

BIBLIOGRAPHICAL NOTE

Barclay: *The Universal Traveller,* by Patrick Barclay, Dublin, 1735. Smollett probably used the London (1735) edition.

Campbell: *Navigantium atque Itinerantium Bibliotheca,* originally edited by Dr. John Harris, revised and enlarged by Dr. John Campbell, third ed., 2 vols., London, 1764. This seems to be an exact reprint of the second ed. (London, 1744–48), which Smollett used.

Churchill: *A Collection of Voyages and Travels,* by Awnsham and John Churchill, third ed., 6 vols., London, 1744–46.

Comp.: *A Compendium of Authentic and Entertaining Voyages,* edited by Smollett, 7 vols., London, 1756.
For full references to individual articles and sources of the *Compendium,* consult the special Index (p. 200) to Appendix I.

Letters: *The Letters of Tobias Smollett, M.D.,* edited by Edward S. Noyes, Cambridge [Mass.], 1926.

MLN: *Modern Language Notes.*

PMLA: *Publications of the Modern Language Association of America.*

Pres. St.: *The Present State of All Nations,* compiled or edited by Smollett, 8 vols., London, 1768–69 (vol. I marked "Second Edition").
For full references to sources of *Present State,* consult Appendix II.

Purchas: *Purchas His Pilgrimes,* by Samuel Purchas, published for the Hakluyt Society, 20 vols., Glasgow, 1905–1907.

Univ. Hist.: *The Modern Part of the Universal History,* compiled and edited by Smollett, Dr. John Campbell, and others, 16 vols., folio, London, 1759–65.

Works: *The Works of Tobias Smollett,* with an Introduction by W. E. Henley, 12 vols., Westminster and New York, 1899–1901. For the reader's convenience I have given all page-references to Smollett's creative works according to this, the most comprehensive modern edition; but, to avoid corruptions of text and modernization of spelling, I have given all quotations from the creative works according to the original editions.
A few references, specially marked, are made to other editions of Smollett's creative works.

CONTENTS

Introduction

THE title of the present book, like all such necessary generalizations, does not quite accurately represent the contents. First, the book does not include a special study of Smollett's *History of England* or of his connections with periodicals, though these points are considered incidentally. Second, the investigation of Smollett's work on compilations is not only significant for a knowledge of Smollett, but also illustrative of a central trend of mind too little recognized by students of the eighteenth century.

This trend, this great intellectual movement, may be summarized by the word *synthesis:* for reasons best explained in a declaration made about 1663, concerning the "business and design" of the Royal Society:

> To examine all systems, theories, principles, hypotheses, elements, histories, and experiments of things naturall, mathematicall, and mechanicall, invented, recorded, or practised, by any considerable author ancient or modern. In order to the compiling of a complete system of solid philosophy for explicating all phenomena produced by nature or art, and recording a rationall account of the causes of things.[1]

In other words, after the "phenomena" have been investigated and analyzed, there must follow an attempt to synthesize: to classify, to systematize, to combine these observations—into a whole, if possible. The intellectual history of the eighteenth century is, in large part, the history of man's attempt to achieve the final synthesis envisioned in the above quotation, a synthesis which the rapid discoveries of natural science at last seemed to place within man's grasp.

Hence, in the middle of the century, the study of natural history —in the original sense: "the systematic study of all natural objects, animal, vegetable, and mineral"[2]—became the vogue in England, not merely for the specialist, but for every man of culture and curiosity. Samuel Johnson kept a chemical apparatus and "was all his life very fond" of chemical experiments;[3] Thomas Gray spent most of his last ten years in the study of natural history, annotating copi-

---

1. Document among Hooke's *Papers,* quoted by C. R. Weld, *A History of the Royal Society* (London, 1848), I, 147.
2. *New English Dictionary,* entry "Natural History," 3.
3. Boswell's *Life* (Powell's revision of Hill's ed., Oxford, 1934), I, 436.

ously the *Systema* of Linnaeus;[4] Adam Smith and Edward Gibbon attended Dr. William Hunter's course in anatomy; Gibbon also took lessons in chemistry and declared his "taste for books of natural history."[5] As W. Powell Jones has shown, England went through a "ferment of interest in natural history in the 1760's";[6] Smollett's own *Critical Review* declared in 1763, "Natural history is now, by a kind of national establishment, become the favourite study of the times."[7]

Nor was the interest confined to the field of "experimental philosophy": this particular vogue is only one aspect of a trend which touched every study connected with man's habits and environment, past and present. Leslie Stephen has said, "The last half of the eighteenth century . . . is specially characterised by its tendency to historical enquiry"[8]—and by the term "historical" he means the study of man's past. But the eighteenth century did not always thus distinguish in its use of the term "history," which was then frequently applied to any "systematic account (without reference to time) of a set of natural phenomena, as those connected with a country, some division of nature or group of natural objects,"[9] as well as to political or social history in the modern sense. Indeed, the term frequently seems to include any fact, past or present, which could throw light on the nature of the physical universe and its inhabitants. Hence Smollett's compilation, *The Present State of All Nations,* is described on the title-page as "Containing a Geographical, Natural, Commercial, and Political History of All the Countries in the Known World." Consequently, in the present study I shall generally use the term "history" in this broader eighteenth-century sense.

In thus linking the study of physical nature with research into man's past, I am not simply playing upon a verbal similarity. The interest in these two subjects which marks the century is the result of one fundamental intellectual outlook: "l'esprit philosophique," "le rationalisme expérimental et pratique, clair, facile à saisir, sui-

---

4. For Gray's interest in natural history see W. Powell Jones, *Thomas Gray, Scholar* (Cambridge [Mass.], 1937), Chap. VII.

5. See F. W. Hirst, *Adam Smith* (New York, 1904), p. 157; and Gibbon's *Autobiography* ("World's Classics" ed., Oxford, 1907), p. 184.

6. W. Powell Jones, "The Vogue of Natural History in England, 1750–1770," *Annals of Science,* II (1937), 351.

7. *Critical Review,* XVI, 312; cited by Jones, *Annals of Science,* II, 347.

8. Leslie Stephen, *History of English Thought in the Eighteenth Century* (New York, 1876), I, 57.

9. *New English Dictionary,* entry "History," *sb.,* 5.

vant de près l'expérience et l'observation," in the words of Gustave Lanson.[10] The Baconian and Newtonian doctrines triumphed over theology and deductive philosophy; the eighteenth century put its trust in experimental science, in the inductive method of discovering general laws. And in their search for data which could produce verifiable laws, the inquiring minds of the century turned equally to the facts of physical science and to the facts of man's past experience.

The trend of thought is clearly shown in Hume. After his "attempt to introduce the experimental method of reasoning into moral subjects,"[11] he turned naturally, almost inevitably, to the study of man's past, in the belief that such study would help to reveal the principles of human behavior; and, holding that a knowledge of the past "would be of public utility by affording men experience, he would be inclined to record the experiments from which they could derive it":[12] hence, his *History of England.* Thus Gibbon went to Hunter's lectures as a recreation from research on ancient Rome; Samuel Johnson worked his chemical apparatus and compiled his *Dictionary;* Gray turned from research in English history to preoccupation with entomology; and Tobias Smollett, physician and close friend of William Hunter, turned from his medical career to the compilation of history.

Interest in all kinds of historical facts was thus spurred by an enthusiastic belief in the immediate possibility of an answer to the problems of the universe; and, in turn, such remarkable interest inevitably spurred the attempt to synthesize, for two reasons: (1) the rapid accumulation of materials made a sort of synthesis possible, and indeed necessary, for the specialist in nearly every field, and (2) the interest of the general public demanded the compilation of materials into some manageable and easily comprehensible form. The middle of the century thus witnessed an astonishing number of achievements in systematization and classification. A typical example is found in the science of biology:

As the materials for biological study accumulated rapidly in the course of the eighteenth century they tended to produce a sense of bewilderment in the absence of a comprehensive scheme for the orderly arrangement or comprehension of the masses of detail. The first requisite, in the

10. Gustave Lanson, "Formation et développement de l'esprit philosophique au XVIIIe siècle," *Revue des Cours et Conférences,* XVII (series 1, 1908–1909), 508.
11. Title-page of Hume's *Treatise of Human Nature.*
12. W. Hunt, *Cambridge History of English Literature* (New York and Cambridge [Eng.], 1907–17), X, 320.

case of Zoology as well as in the case of Botany, was some suitable system of classification.[13]

The need was answered in Linnaeus's *Systema Naturae* (1735) and his manifold subsequent works of classification; in Buffon's *Histoire Naturelle* (1749–1804), "the first work to present the previously isolated and apparently disconnected facts of natural history in a popular and generally intelligible form";[14] in Haller's *Elementa Physiologiae* (1757–60), which is said to mark "the dividing line between modern physiology and all that went before";[15] in Pennant's *British Zoology* (1766), "a pioneer effort at a systematic description of the mammalia";[16] to say nothing of the many lesser efforts at similar syntheses.

Much the same development took place in other fields of inquiry. Bergman's systematic *Werlds Beskrifning* (1766) marked "an epoch in the history of physical geography";[17] Adam Smith (*Wealth of Nations*, 1776) attempted to discover and describe "the principle of rational connection between a vast assemblage of disjected and incoördinate facts and theories";[18] and the sudden burgeoning of political and social histories in England, represented by the works of Hume, Smollett, Robertson, and Gibbon, is, as I have said, but another aspect of the same trend. As Smollett himself notes, materials for the formulation of history (in the modern sense) lay ready, after earlier annalists had performed the drudgery:

The task of collecting, collating, and arranging old papers and records, is but ill suited to the impatience of the English disposition: but, this labour being in a great measure surmounted by those who had no other merit than industry, divers English authors have lately exhibited elegant specimens of historical talents.[19]

Hence, too, came a demand for encyclopedic compilations, such as the popular one provided by Ephraim Chambers, who, in his *Cyclopaedia: or, an Universal Dictionary of Arts and Sciences* (1728), declared that his aim was "so to dispose such a multitude of materials, as not to make a confused heap of incoherent Parts, but one consistent Whole"[20]—an aim followed by the compilers

13. A. Wolf, *A History of Science, Technology, and Philosophy in the Eighteenth Century* (New York, 1939), p. [460].
14. *Encyclopaedia Britannica* (fourteenth ed.), article "Buffon."
15. Sir Michael Foster, cited by Sir William Dampier, *A History of Science* (New York, 1932), p. 203.
16. Thomas Seccombe, *The Age of Johnson* (London, 1914), p. 103.
17. Wolf, *op. cit.*, p. 420.   18. Seccombe, *op. cit.*, p. 92.
19. Smollett, *The Present State of All Nations* (London, 1768–69), II, 224–5.
20. Chambers, Preface to *Cyclopaedia*, cited from fifth ed. (London, 1741), I, ii.

of a greater achievement directly motivated by the work of Chambers,[21] the *Encyclopédie* of Diderot and D'Alembert (1751–65).

Among these works, one should not forget the *Dictionary* (1755) of Samuel Johnson, for, as Ephraim Chambers said,

> . . . the analogy between a *Dictionary* and a *history*, is closer than people at first sight may imagine: the Dictionary relates what has passed, with regard to each of our ideas, in the coalitions, or combinations that have been made thereof: its business is, to deliver the progresses made in the several parts of knowledge under consideration, by an orderly retrospect, and deduction of the terms, from their present complex, to their original simple state. The Dictionary of an art, is the proper history of such art: the Dictionary of a language, the history of that language.[22]

And Johnson's *Dictionary* is not simply the first adequate investigation of English words: it is also to some extent of encyclopedic nature, and would have been even more so, if Johnson could have accomplished his original aim:

> When I had thus inquired into the original of words, I resolved to show likewise my attention to things; to pierce deep into every science, to inquire the nature of every substance of which I inserted the name, to limit every idea by a definition strictly logical, and exhibit every production of art or nature in an accurate description, that my book might be in place of all other dictionaries, whether appellative or technical.[23]

With this mass of syntheses, in such various fields of endeavor, all published between 1728 and 1776, it seems that the eighteenth century, in England, and in the cultured countries of Europe as a whole, deserves to be distinguished as an "Age of Synthesis." In this movement Tobias Smollett played an important rôle.

After the completion of his three earlier novels, *Roderick Random* (1748), *Peregrine Pickle* (1751), and *Ferdinand Count Fathom* (1753), Smollett gave up his attempts to establish himself as a medical practitioner. For his livelihood he turned instead to the booksellers, for whom he had already translated *Gil Blas* (1749)[24] and had contracted to translate *Don Quixote* (1755). From 1754

---

21. See Wolf, *op. cit.*, pp. 38–9.   22. Chambers, *op. cit.*, I, xvii.
23. Johnson, *Works* (Oxford, 1825), v, 42–3.
24. It has sometimes been suspected that this translation was only nominally Smollett's; but Putney has shown that Smollett performed the translation himself; see R. D. S. Putney, "Lesage and Smollett" (unpublished Yale dissertation, 1936), Chap. II. Putney notes that the work really appeared in October, 1748 (*idem*, p. [63]).

until his death in 1771 most of his energy was devoted to drudgeries of Grub Street, comprising incredibly multifarious tasks. He wrote a "Great Part" of and edited the *Critical Review* (1756–), wrote "some pieces" for and edited the *British Magazine* (1760–),[25] and wrote the ill-fated *Briton* (1762–63) in defence of Bute. Along with these projects we know he engaged in numerous occasional tasks of translating and editing, and doubtless he also had a hand in other projects with which his connection is not known.[26]

But these labors were incidental to his huge projects of historical synthesis. The largest single effort of this sort was his famous *History of England* (1757–58) and its *Continuation* (1760–65). Smollett, however, prided himself upon the remarkably short time in which he compiled the main body of this work;[27] even when all his labors of revision and continuation are considered, it seems that only three or four years could have been devoted to this history. More of his time seems to have been spent in the compilation of general history, which, as I have said, included the natural history, as well as the annals, habits, and remains of nations. The chief source of such history was travel-literature.

Smollett's concern with such general history began with his editing of Alexander Drummond's *Travels through Different Cities of Germany, Italy, Greece, and Several Parts of Asia, as far as the Banks of the Euphrates: in a Series of Letters* (folio, London, 1754). Smollett's exact part in this work is not known, but, as Noyes has said, the large sum which he received for preparing it for press indicates that he performed extensive revision.[28] This comparatively brief work was followed by *A Compendium of Authentic and Entertaining Voyages, Digested in a Chronological Series* (7 vols., 12mo, London, 1756), over which Smollett exer-

25. See *Letters*, pp. 81–2; Smollett severed his connection with these periodicals before he left for the Continent in June, 1763: see *idem*, p. 96.

26. One of his largest projects was the translation of Voltaire's *Works* (London, 1761–69) which he supervised in conjunction with Thomas Francklin; for this Smollett says he performed "a small part of the Translation . . . , [probably *Micromegas:* see below, p. 92] including all the notes historical and critical" (*Letters*, p. 82). This statement, of course, may be meant to apply only to the volumes which had appeared by May 8, 1763, the date of the letter in which the statement appears. Eugène Joliat ("Smollett, Editor of Voltaire," *MLN*, LIV [1939], 429–36) shows that Smollett edited only the prose works, which form by far the greater proportion of the edition. See below (p. 23) for minor jobs performed during these years; and see also *Letters*, p. 49, where Smollett speaks of preparing for press a manuscript by one Dr. R———, which Noyes (*idem*, pp. 163–4) conjectures (very plausibly) to be Dr. William Robertson's *History of Scotland* (London, 1759).

27. See *Letters*, p. 81. He evidently spent much time revising the *History* for later editions (see *idem*, pp. 54, 81).

28. See *idem*, pp. 24–5, 134.

cised rigorous editorial supervision, and for which he personally compiled at least one, and probably two, accounts.[29]

Smollett was also associated with one of the monumental works of the century: *The Modern Part of the Universal History* (16 vols., folio, 44 vols., 8vo, London, 1759–65).[30] This was a continuation of the work which had begun to appear in sheets in 1730 under the title, *An Universal History from the Earliest Account of Time to the Present*. The promoters of this venture, as its title indicates, sincerely proposed to compile from original sources a copious, complete account of every nation and country in the world's history. And evidently they achieved considerable success: Fueter declares the work to be "die erste Weltgeschichte, die ihren Namen wenigstens einigermaszen verdient";[31] and Barnes says, "It was the first reasonably complete world history ever written, it was fairly popular, and it helped greatly to introduce a more expansive conception of the history of the human race."[32] The project, however, proved to be too ambitious for speedy completion: the huge mass of materials extended the earlier part far beyond the size of the original plan, and the work accordingly suffered serious delays. As a result, when the section on ancient history was at last completed in 1744, in seven great folio volumes, it was deemed wise to divide the work into two parts, "Ancient," and "Modern," and allow a breathing-spell before continuing with the later portion. The Preface to *The Modern Part* and the gap of fifteen years indicate that the same difficulties were encountered by the compilers of the continuation.

It is impossible to say exactly when Smollett began work on the compilation, but this much is clear: work on *The Modern Part* was under way by December 12, 1751;[33] sometime before 1752 Smollett had procured a job for Peter Gordon on this project;[34] and on March 1, 1754 Smollett announces that he has "made some progress" in a "History of the German Empire"[35] which ultimately appeared in the *Universal History* (1761). As I have shown in an earlier study,[36] it is certain that, with the assistance of his "amanu-

29. See below, Part I, Chap. I, and p. 42.

30. The octavo edition was not completed until 1766.

31. Eduard Fueter, *Geschichte der Neueren Historiographie* (Munich and Berlin, 1936), p. 322.

32. Harry Elmer Barnes, *A History of Historical Writing* (Norman [Okla.], 1937), p. 172.

33. See Samuel Richardson, *Correspondence,* ed. Barbauld (London, 1804), II, 279.

34. See H. P. Vincent, "Tobias Smollett's Assault on Gordon and Groom," *Review of English Studies,* XVI (1940), 184.

35. See *Letters,* p. 28.

36. "Tobias Smollett and the *Universal History,*" *MLN,* LVI (1941), 1–14.

ensis," Smollett contributed to this compilation the histories of the German Empire, the United Provinces, Denmark, Sweden, and the Southern Continent, a total of 1370 folio pages; he also seems to have had some close connection with the histories of Italy, Poland, Lithuania, and Prussia; and he had editorial supervision over some parts of the histories of France and southern and western Africa. In short, he held a position as co-editor with Dr. John Campbell, and, through editorial supervision or personal compilation, seems to have been responsible for nearly a third of *The Modern Part*.

And his connection did not end here. Despite his protestations that he is "resolved to have no new employments with the proprietors in any scheme of abridgement"[37] of this history, he took fifty-eight volumes of it along with him to France in 1763, apparently for the purpose of performing some sort of work;[38] a letter by his wife, written after his death, shows that during his last years in Italy he worked extensively on the *Universal History*, evidently in some task of revision;[39] and the anonymous life of Smollett prefixed to his *Plays and Poems* (1777) says, "He was employed, during the last years of his life, in preparing a new edition of the Ancient and Modern Universal History, ... He lived nearly to compleat this work, and it is said it will soon be published."[40] The revised edition of the whole *Universal History*, in sixty volumes, octavo, was not published until 1779–84; but this must be the edition upon which Smollett was laboring a decade earlier.

Meanwhile, in 1768–69, appeared Smollett's *Present State of All Nations* (8vo, 8 vols.), on which he had made "some Progress" before May 8, 1763, and for which he had contracted sometime prior to 1760; he appears to have compiled a large part of this work himself.[41]

To estimate the significance of all this compilation in Smollett's career and in the movement toward a synthesis of knowledge, it is necessary to survey the state of travel-literature and general history in England, as Smollett began his labors.

37. *Letters*, p. 68.
38. See below, p. 105.
39. See L. M. Knapp, "Ann Smollett, Wife of Tobias Smollett," *PMLA*, xlv (1930), 1040–1.
40. Smollett, *Plays and Poems* (London, 1777), p. xiii. This statement seems to be based on the anonymous life of Smollett published in the *Annual Register* for 1775 (p. 48, second pagination), which, however, says that Smollett was occupied "in abridging the Modern Universal History." Knapp (*loc. cit.*), cites a letter of R. Gough (Dec. 16, 1771): "An 'Abridgement of the Universal History,' whether antient or modern, or only the former, left by Smollett, is to make its appearance this winter." (*Literary Anecdotes*, ed. Nichols, viii, 574.)
41. See below, pp. 105–8.

After the publication of *Purchas His Pilgrimes* (1625) no comparable collection of voyages appeared in English until 1704, when Awnsham and John Churchill issued in four folio volumes their *Collection of Voyages and Travels*. These two collections were seriously defective. Purchas was erratic in the revision of his accounts and did not arrange them according to any regular plan. The Churchills, on the other hand, scarcely attempted to revise or condense: generally they bound up complete accounts without any plan. The eighteenth century could not long be content with such collections.

In 1705 Dr. John Harris made the first extensive attempt to remedy these irregularities, in the two folio volumes of his *Navigantium atque Itinerantium Bibliotheca*. His first volume dealt only with accounts down to the year 1626; in it he began with the circumnavigators, and then arranged various accounts according to the regions to which they related. In his second volume he likewise arranged more recent travels under geographical headings. He made no attempt, however, to reconcile or conflate his accounts, but merely subjected them to erratic condensation.

The *Bibliotheca*, however admirable as a first attempt, was far from satisfactory to one Mead, who in 1717 published a curious treatise entitled *The Construction of Maps and Globes*, giving the opinion that the travel-collections "hitherto published, are very volumenous, and yet altogether would not make one complete Collection." He then proceeds to give directions for the compilation of a truly complete collection of voyages: first, he sees "no necessity for introducing more of each Author than the pure Topography and History abstracted from all Adventures"; furthermore, he declares that "where there are several Travels to the same Countries, a general Collection of their Observations together may serve for all."[42] Obviously the desired result would be, not a collection of voyages, but a compendious, systematic history of all nations.

The synthesis here advocated by Mead was accomplished during the eighteenth century in a succession of huge compilations which gradually reduced the disorderly mass of travel-literature to the form of static, systematized accounts of particular countries. Herman Moll's *Atlas Geographus: or a Compleat System of Geography* (5 vols., 4to, London, 1711–17), Thomas Salmon's *Modern History: or, the Present State of All Nations* (32 vols., 8vo, London, 1725–39), and the great *Universal History* are outstanding among

42. *Construction of Maps,* pp. 209–10.

many lesser attempts. The popularity of such syntheses is evinced by the three editions of Salmon's *Modern History* which appeared by 1746.

Thus, inevitably, the publishers of voyages felt the pressure of the demand for synthesis, and, simultaneously, two large collections appeared which followed in part the plan outlined by Mead many years before. The best of these was, aptly enough, compiled by the editor of the *Universal History*, Dr. John Campbell, who published (1744–48) an elaborate revision of the *Navigantium atque Itinerantium Bibliotheca*, in two great folio volumes. In selecting materials, Campbell explains, he has been careful to exclude "such Pieces as are of dubious Authority, contain Matters of mere Amusement, are filled up with extravagant and uninstructive Adventures, and have nothing to recommend them but Liveliness of Thought and Vivacity of Stile."[43] His primary purpose is clearly not to amuse, but to "afford the Reader as clear, as copious, and as comprehensive an Account of the past and present State"[44] of the world as possible. Accordingly, he inserts a great quantity of ancient history, evidently from his own *Universal History*, collects the observations of various writers on a given subject into one regular chapter, condenses individual voyages to suitable proportions, and, in general, strives to regularize a vast body of matter "in such a manner, as that the Piece may be whole and intire, without any Mark of Patchwork."[45] Thus the collection, though it contains many individual voyages, really follows on a smaller scale the plan of the *Universal History*.[46]

At the same time (1745–47) Thomas Astley published, in four huge quarto volumes, *A New General Collection of Voyages and Travels*, compiled by John Green upon an equally regular plan. Green closely followed Mead's suggestions: first, by grouping accounts according to geographical situation; and second, by dividing each section into two parts: (a) abstracts, which give short journals of particular voyages, and (b) digests, which group the remarks of all writers upon a particular region. By this plan, Green explains,

. . . instead of a great many imperfect Accounts, which the Authors separately afford, he [the reader] will be furnished with one complete Description, compiled from them all. And thus our Collection becomes a System of *Modern Geography and History*, as well as a Body of Voy-

43. Campbell, II, 1056.
44. *Idem*, p. 1048.
45. *Idem*, I, 370.
46. The work was eminently successful, and was reprinted in 1764.

ages and Travels, exhibiting the *Present State of all Nations,* in the most concise, yet comprehensive Manner.[47]

Clearly Green was consciously imitating Salmon's successful *Modern History: or, the Present State of All Nations;* although, by retaining abstracts of journals, Green at least preserved the semblance of a *Collection of Voyages.*[48]

Such, then, was the movement toward a synthesis of general history in which Smollett played his important part. The popularity of voyages and travels themselves was paralleled by a demand for the static arrangement of facts from travel-books in the compendious form of a "Complete System," a "Modern History," or a "Universal History." The compilers of new collections of voyages thus could no longer be content to present isolated narratives at random: they instead condensed, arranged, and coalesced their accounts in a regular and precise fashion, in order to meet the rapidly growing demand for historical compendiums.

Smollett's work of compilation illustrates the progress of this movement. First, in Drummond's *Travels* (1754), he edited an individual account. Next, in the *Compendium of Voyages* (1756) he "digested" accounts according to a chronological plan. Here he as yet preserved the form of a collection of travels, but the trend of the age is shown in his synthetic use of several sources to produce nearly half the accounts in the collection. The *Compendium* thus represents a transition to the static synthesis of *The Modern Part of the Universal History* (1759–65) where, generally, he threw aside the form of voyages and joined Campbell in grouping remarks from various accounts into regular chapters of static history. Finally, in *The Present State of All Nations* (1768–69) he reduced historical materials into a more concise and even more regular form for the convenience of the common reader—a service which he also performed on a larger scale in his revision of the *Universal History.*

The Present State of All Nations, indeed, represents the extreme limit of regularity, as Smollett indicates in his Preface:

> In methodizing the subject, it was judged proper to digest it into separate articles, ranged under certain heads or titles, which not only direct the view, and assist the comprehension, but also serve as pauses of repose to the eye and the attention.

Thus, for example, in discussing the article of *England:* Under the

47. Astley's *Collection,* I, vii.
48. The original plan was never completed, for the collection includes only accounts of Africa and part of Asia.

first head, its *Geography* is ascertained: its *Situation, Extent,* and *Boundaries.* The second contains a description of *the Face of the Country, its Mountains, Forests, Lakes, Rivers,* and *Waters.* The third takes cognizance of *the Air and Climate.* The fourth explains *the Nature of the Soil, and its Productions, Mineral, Vegetable,* and *Animal.* The fifth investigates its *Constitution, Government,* and *Laws.* The sixth gives an analysis of its *Religion,* branched out into various *Sects* and *Societies.* . . . In a word, every particular which the mind can be supposed to contemplate as a distinct object, is here referred to its proper class; . . . .[49]

The significant aim stated in the concluding sentence is followed rigidly throughout the compilation. The account of each country begins with a general discussion in which each fact is placed precisely in its proper section. The particular description of the various parts of each country follows, with each geographical or political division distinctly marked by a separate heading or a new paragraph. Systematization can go no further.

Of the years between *Count Fathom* and *Humphry Clinker* Herbert Read has said:

. . . these seventeen years were years of the most unremitting literary labour, and to omit to reckon them in any estimate of Smollett is as though we were to ignore in Milton's case the twenty years that elapsed between *Lycidas* and *Paradise Lost.*[50]

No man could for so long engage in such labor, without bearing its indelible imprint upon his habits of thought, his method of expression, and his general interests. It is significant, then, that the products of Smollett's later creative period (1766–71) all represent radical departures from the picaresque tradition which Smollett had followed in his three earliest novels.

The contrast is typically illustrated by the scenes in Scotland with which Smollett began and ended his career as a novelist. *Roderick Random* opens with the hero's life in Scotland, but, as Robert Chambers has noted, the hero "only intimates that he was born in 'the northern part of the United Kingdom,' indicates Glasgow as 'a town not many miles distant, famous for its colleges,' and passes through seven Scottish chapters without ever specifying a Scottish locality."[51] The contrast with *Humphry Clinker* is obvious:

49. Smollett, *Pres. St.,* I, v–vii.
50. Herbert Read, "Tobias Smollett," in *Reason and Romanticism* (London, 1926), p. 192.
51. Robert Chambers, *Smollett: his Life and a Selection from his Writings* (London and Edinburgh, 1867), p. 17.

nearly an eighth of the later novel is concerned with detailed description and discussion of Scotland. Clearly, in the Scottish scenes of *Roderick Random* Smollett is absorbed in the adventures of his hero, and has no interest in historical details; whereas in the corresponding scenes of his last novel these details have become at least equal in importance with the characters. The same concentration upon the picaresque fiction marks even the account of Roderick's expedition to Carthagena. As I have shown in a recent article,[52] the historical details are here used primarily as a string on which to hang the largely fictitious adventures of Smollett's hero; and even the slender descriptions of naval and military manoeuvres are warped by Smollett's satirical tone and purpose in the novel as a whole. Comparison with Smollett's later "Account" of this expedition in his *Compendium of Voyages* shows such radical differences in treatment that the corresponding chapters of the novel can never be accepted as historical, except for a few passages on hardships which remain the same in both. This section in the novel, so often regarded as historical narrative, is not intended as such: it is an inseparable portion of a romance in the manner of Le Sage.

The same contrast appears when *Peregrine Pickle* and *Ferdinand Count Fathom* are compared with *Humphry Clinker*. Like Roderick, both Peregrine and Count Fathom travel extensively, for constant travel is an essential ingredient in the picaresque formula; in fact, Peregrine makes an educational tour to France and the Low Countries which is based on Smollett's own travels to these places. Nevertheless, here again Smollett is not interested in the usual materials of the travel-book: he concentrates upon the picaresque experiences of his hero. In all three earlier novels, then, Smollett is following the tradition of Le Sage, which he acknowledges in his Preface to *Roderick Random*.

But in *Count Fathom*, I think (and other readers, such as Hannay,[53] have felt the same), Smollett shows signs of having used up the resources of this tradition. Evidently seeking new inspiration, he attempts a variety of unusual materials: the "horror-tale" in the German forest; the "fairy-tale" of the wicked Count Trebasi and his forbidden castle; the "Gothic" scenes at Monimia's "tomb"; the fantastic narrative of Don Diego.

Apparently Smollett himself felt that his inspiration had flagged, since seven years elapsed before the publication of his fourth novel, *Sir Launcelot Greaves*, which appeared serially in the *British Mag-*

52. "Smollett and the Expedition to Carthagena," *PMLA*, LVI (1941), 428–46.
53. See David Hannay, *Life of Tobias George Smollett* (London, 1887), p. 90.

azine (1760–61); and this he evidently forced himself to write in an effort to give his magazine a favorable start. Sir Walter Scott alleged, apparently on good authority, that some installments of *Sir Launcelot Greaves,* "when post-time drew near," were hastily composed within "half an hour or an hour."[54]

Though it is the worst of Smollett's novels, *Sir Launcelot Greaves* is worthy of careful reading, not only for its frequent amusing incidents, but also because it contains many elements essential to an understanding of Smollett's development as a novelist. It is a transitional novel: in date it comes almost in the middle of the gap (1753–66) between what may be called Smollett's earlier and later creative periods. It is a strange amalgam of echoes from Smollett's earlier period and hints of his later interests, loosely hung together by the unfortunate imitation of Cervantes. Smollett must have been desperately in need of a model, to choose the Quixotic idea, which he himself seems to mistrust, through the words of Ferret in this very novel:

"What! (said Ferret) you set up for a modern Don Quixote?—The scheme is rather too stale and extravagant.—What was an humorous romance, and well-timed satire in Spain, near two hundred years ago, will make but a sorry jest, and appear equally insipid and absurd, when really acted from affectation, at this time a-day, in a country like England."[55]

The same urgent need for a model appears in the best character of the book, Captain Crowe, who is so obviously a repetition of Trunnion in *Peregrine Pickle* that one wonders how Smollett dared commit such self-plagiarism; in particular, Crowe's scare in the church is patently reminiscent of a similar trick played upon Trunnion.[56] Other parts of the novel are equally evident remains of Smollett's earlier period: the whole affair between Aurelia and Greaves is carried on in the tiresome, stilted manner which frequently marks the raptures of Roderick and Narcissa, Peregrine and Emilia, Renaldo and Monimia; the scene with the fortune-teller, Dr. Grubble, is an echo of Peregrine's collusion with Cadwallader Crabtree;[57] the name Ferret is repeated from *Ferdinand Count Fathom,* and, as Saintsbury says, the night's turmoil at the Black Lion is "the very refuse of the cut-and-dried stock-in-trade of the adventure novelist."[58]

54. "Prefatory Memoir to Smollett," in *Ballantyne's Novelist's Library* (London, 1821–24), II, xxiii.

55. *Works,* x, 15.

56. Cf. *Works,* x, 76 f.; v, 85 f.   57. Cf. *Works,* x, 251 f.; VII, 1 f.

58. George Saintsbury, Introduction to *Sir Launcelot Greaves,* in Smollett's *Works* (Navarre Society ed.), x, xii. See *Works,* x, 78 f.

But, combined with these efforts to revive old materials, new materials occur which provide some of the best parts of the novel —some of the best, indeed, that Smollett ever wrote: the election incident, the unmasking of Justice Gobble, the political misanthropy of Ferret, Greaves's denunciation of English madhouses, even parts of the prison sequence (though this sort of scene was a favorite with Smollett, occurring in all three previous novels, as well as in *Humphry Clinker*).[59] These parts are not "new" in the sense that they represent ideas never used before by Smollett. They are "new" because Smollett approaches them with a different focus and emphasis: they form set pieces with primarily political and historical purposes. Instead of concentrating upon the adventures of his hero, in these parts Smollett seems interested in giving a set picture of contemporary conditions. He had, of course, used such topical materials in his earlier novels, but seldom with such concentration, such overtly topical aims. These incidents point the way to the distinctive content of Smollett's later creative period: topical, historical materials.

For Smollett's next creative work, *Travels through France and Italy* (1766), is not a novel, but a travel-book, containing many amusing experiences, but primarily concerned with political observations, antiquarian notes, and every variety of historical detail: indeed, nearly a fourth of the book is taken up with "a sort of natural History"[60] of Nice. His penultimate creative work forms an equally sharp contrast with the picaresque tradition: *The History and Adventures of an Atom* (1769) is almost entirely concerned with history—not only English, but Japanese. Hence, *Humphry Clinker* is by no means an anomaly in Smollett's career: it is a fulfillment of the new inspiration partially glimpsed in *Sir Launcelot Greaves;* it is an adaptation to novel-form of the topical and historical interests which produced his *Travels* and *Adventures of an Atom.*

The explanation of this shift of interests in Smollett's later period must already be evident: it lies, certainly, in his preoccupation with these new materials during his "fallow" years. The political quarrels incidental to the *Critical Review* and the overt political propaganda of the *Briton* help to account for much of Smollett's increased interest in political affairs, as manifested in all three later works. But the dominant cause of his change in focus lies, I believe, in his immense compilations of history. Year after year he had compiled or edited the stubborn facts of history, taken from annals

59. See *Works*, x, 97 f., 108 f., 119 f., 228–32, 268–9.
60. See below, pp. 70–1.

of England, Sweden, Germany, Holland, and other countries—
from travel-books relating to practically every country in the
known world. Sheet upon sheet the histories rolled from the press:
*Compendium of Voyages, History of England, Universal History,
Present State*—to say nothing of histories reviewed for the *Critical*
or of assistance rendered to Drummond, perhaps Robertson, perhaps others. After Smollett's saturation in historical details, a shift
of interests was inevitable. He emerged from his labors of compilation for the booksellers only to compile his own travels through
France and Italy, through England and Scotland, and to give another, satirical account of recent English history.

With this change in interests came a change in style, already
apparent in *Sir Launcelot Greaves*. There is a change from elaboration to simplicity, from expansiveness to succinctness, from tur-
gidity to precision. Here again, I think, the cause is obvious. During the gruelling labor of these years Smollett had probably edited
more copy and compiled more history per hour than any other man
of his day; and by this constant practice in setting down facts
with order and clarity, Smollett's manner of expression was ham-
mered down to the sharpness of a die. The generally recognized
superiority of *Humphry Clinker* over the novels of the early period
rests, I believe, in large part, on superior precision, economy, and
clarity of style.

Thus it appears that Smollett's labors of historical compilation
played an important part in a great intellectual movement, and also
exerted a dominant influence upon Smollett's later creative works.
Yet these compilations have been almost entirely neglected by students of Smollett and the eighteenth century. It seems essential
to examine in detail at least one of these works, in order to discover
Smollett's methods of revision, to illustrate more thoroughly the
movement toward synthesis, to learn something of Smollett's capacity as editor and historian, and to understand why these compilations exerted so great an influence upon his later creative period. The *Compendium of Voyages* seems best for such an investigation: (a) it illustrates the beginning of the process of synthesis,
both for Smollett and for the whole movement; (b) it is small
enough to be manageable; (c) it exerted a marked influence upon
later collections of voyages and travels.

The last statement warrants considerable illustration—much
more than the present demands of space will allow. Briefly, then,
it must be said that the *Compendium* appears to have inaugurated
a succession of concise, orderly, convenient, and inexpensive col-

lections, designed to make these important historical materials available to the mass of readers. The *Compendium* was not actually the first general collection of travels in duodecimo format, but, since it was projected as early as May 5, 1753,[61] it may have been the first to be planned. In 1754, however, a meagre compilation in three duodecimo volumes was published under the title, *A New Universal History of Voyages and Travels*. This is a limited and badly written collection, mostly pilfered from Campbell's *Bibliotheca*, and appears to be a hasty attempt to anticipate Smollett's collection. But such a wretched work achieved no reputation, and is hardly comparable to Smollett's compilation of seven volumes. One may assert, then, that the *Compendium* was the first comprehensive collection of travels to appear in duodecimo size.

The *Compendium* enjoyed considerable popularity, for it attracted enough attention to warrant the beginning of a French translation;[62] it was reprinted in 1766, and, according to Cox,[63] issued in a third edition with two extra volumes in 1784. But the best tribute to the success of the collection lies in its imitators. In the next year after its publication there appeared a work significantly entitled *A Compendium of the Most Approved Modern Travels*, published in both London and Dublin, in four duodecimo volumes. This work contains nothing from Smollett's collection, but manifestly (as the *Monthly Review* remarked at the time) "is a suitable, and seems an intended, Companion to the Compendium of Voyages."[64]

The combined popularity of these two collections evidently suggested to John Newbery the project of publishing a larger collection which would include the best parts of each *Compendium*, together with additional accounts of great popular appeal. Accordingly, from 1759 until 1761 Newbery published the first edition of the most popular collection of voyages in the eighteenth century: *The World Displayed; or, a Curious Collection of Voyages and Travels*, in twenty volumes, with a peculiar format of eighteens,[65]

---

61. See below, p. 23. 62. See below, pp. 18–19.

63. E. G. Cox, *A Reference Guide to the Literature of Travel* (*University of Washington Publications in Language and Literature*, ix, x, Seattle, 1935–38), i, 16.

64. *Monthly Review*, xvii (1757), 279. The publisher of the Dublin edition, J. Smith, also issued in 1757 a thin duodecimo volume entitled *A Compendium of the Travels of Mr. Hanway, Sir John Mandeville, and Mr. Lionel Wafer, and a description of Greenland*. The collection, from its title, seems to have been inspired by Smollett; and the accounts of Wafer and Greenland seem to have come from his *Compendium*.

65. For a detailed description of this remarkable work see A. T. Hazen, *Samuel Johnson's Prefaces & Dedications* (New Haven, 1937), pp. 218–21.

which reduced each volume to about two-thirds the size of one in Smollett's *Compendium*.

Newbery hired Samuel Johnson to write the introduction on pre-Columbian discoveries; and then, without acknowledgment, he opened his collection with two accounts drawn, with slight alterations, from Smollett's *Compendium:* the account of Columbus, which covers almost the whole of Newbery's first volume; and the account of Cortes, which comprises the entire second volume. In later parts of the collection he also consulted Smollett's accounts of Pizarro, Gama, Cabral, Dampier, Rogers, and James.[66] By a cannier choice of materials and handier size *The World Displayed* achieved much greater success than Smollett's *Compendium*. The opening volumes of Newbery's collection, derived largely from Smollett's accounts, were reprinted in a second edition before the last volume was published; by 1779 the collection had gone into a sixth edition; and it was still being reprinted in Dublin as late as 1814–15. In 1795–96 a first American edition was published in Philadelphia, which attributed the compilation to Smart, Goldsmith, and Johnson. In 1764 the whole work was translated into German.[67]

The astonishing popularity of *The World Displayed,* together with the more modest reputation of Smollett's *Compendium,* naturally led to the publication of other duodecimo collections, of which one of the earliest appears to have been Samuel Derrick's *Collection of Voyages* (2 vols., London, 1762).[68] The most important of these later compilations, however, was the work of John Barrow, who in 1765 issued, in three duodecimo volumes, *A Collection of Authentic, Useful, and Entertaining Voyages and Discoveries, Digested in a Chronological Series,* which not only represents a very close imitation of Smollett's title, plan, and format, but also owes about half its contents to Smollett's accounts.

So patent was Barrow's plagiarism that one Targe, who had al-

66. This and the following statements of indebtedness must be understood in a restricted sense: I have been forced to limit comparison to selected portions of each account. Accordingly, a statement that a compiler used the *Compendium* means only that Smollett's accounts were consulted; in most cases the *Compendium* appears to be the chief or only source; but some accounts also show extensive use of other sources.

67. In 1759, the year in which *The World Displayed* began to appear, W. H. Dilworth also pilfered from the *Compendium* two volumes in his popular series of pocket-sized histories: *The History of the Conquest of Mexico, ... To which is added, The Voyage of Vasco de Gama,* and *The Conquest of Peru, ... Together with The Voyages of the first Adventurers . . . for the Discovery of Florida,* each published in a thin duodecimo volume.

68. I have not seen a copy of this work.

ready begun a French translation of Smollett's anonymous *Compendium*, assumed that Barrow's *Collection* was a new edition of Smollett's work. In completing his translation, Targe therefore substituted Barrow's longer account of Anson's voyage for Smollett's brief condensation, and, to the twenty-six accounts translated from the *Compendium*, added ten new accounts from Barrow, as well as a few minor items from other sources. Finally, since Barrow's *Collection* is attributed on the title-page to "John Barrow, Esq. Author of the Geographical Dictionary," Targe accredited Barrow with the original of the entire translation, which was pub lished in Paris in 1766 in twelve duodecimo volumes, with the following title: *Abrégé Chronologique ou Histoire des Découvertes Faites par les Européens dans les différentes parties du Monde, Extrait des Relations les plus exactes & des Voyageurs les plus véridiques, Par M. Jean Barrow, Auteur du Dictionaire Géographique.*[69]

In his Preface to this translation Targe unwittingly relates the history of his error, with statements which provide further proof of the *Compendium's* reputation:

La premiere Edition de l'Ouvrage, dont on donne aujourd'hui la traduction, parut à Londres en 1756, sans nom d'Auteur; & je formai dès-lors, le projet de le faire passer en notre Langue. D'autres occupations m'en ayant totalement détourné, ce que j'en avois commencé, seroit peut-être resté long-temps dans l'oubli, si le même Ouvrage n'avoit reparu en 1765, avec le nom bien connu de M. Barrow, qui a ajouté dans cette nouvelle Edition, plusieurs Découvertes importantes. Il mérite sans doute tout le succès qu'il a eu en Angleterre. . . . [Les Anglois] ont trouvé quelque avantage à voir une Histoire des progrès de la navigation dans l'ordre Chronologique, suivi par M. Barrow: ils ont vu avec plaisir quelques détails intéressants, qui ne se trouvent pas dans les grands Voyages, & qui sont dégagés des variations de l'aiguille aimantée, des Journaux minutieux de tous les changements de temps, & de beaucoup d'autres parties, trèsbonnes pour instruire des Navigateurs; mais inutiles pour ceux qui ne veulent pas entreprendre de faire les mêmes Voyages.

69. Sabin, in his *Bibliotheca Americana* (1, 485), translated Targe's title into English and listed this hypothetical work as the first edition of Barrow's *Collection*, under the date of 1756. This error is followed by the life of Barrow in the *Dictionary of National Biography*, by the new *Cambridge Bibliography of English Literature*, and by Cox (*op. cit.*, 1, 16), who states that a German translation of Barrow's *Collection* appeared in 1767. Whether this translation is really from Barrow, or from Targe, I have not been able to determine. In either case, however, the essential point remains: Smollett's accounts reached a German audience in another translation, in addition to that of *The World Displayed*. In England Barrow's *Collection* was reprinted in 1783.

The influence of the *Compendium* was not confined to duo-decimo collections: in a peculiar way it also inspired the compilation of John Knox's larger work, *A New Collection of Voyages, Discoveries and Travels* (7 vols., 8vo, London, 1767). For, while explaining his purpose and plan in the Preface to this collection, the compiler repeats almost verbatim, without acknowledgment, two paragraphs from Smollett's Preface to the *Compendium.*[70] It is tempting to suggest that Smollett himself wrote this Preface to Knox's *Collection;* for it is difficult to see why any other compiler should have copied the passage. But the compiler vilifies all previous small collections, and uses the *Compendium* only for the accounts of Columbus, Cortes, and Pizarro, which begin the work, and for a few selections from the account of Nieuhoff. The remainder of the collection reveals no evidence of Smollett's hand. But, at least, it is clear that the anonymous author of this preface consciously modelled his compilation upon Smollett's *Compendium.*

In 1768 Edward Cavendish Drake used Smollett's *Compendium* more extensively than any previous editor, in compiling his folio volume entitled *A New Universal Collection of Authentic and Entertaining Voyages and Travels,* which in thirteen accounts reveals very great, if not total, indebtedness to the *Compendium.*

The respectable popularity of the *Compendium* itself was therefore the least significant result of Smollett's labors. The importance of the *Compendium* lies in the fact that within a dozen years after its appearance, it had inspired the publication of at least nine separate English works, seven of which used Smollett's accounts[71] and eventually disseminated their materials to thousands of English readers on both sides of the Atlantic; moreover, at the same time, readers also perused Smollett's accounts, directly or indirectly, in French and German translations. Smollett's first compilation of general history was therefore of some consequence. After the mass of readers had thus been introduced to a higher level of organization and style in such compilations, publishers could no longer hope to win favor with slovenly collections of voyages.

70. Cf. Knox's *Collection,* I, v-vi; *Comp.,* I, [i]–ii.

71. Some of the accounts in later collections which reveal indebtedness to Smollett may, of course, have been taken from *The World Displayed* or other works derived from Smollett, and not directly from the *Compendium.*

PART I

SMOLLETT'S COMPENDIUM OF VOYAGES

I

Evidence of Smollett's Editorship

PREVIOUS students of Smollett have always dismissed his connection with the *Compendium of Voyages* with some such cautious conjecture as, "His function was chiefly editorial"; it has been generally assumed that Smollett's hirelings produced the work and that the "Compiler" really did little more than select the voyages to be included. The present study will show that the choice of materials was in itself a task upon which Smollett expended great care and labor; that in addition to this Smollett was intimately concerned with the entire arduous process of revision; and finally, that as a result of this rigorous editorial supervision, the *Compendium* excels in polish, precision, and order any similar work produced before 1756.

Smollett signed the contract for the *Compendium* on May 5, 1753[1] and agreed therein to complete the whole by August 1, 1754; but, probably because he was harassed by other engagements, he did not fulfill his promise: the compilation, nearly two years late, was at last published anonymously on April 29, 1756, in seven volumes, duodecimo.[2] Indeed, it seems little short of miraculous that the *Compendium* appeared at all, when we consider the amount of work which Smollett performed between the signing of the contract and its fulfillment. In 1754 he published a translation from the French entitled *Select Essays on Commerce*, and edited Drummond's *Travels* and the second volume of Dr. Smellie's *Cases in Midwifery;* he completed his translation of *Don Quixote* (1755); wrote part of his account of the German Empire for the *Universal History*, and perhaps performed some other tasks for that compilation;[3] at least projected his *History of England;* and took a leading part in the foundation of the *Critical Review*.[4]

The very delay in publication thus appears to be a tribute to Smollett's editorial fidelity: despite these numerous activities he evidently would not permit the *Compendium* to go forth without his supervision. On the other hand it must be admitted that most of the labor of compilation was really done by his assistants; for

1. See *Letters*, pp. 23–4.
2. See *London Evening Post*, April 20–22, 27–29, 1756.
3. See above, pp. 7–8.　　　　4. The first issue appeared in March, 1756.

indisputable proof of this fact is found in a letter which one Richard Smith wrote to him from America in 1763. Here, amid other matters, Smith mentions his suspicion that "The Voyages which go under your Name[5] . . . are only nominally yours or at least were collected [by your] understrappers."[6] Since Smith obtained his information from James Rivington, one of the publishers of the *Compendium*, the latter alternative may be accepted as substantially correct, though the first needs great qualification, as the subsequent study will show.

In his letter answering Smith's queries Smollett lists among his works "a very small part of a compendium of voyages."[7] It has been generally assumed that this part is simply the "Account of the Expedition against Carthagene" which Smollett undoubtedly wrote.[8] Before accepting this conclusion, however, one must recall that in the same letter to Smith, Smollett includes among his works "a small part of the modern Universal History";[9] and we have seen the great extent of his labor on this project.[10] Smollett was thus inclined to disparage his hack work, since he felt it beneath his dignity: the *Select Essays on Commerce*, for instance, he dismisses as "no other than a paltry bookseller's job, in which my name ought not to be mentioned."[11] Hence, we may well suspect that his work on the *Compendium* was no less thorough than that which he performed for the *Universal History*.

More specific evidence of Smollett's actual procedure is found in the review of Rolt's *History of South America* which he wrote for the *Critical* in March, 1756,[12] just as he was finishing his work with the *Compendium*. He begins this review by attributing the bad repute of British learning to wretched publications by booksellers,

. . . who cannot distinguish authors of merit, or if they could, have not sense and spirit to reward them according to their genius and capacity.

---

5. Since the publication was anonymous, this reference seems to prove that Smollett's editorship was widely recognized.

6. *Notes and Queries*, CLXIV (1933), 316.   7. *Letters*, pp. 81–2.

8. See my article, "Smollett and the Expedition to Carthagena," *PMLA*, LVI (1941), 428–46.

9. *Letters*, p. 82.   10. See above, pp. 7–8.   11. *Letters*, p. 28.

12. *Critical Review*, I, 97–106. The style and content of the article as illustrated below are sufficient to establish Smollett's authorship: but more tangible evidence is found in the passage (p. 100) in which the reviewer attacks Rolt's ignorance of Spanish, as revealed by many misspelled names; here the author cites seven examples of these errors, and gives the correct spelling: four of these are the names of places at Carthagena, corrected in accordance with Smollett's "Account" in the *Compendium*, except for capitals, hyphens, and one vowel, all of which may be attributed to the difference in printers.

Without considering the infinite pains and perseverance it must cost a writer to form and digest a proper plan of history; compile materials; compare different accounts; collate authorities; compose and polish the stile, and complete the execution of the work; he furnishes him with a few books, bargains with him for two or three guineas a sheet; binds him with articles to finish so many volumes in so many months, in a crouded page and evanescent letter, that he may have stuff enough for his money; insists upon having copy within the first week after he begins to peruse his materials; orders the press to be set a going, and expects to cast off a certain number of sheets weekly, warm from the mint, without correction, revisal, or even deliberation. Nay, the miserable author must perform his daily task, in spite of cramp, colick, vapours, or vertigo; in spite of head-ach, heart-ach, and *Minerva's* frowns; otherwise he will lose his character and livelihood, like a taylor who disappoints his customer in a birth-day suit.[13]

This appears to be a description of Smollett's agonies in preparing the *Compendium* for the press, for he had published no other historical compilation. Here, I think, is revealed the clash between Smollett and his employers, with the editor endeavoring to produce a work which shall meet his high standards, and the publishers clamoring for the copy nearly two years overdue. But in spite of such insistent demands Smollett has striven to avoid disgracing the British name with another "raw, crude, hasty, superficial production," such as Rolt's, "without substance, order, symmetry or connection, like the imperfect rudiments of nature in abortion"; and he therefore proceeds "to declare this pretended history of *South-America,* a very trivial, insipid, injudicious and defective performance, without plan, method, learning, accuracy or elegance"[14]—a work, in short, containing all the faults which, as we shall see, Smollett has avoided in his own compilation.

The explicit reason for these denunciations is found in Smollett's Preface to the *Compendium,* where he outlines his editorial policy. To attain continuity (so lamentably lacking in Rolt) he explains that he has arranged his voyages "in chronological order, so as to form, as it were, The Annals of Navigation." This careful, orderly procedure is not confined to the general plan: it penetrates the whole compilation:

One of his [the compiler's] principal views in undertaking the work, was to disincumber this useful species of history from a great deal of unnecessary lumber, that tended only to clog the narration and burthen the memory.

[Other collections of voyages] . . . are generally so stuffed with dry

13. *Critical Review,* I, 97–8.   14. *Idem,* p. 98.

descriptions of bearings and distances, tides and currents, variations of the compass, leeway, wind and weather, sounding, anchoring, and other terms of navigation,that none but mere pilots, or seafaring people, can read them without disgust.

Our aim has been to clear away this kind of rubbish in such a manner as to leave the narrative less embarrassed, but more succinct: we have not only retrenched the superfluities, but endeavoured to polish the stile, strengthen the connexion of incidents, and animate the narration, wherever it seemed to languish.

The parallel between this procedure and that described or implied in the above review is sufficient to indicate that Smollett's connection with the *Compendium* has been much more than nominal.

Further evidence of Smollett's rigorous supervision is found in the review of the *Compendium* which appeared in the *Critical* for May, 1756.[15] It seems highly probable that Smollett wrote the review himself: (a) it contains the same remarks on the value of travel-books in general and of the *Compendium* in particular, as are found in Smollett's Preface to the compilation; (b) it gives particular praise to Smollett's "Account of the Expedition against Carthagene" and quotes at length his violent attack on the leaders of this expedition; (c) Smollett's penchant for reviewing his own work is evident from the articles which he seems to have written on his own parts of the *Universal History*.[16]

This review solemnly announces that the voyages "seem to have been selected with judgment, and by being digested in a chronological series . . . are capable of giving the reader more satisfaction as well as more improvement than works of this nature can generally pretend to."[17] The author then proceeds to quote the compiler's Preface and gives verbatim the part on "unnecessary lumber," after which he adds an enlightening comment:

This rubbish (. . . [the compiler] informs us) he has taken the pains to clear away, which, though it must have been a disagreeable task to the Compiler, was, no doubt, extremely necessary; and we hope the favourable reception of the public will make him amends for his trouble.[18]

Thus it seems that Smollett's plan for the *Compendium* was carefully considered and laboriously fulfilled; but more specific evidence must be examined in order to discover his hand in the actual manuscript.

15. *Critical Review*, I, 309–12.
16. See my article, "Tobias Smollett and the *Universal History*," MLN, LVI (1941), 12–14.
17. *Critical Review*, I, 309–10.   18. *Idem*, p. 310.

Some evidence of particular revision by Smollett is found in the above review of the *Compendium,* where the author picks out for praise the history of the conquest of Mexico, and asserts that "The voyages of Sir *Francis Drake,* (in this collection) are likewise remarkably entertaining."[19] Most significantly, he quotes the long "character" of Drake from this account, declaring that he believes it "to have been drawn by the Compiler."[20] No doubt this attribution is made on good authority. The only other voyage honored by quotation is Smollett's own "Account of the Expedition against Carthagene." The fact that the last two accounts are thus equally praised and quoted leaves little doubt that Smollett at least revised carefully the voyages of Drake; and it seems probable that he also corrected the account of Mexico which is recommended so highly. The acknowledged source for the last narrative is the history of Antonio de Solís; and Smollett, in two footnotes which he wrote for his edition of Voltaire, twice corrects Voltaire's account of Montezuma by citing the authority of Solís for minute details which are included in the *Compendium.*[21] The nature of these details, and one striking verbal parallel, make it almost certain that Smollett either copied or remembered this material from the *Compendium.*

Further evidence of Smollett's hand in the revision is found in the review of Dr. Patrick Browne's *Civil and Natural History of Jamaica* which Smollett wrote for the *Critical* in June, 1756.[22] In this article, after correcting some errors of Browne relating to the discovery of America by Columbus, Smollett continues:

We have likewise read, in the journals published by his own son, that he knew nothing at all of *Hispaniola* until he was informed by the inhabitants of *Cuba;* and that instead of landing upon *Hispaniola* on the 18th of *October,* as the doctor affirms, he did not reach the coast of that island until the 6th day of *December.*[23]

It seems manifest that Smollett is here using information acquired in the course of preparing the account of Columbus for the *Compendium,* since the introduction to this account stresses the fact that the source "was originally written by the son of Columbus."[24] The facts in the *Compendium,* of course, agree with Smollett's cor-

19. *Critical Review,* I, 311.   20. *Ibid.* See below, p. 61.
21. Cf. Voltaire, *Works* (London, 1761–69), IV, 202, 206; *Comp.,* II, 9, 88–9.
22. *Critical Review,* I, 389–409. It is difficult to believe that Smollett would have allowed anyone else to review a history of the island in which he had resided and from which his wife and her fortune originated; and it is so patently written by a satirist and zoologist familiar with the island that the attribution to Smollett seems certain.
23. *Idem,* p. 391.   24. *Comp.,* I, [1].

rections of Browne. Moreover, in two other notes to his edition of Voltaire, Smollett adds some detailed corrections relating to Columbus which, like those on Montezuma, seem certainly to be derived from the *Compendium.*[25]

Even more tangible evidence is found in the occasional addition of medical information to the accounts of Baldaeus and Rowe, and the "Voyage to the North of Europe."[26] These few facts can only be attributed to Smollett, unless we make the improbable supposition that he hired a physician as one of his assistants.

Thus far, then, Smollett has been connected with eight of the twenty-seven accounts in the *Compendium:* the "Account of the Expedition against Carthagene"; the accounts of Columbus, Sir Francis Drake, and Sir Thomas Rowe; the "Conquest of Mexico"; Baldaeus's accounts of Coromandel and Malabar, and Ceylon; and the "Voyage to the North of Europe." These eight articles comprise over one-third of the collection.

Final proof of Smollett's personal revision of the copy is found in the great number of links between various accounts in the *Compendium.* Exclusive of several cases which cannot be traced with certainty, there are fifteen instances in which the reader is referred to another article in the collection; five of these concern accounts with which Smollett has already been connected. Twice the citation is to specific pages and once to the volume; since these specific references occur only in the last volume, it seems that they were added by the editor as he perused the final pieces of copy with the printed sheets of the earlier volumes before him. Nine times the reader is simply referred to a particular account, and three times to facts that can be specifically located; six of these references show an accurate knowledge of the sequence of voyages in the collection as a whole. These cross-references are so related that, as one may see in the diagram below,[27] at least eleven of them appear to

25. Cf. Voltaire, *Works,* IV, 184–5; *Comp.,* I, 2–4.
26. See *Comp.,* III, 184, line 35–p. 185, line 2; V, 39, lines 10–12, 18–20; p. 69, lines 4–15; p. 239, line 3.
27.

"Gemelli"
↑   ↑
"Drake"←"Peru"←"Rogers"→"Nieuhoff"→"Baldaeus"
↓   ↑   ↓
"Florida"→"Mexico"   "Anson"←→"Dampier"→"Wafer"

"Peru," II, 192, refers to "Drake"; 217, refers to "Mexico." "Florida," II, 265, refers to "Mexico." "Iceland," IV, 37, refers to subject found in "Monk," III, 256–7. "James," IV, [42], refers to "Rowe." "Nieuhoff," IV, 192, refers to subject found in "Dampier," VI, 122; 213, refers to subject found in "Gemelli," VI, 311–12; 217, refers to "Baldaeus." "Dampier," VI, 5, refers to "Wafer"; 72, refers to "Anson."

have been done by one hand; moreover, the whole of each account concerned had apparently been read by the person who made the references, for they are scattered in various positions throughout the accounts. Accordingly, the person who added these eleven links evidently perused a total of 1,601 pages out of a total of 2,205 in the entire collection. It is absurd to suppose that one understrapper was entrusted with the responsibility for such a large proportion of the work: one can only deduce that Smollett added the links as he was revising the copy handed to him by his assistants.

Indeed, without the foregoing evidence one who has read the entire *Compendium* and studied its methods of revision is easily convinced that Smollett guided the whole compilation. Such consistent order and polish could have been accomplished only under the supervision of a single scrupulous editor. It is clear, then, that Smollett's editorship of the *Compendium* was not merely nominal, but was a serious personal task performed with exactitude. Smollett's own words and phrases undoubtedly form "a very small part of a compendium of voyages"; but that small part, like the catalytic agent in a chemical process, has been essential in transmuting a crude, chaotic mass to an orderly, succinct, and fluent "history."

In turning to study the methods used in assembling the *Compendium* it is thus essential to remember that the compilation was performed under Smollett's immediate orders; that in the majority of instances, revisions were at least approved by his editorial eye; and finally, that some proportion of the final recension was undoubtedly the work of his own hand, as he labored to add vigor and polish to the copy prepared by his less gifted hirelings. Hereafter, for convenience, I shall frequently refer to acts of compilation as done by Smollett; I do not thus imply that these acts were necessarily performed by Smollett alone, but that he was at least editorially responsible for them.

"Rogers," VII, 157, refers to "Nieuhoff" and gives pages; 251, refers to "Gemelli"; 255, refers to "Peru," and gives volume. "Anson," VII, 305, refers to "Rogers"; 352, refers to page which occurs in "Dampier."

II

The Sources of the Compendium

SMOLLETT promised in his agreement with the publishers to compile the *Compendium* "from the best books on these subjects extant."[1] His reputation as an editor will thus depend largely on his fulfillment of this obligation. Did he attempt to record the best available information on a given topic? Did he make fresh accounts, or simply lift them from previous compilers? Did he acknowledge his sources?

In answering these questions we must first admit that Smollett followed the mellow tradition of Grub Street by refusing to acknowledge any immediate sources: he never referred to specific editions and never admitted the use of a translation, though he consulted foreign works exclusively in English versions. Out of at least forty-six sources[2] used in the compilation, only eighteen are acknowledged in any way.

In six instances the source for an entire account is formally cited at the beginning; of these six references, three are accurate and three are deceptive. In the opening of "The Conquest of Mexico" Smollett devotes a whole paragraph to an explanation of his choice of "the learned Antonio de Solís"[3] as his authority for the account. This statement is accurate as far as it goes, but Smollett leaves the reader free to infer that he has used the Spanish original of Antonio de Solís y Ribadeneyra's *Historia de la Conquista de México* (1684); whereas he has used the English translation by Thomas Townsend, in the edition revised by Nathanael Hooke (1738). Similarly, at the beginning of the history of Columbus Smollett emphasizes the authenticity of his source, the account of Ferdinand Columbus; and he also devotes an introductory page to discussion of the merits of Gemelli's journal. In both these cases Smollett has used the English translations in the *Collection of Voyages and Travels* published by Awnsham and John Churchill, but he nowhere admits this indebtedness.

In each of the three other instances where the source is thus

1. *Letters*, p. 23.
2. I have counted as separate sources the individual voyages or chapters in a collection, except when facts are gleaned from a number of chapters by use of an index.
3. *Comp.*, I, [179].

formally acknowledged, the reference conceals insertions from other sources. Smollett attributes the description of Malabar and Coromandel and the account of Ceylon entirely to Baldaeus in the heading of each article, and at the beginning of the first devotes a page to a panegyric on the author. The greatest part of the material, including this exordium, is taken from the Churchills' translation of Baldaeus; but at various intervals throughout the accounts Smollett inserts, without acknowledgment, a total of nearly twenty pages of descriptive matter, chiefly from Campbell's edition of the *Navigantium atque Itinerantium Bibliotheca*.[4] He likewise states in the title that the "Voyage to the North of Europe" is "Extracted from the Observations of a Gentleman, employed by the North-Sea Company at Copenhagen, to make Discoveries," and he introduces the account with a formal discussion of this source. The article is actually taken from the account already "extracted" by Campbell in the *Bibliotheca;* moreover, without acknowledgment, Smollett adds a total of about four pages from other sources.[5] In the same manner Smollett acknowledges "the history of Osorio, bishop of Sylves"[6] as his authority for the account of Vasco da Gama's first voyage to India; and then, without acknowledgment, he adds a page of preliminary material on Portuguese discoveries under John II, taken almost verbatim from the "Introductory Discourse" to the Churchills' collection.[7] The remainder is found in the English translation of Osorio's *De Rebus Emmanuelis* (1571) performed by James Gibbs and published in 1752. The account of Cabral's first Indian voyage, immediately following the account of da Gama, is also taken from Osorio, but this time the authority is not acknowledged: apparently Smollett did not want two articles to be traced to the same history.

Seven other sources are allowed incidental acknowledgments; but only four of these actually admit the extent of the indebtedness. The journals of Edward Pelham and Sir Thomas Rowe, Father Sepp's account of Paraguay, and a letter by Thomas Coryat are all accurately cited as authorities for the sections concerned.[8] In the three other incidental acknowledgments Smollett betrays a source by occasional reference to substantiate a particular fact, but nowhere admits a larger use of this source. In his account of Anson's voyage he mentions "Mr. Walter" three times,[9] but does not acknowledge him as the source for the whole, whereas the entire ac-

4. See below, pp. 37–8.   5. See below, p. 36.   6. *Comp.*, I, [130].
7. Cf. *Comp.*, I, [130]–1; Churchill, I, xxi.
8. See *Comp.*, IV, 10; III, [237] (misprinted 189); VII, 179; III, 249.
9. *Comp.*, VII, 302, 306, 341.

count, except for a few incidental details, is taken from Richard Walter's famous narrative of Anson's expedition, published in 1748. Similarly, Lediard's *Naval History* (1735) is cited to support some statements at the close of Raleigh's West Indian voyage of 1592;[10] but Smollett makes no mention of the fact that Lediard has also been consulted for the accounts of the five Virginian voyages and the expedition to the Azores, which precede this reference. He also refers to Captain James's journal once,[11] but makes no acknowledgment of a source for the complete article on James, which is apparently taken from the journal as printed in the Churchills' collection.

Finally, in five voyages, the ultimate source is implicit in the name of the traveller: the accounts of Wafer and Dampier were available in Knapton's collection of 1729, Rogers's *Cruising Voyage* could be found in the second edition of 1726, and the accounts of Monk and Nieuhoff were accessible in the translations published by the Churchills.

These are the only helpful hints which Smollett gives concerning his authorities: for the remaining twenty-eight sources the only clues are verbal echoes.

One might attempt to excuse Smollett's neglect of acknowledgments with the plea that they would tend to distract and annoy the ordinary reader, for whom the collection was made. This apology, however, is refuted by the fact that Smollett has no objection to sprinkling his pages with weighty allusions to authors whom he apparently did not consult on this occasion. Thus he suppresses the fact that he is using Isaac de La Peyrère's description of Iceland, from the Churchills' collection, while he repeats La Peyrère's citations of Jonas, Blefkenius, Ortelius, and Wormius. He conceals his use of Oldys's life of Raleigh, and yet rifles the footnotes of his source to obtain references to Monson, Camden, Theobald, Mandeville, and Herrera.

He also gives long disquisitions on the relative merits of authorities whom he does not appear to have consulted in making the compilation, and even discusses one source which never existed. Take, for example, such generous acknowledgments as these, which relate to the discovery of Florida by de Soto:

From hence, after a tedious march, he came to Tulla, where *we are told by Ramusio, in the third volume of his collection of voyages,* the cacique, attended by eighty people, received and treated him very civilly; *but we rather chuse to follow Herrera, who in his history of America tells*

10. *Comp.*, III, 137–8.   11. *Comp.*, IV, 60.

us, that the people of Tulla opposed him and were all put to the sword; as these two accounts are point-blank contrary, it were in vain to attempt to reconcile them; but this much may be said for Herrera, that he seems all along very well acquainted with the American affairs; and tho' both were men of veracity, the latter is the more exact in general.[12]

But no account of de Soto's expedition appears in Ramusio's third volume, nor indeed in any of his volumes.[13] Smollett used the account of this exploit given by Purchas, which does not come from Ramusio, but from Hakluyt. Why then the reference to Ramusio? In the preceding account of the expedition of Narvaez to Florida, Smollett had also bilked the reader with an allusion to Ramusio.[14] In this article he had used an account by Purchas which immediately precedes the section on de Soto. Purchas refers to this account of Narvaez as "translated out of Ramusio"; and in the margin he adds, "Ramus. vol. 3."[15] It is obvious that the compiler did not notice the attribution to Hakluyt in the succeeding account of de Soto and assumed that it also came from Ramusio. But what of the reference to the *Historia General de los hechos de los Castellanos* (1601–15) by Antonio de Herrera y Tordesillas? Has he really consulted this author, available in Stevens's translation of 1725–26? Not at all: the allusion is lifted from the account of the discovery of Florida in Patrick Barclay's *Universal Traveller* (1735).[16]

Similarly, in the "Conquest of Peru," this extended commentary occurs:

> Herrera and De la Vega give very different accounts of the administration of Nunez, but we shall rather chuse to adhere to the relations of the latter, as he seems to speak very cooly every where, and shews no rancor against any party, neither does he pretend to vindicate any ill action on either side; on the contrary, Herera [*sic*] tho' [*sic*] the whole, plainly manifests a fixed enmity to Pizarro's family; and what would induce us to credit La Vega still more, is, that he lived on the spot at the same time that the things happened, concerning which he writes.[17]

One would hardly doubt that Smollett had used both Herrera's *Historia General* and Garcilasso de la Vega's *Commentarios Reales*

12. *Comp.*, III, 24 (my italics).
13. The reference, of course, is to the compilation by Giovanni Battista Ramusio entitled *Delle Navigationi et Viaggi* (Venice, 1550–59).
14. *Comp.*, II, 272.   15. Purchas, XVII, 437.
16. See Barclay, p. 174. The same situation occurs in the preceding account of Narvaez, where the reference to Ramusio cited above is linked with another allusion to Herrera; the latter is also borrowed from Barclay (p. 164).
17. *Comp.*, II, 248.

(1609, 1616), since the latter was also available in an English translation. The whole passage in the *Compendium*, however, is lifted from Barclay.[18]

An abundance of similar examples could be found throughout the *Compendium;* but these are sufficient to prove that Smollett lacked candor in his use of sources. One can only say that he was no worse than the majority of his contemporaries.

The questions of accuracy and scope remain untouched: an editor may neglect acknowledgments and yet possess the industry and intelligence to consult the best extant accounts. If Smollett sought to assemble all the best information on a given topic, he performed the essential function of an editor. It is therefore necessary to examine the nature of his sources.

In selecting Osorio's *History of the Portuguese* as the source for his accounts of da Gama and Cabral, and Solís's *Conquest of Mexico* as his authority for the article on Cortes, Smollett chose the best compendious relations of these events published in his day. His honesty and thoroughness are emphasized by the fact that both Barclay's *Universal Traveller* and Campbell's *Bibliotheca* contained adequate narratives of the conquest of Mexico, which could have been revised to suit his purposes. Smollett preferred to make a new selection of material.

To compile his history of Anson's expedition Smollett could have chosen any one of at least five different accounts: the original but faulty narratives of Philips[19] and Thomas;[20] a long account in Campbell's *Bibliotheca;* Walter's official narrative; and an abstract of Walter's account in *A New Universal History of Voyages and Travels.*[21] Smollett chose to condense his article directly from Walter's classic of travel-literature.

It is equally significant that Smollett was the first to attempt the task of reducing the whole of three gigantic accounts in the Church-

18. See Barclay, p. 133. A longer passage of this kind occurs in the narrative of the Inca's murder by Pizarro, where Smollett devotes over a page (*Comp.,* II, 205–6) to a contrast between the relations of Herrera and Garcilasso de la Vega. This is taken entirely from Barclay (pp. 113–14) except for one short sentence, which comes from Campbell (II, 149).

19. John Philips, *An Authentic Journal of the late Expedition under the Command of Commodore Anson* (London, 1744). I find a record of two other accounts published this year, which may or may not be taken from Philips: *An Authentic Account of Commodore Anson's Expedition;* and *A Voyage to the South Seas . . . by Commodore Anson.* I have not been able to examine the last two books.

20. Pascoe Thomas, *A True and Impartial Journal of a Voyage to the South Seas . . . under the Command of Commodore George Anson* (London, 1745).

21. See above, p. 17.

ills' collection: Gemelli's *Voyage round the World*, Nieuhoff's *Voyages and Travels into Brasil and the East-Indies*, and Baldaeus's accounts of Malabar, Coromandel, and Ceylon. Such an array of almost eleven hundred folio pages was sufficient to intimidate even the intrepid Dr. John Campbell, who omitted all these from his *Bibliotheca*, despite its capacious format. Here is one massive proof of Smollett's desire to popularize all the best information, for these accounts contain immense quantities of valuable history, otherwise inaccessible to the general reader.

Smollett's extensive use of the Churchills' collection is in itself sufficient evidence of his wish to base his compilation on original material; for they collected complete accounts almost exclusively and printed them usually with separate title-pages; Purchas, Harris, Barclay, and Campbell, on the other hand, condensed or merged such complete accounts. It is therefore important to notice that Smollett used the Churchills' collection to compile thirteen articles, and that in every case but two the Churchills' account was the principal source; whereas Campbell's *Bibliotheca* was consulted for only nine accounts, *Purchas His Pilgrimes* for four, Barclay's *Universal Traveller* for two; and, most significantly, each of the last three collections was used only twice as a major source. For the voyages of Columbus and James, Smollett could have found adequate reductions in Campbell's *Bibliotheca;* but in both cases he used the Churchills' full narrations. For his four short adventurous narratives relating to Greenland and Spitzbergen, and his description of Iceland, he could have used accounts already condensed in Harris's original *Bibliotheca* of 1705; but again he went to the longer accounts given by the Churchills. And although he used the *Pilgrimes* for some letters in the account of Sir Thomas Rowe, he scorned Purchas's synoptic version of Rowe's journal, and consulted the original as published by the Churchills.

Smollett apparently was forced to depend upon Campbell's condensation for the "Voyage to the North of Europe," since this was, as far as I can discover, its first appearance in English. Purchas's compendious account of Magellan's voyage had been used in some form in almost every subsequent collection except the Churchills', and, in particular, was reduced very slightly by Campbell; yet Smollett astutely went back to the ultimate English source in Purchas. It is obvious that Smollett consulted other collections only when the Churchills did not give the desired account; and even when he depended upon previous condensations, he sought out the best versions available. The same policy was followed by Smollett in his treatment of more recent voyages: Campbell provided adequate synopses of the circumnavigations of Dampier and Rogers, but in each case Smollett went back to the original.

Such evidence indicates that Smollett strove honestly to compile his collection from the best sources available in English, and that he did not follow the ordinary practice of stealing ready-made abstracts from other compilations. His constant aim was to present all the essential information relative to a given topic; and he therefore refused to trust the judgment of other editors.

Furthermore, only fourteen of the twenty-seven articles in the *Compendium* are limited to a single source. In the majority of instances this use of an additional authority is merely incidental, as in the account of Dampier's circumnavigation, which opens with three paragraphs on Dampier's early life, taken from Campbell's *Bibliotheca*.[22] Similarly, at the beginning of "Some Authentic Memoirs relating to the Affairs of Russia," Smollett adds two pages[23] of information about the country in general, taken from Salmon's *Geographical Grammar*.[24]

More striking evidence of an earnest desire for complete information is found in the additions made to the Churchills' account of Sir Thomas Rowe. The Churchills give almost everything in Purchas's chapter on Rowe, and a great deal more; but "almost" was not enough: the compiler also scanned Purchas carefully in order to be certain that nothing of importance had been lost. He found in one spot a letter of the Mogul to King James, while thirty pages later he discovered an amusing passage which relates the Mogul's quandary over placing his seal on this letter. These two related matters were plucked forth and tacked on at the end of the material from the Churchills.[25] As if this industry were not sufficient, the concluding paragraph gives some additional facts from the first letter of Thomas Coryat, in the succeeding chapter of the *Pilgrimes*.[26]

It seems highly improbable that any understrapper would have made such additions of his own accord: Smollett apparently consulted the supplementary accounts himself or directed some as-

22. Cf. *Comp.*, VI, 2–3; Campbell, I, 85.
23. *Comp.*, V, [198]–200. The "Memoirs" form an appendix to the "Voyage to the North of Europe."
24. See Appendix I, 21, b. A few additional details, totalling about two pages, are also scattered throughout this account; these have been taken from still another source, which it is difficult to locate with certainty.
25. Cf. *Comp.*, III, 248–9; Purchas, IV, 436–7, 467.
26. Cf. *Comp.*, III, 249; Purchas, IV, 475–6.

sistant to do so. This theory receives strong substantiation from surprisingly extensive additions to the account of Rogers's voyage. At one point the original launches into a short history of the exploration of the Amazon[27] which should, one might think, be quite sufficient for material which really has nothing to do with Rogers. But Smollett was compiling a history of exploration, and for his purpose evidently found this sketchy account inadequate. He therefore went to Campbell's *Bibliotheca* for about seven pages of additional information, which was incorporated with material given by Rogers, to produce a succinct history covering ten pages of the *Compendium*.[28] At the beginning of this section the editor adds an introductory paragraph in which he mentions his previous account of Nieuhoff, gives in a footnote the specific pages in Nieuhoff's account to which he refers, and stresses the importance of this digression on the Amazon. This strongly suggests that Smollett inserted the narrative himself when he corrected the copy and saw the faulty nature of the account prepared by his assistant.

Further evidence of what I believe to be Smollett's hand is found in the same voyage, where, immediately after this section on the Amazon, Rogers's description of the Plata basin is augmented by use of Father Sepp's account of Paraguay, as translated in the Churchills' collection.[29] It is impossible to ascertain the exact indebtedness of the *Compendium* to Sepp's original account, since Rogers had already derived his description of the region almost entirely from Sepp. But verbal echoes prove that the description in the *Compendium* is an amalgam of the two sources. It seems that the understrapper, ordered to prepare copy for the voyage of Rogers, had of course compiled his account of the basin from the description given by Rogers; but Smollett, in reading over the copy, feared that something significant might have been lost, and therefore collated, or ordered someone to collate, the copy with Sepp's original account.

This practice of inserting additional material is most extensive in the accounts of Malabar, Coromandel, and Ceylon, where, as I have said, the whole is attributed to Baldaeus, but actually a total of about twenty pages is added, chiefly from Campbell's *Bibliotheca*. Smollett apparently detailed an assistant to prepare the material from Baldaeus, and then, as he read over the copy, became dissatisfied with Baldaeus's summary treatment of some topics. He therefore added, or directed someone to add, sufficient matter to satisfy his desire for all the best information, but, either

27. See Rogers, pp. 63–71.   28. Cf. *Comp.*, VII, 158–69; Campbell, II, 209–12.
29. Cf. *Comp.*, VII, 174–82; Rogers, pp. 74–89.

through oversight or intention, omitted to alter the original acknowledgment of Baldaeus. Most of these additional facts appear to have been gleaned from the *Bibliotheca* by consulting the index. It seems that the compiler performed the labor of looking up about a dozen topics, with a total of more than a hundred page-references.[30]

Such was Smollett's endeavor to assemble all the significant facts relative to a given subject: he not only sought the best single sources available in English, but filled out these original accounts with additional details from a variety of other books. Down to tiny changes in details of size, longitude, and latitude, Smollett strove to present the best information on these topics available in his day.

Although in the great majority of cases Smollett used the most comprehensive sources available in English, he did not always do so. In four accounts he resorted to a much easier method, which was nevertheless equally efficient in obtaining essential information. This method consisted in the conflation of secondary sources: a procedure best illustrated in the "Conquest of Peru."

Here Smollett was faced with a peculiar problem, for no history such as that of Solís existed for this exploit. The only comprehensive sources in English were Herrera's history, in which the remarks on Peru are scattered through four volumes of Stevens's translation, and Garcilasso de la Vega's *Royal Commentaries,* which presents a huge mass of ill-sorted facts. Obviously Smollett had no time to compile an original history from such unwieldy accounts: he therefore solved his problem satisfactorily by fusing the two short and independent histories of the conquest of Peru which he found in Barclay's *Universal Traveller* and Campbell's *Bibliotheca.* Smollett's version covers nearly eighty pages; of these, the first twenty follow Campbell almost exclusively, since Barclay is very brief in his account of Francisco Pizarro's preparations and early

30. See entry for "Elephants" and cf. *Comp.*, v, 72, line 17–p. 73, line 10: Campbell, I, 839; *Comp.*, v, 73, line 11–p. 76, line 23, lines 29–34: Campbell, I, 459–63; *Comp.*, v, 76, lines 24–8: cf. Campbell, I, 745. Also cf. "Tygers," *Comp.*, v, 76, line 35–p. 78, line 27: Campbell, I, 466–7; "Crocodile," *Comp.*, v, 81, lines 12, 27–38: Campbell, I, 484; "Serpents," *Comp.*, v, 82, lines 16–20, line 27–p. 83, line 5, lines 29–33: Campbell, I, 475; "Ambergrease," *Comp.*, v, 85, lines 12–18, p. 86, lines 1–16: Campbell, I, 540–1; "Pearl Fishery," *Comp.*, v, 86, line 17–p. 87, line 17: Campbell, I, 482–3. The compiler seems also to have consulted Campbell's entries for "Diamonds," "Coral," "Goa," "Amadabat," "Cambaya," "Surat," "Agra," and "Diu"; but these topics, and a few others, appear to have been elaborated by use of some additional source which I have not been able to identify; hence, in these cases the indebtedness to Campbell must remain conjectural.

disappointments. For approximately the next forty pages, up to the death of Francisco Pizarro, the sources are mixed in nearly equal proportions, since, in this crucial part of the conquest, Barclay and Campbell are equally comprehensive. After this, however, Campbell gives a very short summary of events up to the close of Pedro de la Gasca's career in Peru: the last twenty pages in the *Compendium*, therefore, are almost entirely from Barclay. Finally, Smollett's history is balanced by the addition of an initial biographical paragraph on Francisco Pizarro and eight final lines on the later life of Gasca.[31] Such symmetry is the proper measure of the editorial precision displayed throughout the account. Into the same space which Barclay and Campbell each required to present their faulty accounts, Smollett has compressed the essential facts of both, with vigor and conciseness beyond the grasp of mere industry.

In compiling the "Discovery of Florida" Smollett met with an even more difficult problem, for again no history such as that by Solís had been written on the subject; furthermore, Barclay's *Universal Traveller* was the only collection which contained a compendious account of these events, and even this was inadequate. With great care, therefore, Smollett supplemented Barclay's brief history with extensive additions from other sources. He opens the article with the addition of a few lines on Cabot's original discovery, perhaps from general knowledge, perhaps from use of the index to the *Bibliotheca*.[32] Next, he adds a few facts relating to Ponce de Leon and Cordova, apparently from Campbell.[33] On his third page, then, Smollett plunges into a longer account of the fatal expedition of Narvaez, which covers ten pages. Since Barclay devotes less than a page to this disaster, Smollett uses almost exclusively the "Relation of Alvaro Nunez" in *Purchas His Pilgrimes*. After this, Barclay gives at greater length an account of de Soto's expedition, equal in size to about thirty pages in the *Compendium*. Smollett might well have been content with this; but, as in the "Conquest of Peru," he found it necessary to add an equal proportion of another source: the narration of de Soto's disaster given by Purchas. All these sources are collated and pieced together as judiciously as they are in the account of Peru, while the whole is condensed and polished in the same manner.

The plan of presenting three consecutive histories of the explora-

---

31. It seems impossible to trace these few facts to any specific source. A few additions are also made in the account of the death of Gonzalo Pizarro.

32. Cf. *Comp.*, II, [263]; Campbell, II, 191.

33. Cf. *Comp.*, II, [263]–5; Campbell, II, 56–9.

tion of Mexico, Peru, and Florida was apparently suggested to Smollett by Barclay, who gives separate accounts of each in this order. Smollett, had he wished, could have transferred these accounts bodily to his collection, just as his predecessor two years before had taken over Campbell's work bodily in the *New Universal History of Voyages and Travels*. But Smollett would not use such methods, although they were common practice: he desired to produce the best histories of these exploits which had thus far appeared in any English collection.

A similar method of compilation was used in preparing the accounts of Drake and Raleigh. In each case Smollett chose as his basis the best extant biography of his protagonist, and compared it with other secondary sources in order to obtain all the essential information relative to the subject.

For the life of Raleigh he was fortunate in having before him the scholarly biography by William Oldys, published in 1736; but Oldys, of course, was not writing a detail of voyages and was therefore comparatively brief in his accounts of the lesser expeditions instigated by Raleigh. Smollett filled out these accounts by using Thomas Lediard's *Naval History of England* (1735), in which he could find longer synopses of these expeditions.[34] So careful was his search for facts that he also collated these two sources with the scanty accounts of the Virginian voyages and the first voyage to Guiana given in Campbell's chapter on the discoveries of the English in America,[35] though the new material to be found in Campbell was very slight indeed. The exact amount of indebtedness to each of these three sources is in many places impossible to establish, since they sometimes treat the same facts in nearly the same words; but frequent divergences in detail and phraseology make it certain that all three were carefully consulted. As in the accounts discussed before, the material from the sources is entirely rewritten, rearranged, and fused to form a smoothly ordered narrative which contains every significant fact.

As the source for his account of Drake's exploits Smollett had no such authoritative biography as that by Oldys: the most comprehensive attempt at a life of Drake was the wretched compilation by Nathaniel Crouch, entitled *The English Hero: or Sir Francis Drake Revived* (1687). This slovenly work could not possibly satisfy Smollett's demands for accuracy and comprehensiveness. Fortunately Campbell had provided an excellent short account of Drake in his *Bibliotheca,* under the heading, "The Voyage of Sir Francis Drake round the Globe"; this is really a biography, though

34. See Appendix I, 9, b.   35. See Appendix I, 9, c.

the account of the circumnavigation preponderates. For the opening portion on Drake's early life Smollett therefore supplements the account of Crouch with facts from Campbell, including learned references to Camden and Stowe.[36] But for the first voyage to the West Indies under Hawkins neither Campbell nor Crouch gives more than bare mention; consequently, Smollett turns to Purchas's synoptic relation of this voyage in his chapter on "The first Voyages made to divers parts of America by Englishmen."[37] After the early life is thus satisfactorily filled out, Smollett follows Crouch exclusively for the long account of the voyage to Panama in 1572. At the close of this section Smollett borrows a biographical paragraph from Campbell to serve as a transition to the account of the circumnavigation.[38]

For the great voyage around the world two original accounts exist: one attributed to Francis Pretty, and the other written by Francis Fletcher. Crouch based his version on Fletcher; Campbell, however, chose to follow chiefly the other narrative; Smollett, accordingly, could obtain nearly all the facts simply by collating the accounts of Crouch and Campbell. But he was not satisfied with this labor: he also compared these two accounts with the one given by Purchas,[39] who condensed very slightly the narrative attributed to Pretty. Crouch provides a basis for the remainder of the account of Drake, but the gaps in his narrative are filled by facts from Campbell and from the summary of Drake's exploits given by Purchas under the heading, "A briefe Historie of Sir Francis Drake's Voyages."[40]

Thus, although Smollett consulted no original sources for the account of Drake, he laboriously assembled all the significant facts, subjected them to a rigorous scrutiny, and, finally, fused them into a vigorous and fluent narrative. The account is ostensibly divided into two articles, dealing, respectively, with the Indian voyage of 1572, and the circumnavigation. But these are so elaborated that they really form a compendious biography, the most comprehensive of the many "lives" of Drake which had thus far appeared.

36. Cf. *Comp.*, III, [65]–6; Campbell, I, 14.
37. Cf. *Comp.*, III, 66–7; Purchas, XVI, 108–9.
38. Cf. *Comp.*, III, 83; Campbell, I, 15.   39. See Appendix I, 8, d.
40. Purchas is used for one detail at the end of the voyage of 1585 (cf. *Comp.*, III, 114, lines 21–3; Purchas, XVI, 121); for a paragraph on the expedition to Cadiz (cf. *Comp.*, III, 115, lines 7–21; Purchas, XVI, 122–5); for the voyage of 1595, where the narrative represents a conflation of Purchas and Crouch (cf. *Comp.*, III, 116–18; Purchas, XVI, 125–31, Crouch, pp. 166–72); and for a few facts concerning the character of Drake (see below, pp. 61–2). Campbell is also consulted for Drake's character and for some facts relative to the Armada (cf. *Comp.*, III, 115, line 22–p. 116, line 8; Campbell, I, 21).

Smollett's personal connection with this account of Drake has already been established by the "character" which the *Critical Review* quotes as "drawn by the Compiler."[41] The study of its sources now suggests that the entire account may have been compiled by Smollett himself: it represents the most exacting collation of sources in the *Compendium;* it contains a greater proportion of editorial comment than any other article except Smollett's own "Account of the Expedition against Carthagene"; and, finally, Smollett's intimate concern with the choice of materials for the account is proved by this passage added at the close of Drake's voyage of 1585:

Altho' no more is required of us, nor indeed in our plan of this work have we promised more than such voyages as were made by the most remarkable adventurers; yet we should think it an affront to the curiosity of an intelligent reader, as well as a piece of injustice to his memory, who, had he lived in the days of Rome, had been raised to the rank of a demi-god, not to give some account of his defeating the Spanish Armada, fitted out for no less a purpose than the total destruction of the English nation.[42]

If Smollett did not compile the whole account, it is evident that he supervised its composition very closely.

After this study of Smollett's sources for the *Compendium*, it is possible to realize the integrity of his editorial standards. In only two brief accounts has he accepted, as his sole authorities, abridgments made by other English editors;[43] and in both cases these appear to have been the longest accounts of the subjects available in English at that time. In every other case he has formed a new account by any one of four different methods: (1) in eleven accounts[44] he has used the original narrations alone (foreign voyages in English translations, of course); (2) in six accounts[45] he has not only consulted the original English relations, but has augmented the originals with material from various other authorities; (3) in three accounts[46] he has revised the narratives presented by excellent foreign historians; (4) in five accounts,[47] where he does use summaries by English authors as principal authorities, these are supplemented or verified by the consultation of one or more additional sources in each instance.

Thus Smollett's fundamental integrity is proved by his indus-

41. See above, p. 27.   42. *Comp.*, III, 114–15.   43. See Appendix I, 7, 14.
44. See Appendix I, 1, 11, 12, 13, 15, 16, 17, 18, 22, 25, 27.
45. See Appendix I, 10, 19, 20, 23, 24, 26.
46. See Appendix I, 2, 3, 4.   47. See Appendix I, 5, 6, 8, 9, 21.

trious endeavor to assemble the best available information relative to a given topic. To be sure, he did not consult books in foreign tongues; but there is no reason why he should have done so, when such ample materials were available in English. It was Smollett's task to select the most significant and authentic accounts from a vast, disorderly accumulation of materials; this duty he performed with admirable fidelity. By his choice of "the best books on these subjects extant" in English, he fulfilled his fundamental obligation as an editor.

III

Condensation and Regularity

WHEN Smollett, in the Preface to the *Compendium*, refers to voyages as "this useful species of history," he reveals the touchstone by which he chose the materials to be included in his duodecimo format. "History," as I have said, was in Smollett's day a comprehensive term for all facts relative to the environment, the nature, the practices, and the exploits of man: it included natural, as well as social and political history. In this sense, then, Smollett's compilation might be called an attempt to achieve a "universal history" in miniature; for on the title-page he promises "A clear View of the Customs, Manners, Religion, Government, Commerce, and Natural History of most Nations in the Known World."

If this aim is to be achieved, the *Compendium* obviously can give but short shrift to adventures outside the main streams of conquest and exploration. The adventures of the privateers are excluded, except for the celebrated accounts of Dampier and Rogers, which are unusually rich in historical observations. Individual accounts of shipwrecks are excluded with the exception of a single perfunctory narrative of two pages.[1] Reports of privation are neglected except for three short journals, covering a total of twenty-five pages,[2] and the voyage of Captain Thomas James, thirty-six pages in length. To these may be added two accounts in which adventure serves primarily to present description. The first of these is "The Voyage of Captain John Monk. To Which are prefixed, Some curious Memoirs, relating to Old and New Greenland." Here the "prefixed" description covers twenty-seven pages, while the actual adventures of Monk are relegated to the last seven pages, almost as an afterthought. The second is "The Voyage of Mr. Lionel Wafer to the Isthmus of America," in which the adventures of Wafer are given only in the first twelve and the last thirteen pages, while in the middle comes a detailed description of the Isthmus, covering forty-two pages. Thus the accounts devoted primarily to minor exploits include less than one hundred pages out of a total of over twenty-two hundred in the *Compendium*.

This neglect of individual experiences is manifested consistently

1. See Appendix I, 15. 2. See Appendix I, 12, 13, 14.

throughout such voyages as those of Rogers, Gemelli, Baldaeus, and Nieuhoff, in which the traveller himself is not a great figure, whereas his historical observations are of prime significance. The personal experiences of such authors are therefore used chiefly to frame this essential matter and to provide occasional diversion for the jaded reader. In the revision of Baldaeus's account even the slight evidence of an itinerary in the original is removed, and the *Compendium* presents purely historical facts in the manner of the *Universal History*. In accounts of other travels at least the semblance of a voyage or tour is retained in order to introduce or connect the static passages; but generally, in accounts which are not of epic significance, Smollett permits only an outline of personal experiences, and frequently retains only the facts of distance or the names of places passed.

Striking evidence of Smollett's preference is found in the voyage of Rogers: the *Compendium* skips eleven pages on the trip round Cape Horn,[3] and fills the gap with additions to the accounts of the Amazon and the Plata, from Campbell and Sepp.[4] After these additions the compiler returns, rather guiltily, to mollify the reader:

Fearing that we have trespassed too long upon the patience of our reader in describing la Plata and the River of the Amazons, we shall hasten after our concert ships now on their way to Juan Fernandez, ...[5]

Smollett may well feel the necessity of thus reminding us that this is really a collection of voyages.

Many of these excisions, of course, remove only immaterial details of daily routine; but Smollett does not stop here: imbedded in the journeys are exciting adventures which are frequently omitted or violently reduced. Preference for description over adventure is particularly obvious in cruising voyages such as those of Anson or Rogers, where interesting incidents abound. Thus, for example, in the condensation of Anson's voyage, an entire chapter of eight pages, concerned with the voyage from Madeira to St. Catherine's, is reduced to a half-page, whereas the descriptions of these two places are allowed to occupy nearly as much space as they do in the original.[6] Similarly, Walter devotes nearly twenty pages to a narrative of the imminent loss of Anson's only ship at the island of Tinian, while Smollett allows barely a page; but for Walter's eight-page description of the island, he allows one and a half pages.[7]

3. Rogers, pp. 101–9, 121–3.   4. See above, p. 37.   5. *Comp.*, vii, 182.
6. Cf. *Comp.*, vii, 281, 287–91; Walter, pp. 16–17, 34–48.
7. Cf. *Comp.*, vii, 353–6; Walter, pp. 308–15, 318–36.

When such experiences are thus condensed, it is almost super-fluous to add that isolated anecdotes of all kinds are even more drastically treated. In Gemelli's tour, for example, scores of amusing anecdotes are interspersed at random, most of which provide grateful relief from the overwhelming mass of historical details. Smollett, however, removes nearly all of them.

It is evident from such omissions that the personality of an author is particularly vulnerable to Smollett's pruning. The first person is retained in only two accounts, the adventures of Wafer, and the "Voyage to the North of Europe"; in all the rest the individual narrator, if he appears at all, is relegated to a vague third person and the emphasis is placed on the objective fact. This excision of personal coloring is generally achieved by removal of the spectator and retention only of the fact observed, or by the formation of a general statement from some specific experience or anecdote of the traveller.

Equally important, of course, is the omission of personal comment: moralizing, conjecture, in fact any remarks not specifically related to the presentation of concrete, authenticated facts. Accordingly, in Roman Catholic writers such as Gemelli and Solís, frequent accounts of miracles are rigidly excluded, apparently because of Smollett's notorious lack of sympathy with "fanaticism." Gemelli, in particular, is censured as "too apt to believe some ridiculous reports of knavish or credulous priests and missionaries."[8]

The rococo Solís naturally suffers severely under the knife, for practically all his decorative digressions are excluded, along with his frequent moralistic interpolations. Thus, in the description of Mexican temples, Solís constantly interjects remarks on the wickedness of idolatry; not one word of all this piety is retained in the Compendium, which presents the temples purely as physical facts.[9] Similarly, in condensing Gemelli's description of the ruins of Persepolis, the compiler deletes the great amount of conjecture, appreciation, and moralizing which Gemelli inserts. Meanwhile, the figures, the physical details of shape and size are retained exactly; with the result that a personal account is transformed into a scientific catalogue.[10] To achieve the purpose of the Compendium the bare fact must thus be set forth with perfect clarity and conciseness; there must be nothing to confuse the common reader.

Although Smollett thus strives to retain all useful particulars, he is careful to exclude facts which clog the description or narra-

8. Comp., VI, [123].   9. Cf. Comp., II, 11–13; Solís, I, 398–402.
10. Cf. Comp., VI, 301–5; Churchill, IV, 163–7.

tion. Lists and documents are usually removed; foreign names are generally omitted, if the English substitute can be given; references to authorities are retained in relatively few places. Other reasons may also motivate omission: flagrant indecency is seldom countenanced; repetitious passages are usually removed; and many accounts are omitted in which the writer does not speak from personal observation.

But even after all this "unnecessary lumber" has been cut away, a bulk of concrete detail remains which is still far too large for Smollett's duodecimo capacity. This residue is pared down to proper size by rigorous selection and epitome, skillfully performed to preserve all the essential information. Usually, descriptions are not extensively rewritten; instead, the compiler forms a mosaic of passages chosen from the mass in his source. He has obviously read over the whole description carefully in order to pick out the most significant portions; but the expressions of the original are generally retained. Industry and accuracy are the chief qualifications for successful description of the present state of nations; hence, in such descriptive parts the expressions of the sources tend to be fairly satisfactory.

Much more subtle gifts, however, are required to relate heroic exploits in a concise, vivid style; thus most of Smollett's sources, being usually the crude work of mariners or hacks, are lamentably deficient in narrative vigor. Consequently, narrative parts of the *Compendium* seldom retain whole sentences from the original: in most cases it is impossible to find repetition of more than isolated clauses and phrases; and frequently the only verbal echoes consist of scattered words. It is in the accounts of the great conquering explorers that Smollett's hand can, I think, most surely be detected. The novelist's sense for trenchant expression is demanded on nearly every page, and apparently Smollett lost few of his opportunities: at any rate, the accounts of Columbus, Cortes, Pizarro, de Soto, Drake, and Raleigh constitute the most forceful and polished contributions to the collection. Their vigor is attained chiefly by dexterous epitome, substantial, yet smooth and concise.

By such methods Smollett effects astonishing reductions: the travels of Gemelli and Nieuhoff, totalling nearly nine hundred folio pages, are pared down to approximately one-fourth the original size; Townsend's two-volume translation of Solís is reduced to one-third the original size; and most of the shorter accounts represent proportional reductions. All this drastic condensation, as we have seen, is not produced by hasty, random omissions, but is performed with great care to preserve every essential historical fact. Thus

Smollett has fulfilled his promise "to disincumber this useful species of history from a great deal of unnecessary lumber," in order that the accounts may be "less embarrassed," and "more succinct."[11]

Had Smollett's revision extended no farther than such condensation, a large part of his *Compendium* would have remained irregular and confused, for most of his sources showed little sense of order and continuity: they were largely simple records of heterogeneous remarks given usually in the order of occurrence. To meet the trend of the times, with its increasing insistence on classification and synthesis, these scattered facts must now be marshalled into order; like must be grouped with like; all confusion of topics must be remedied.

The first step toward order is the separation of intermingled strands of narrative and description, beginning with the relocation of large sections of material, as in the "Voyage to the North of Europe," where Smollett explains:

. . . we shall pursue the account in the same natural order in which he [the original author] has delivered it, except his memoirs concerning Russia, which as they break in upon the thread of his narration, we shall divide from the main body of it, and insert by way of appendix.[12]

Accordingly, these memoirs are removed from the middle of the account in Campbell's *Bibliotheca*, where they occur without any division from the narrative of the traveller, and are placed at the close of the travels under a separate heading: "Some Authentic Memoirs relating to the Affairs of Russia." In treating Monk's voyage the position is reversed: the Churchills give first the account of Greenland, then the actual voyage, and lastly the account of Spitzbergen and the whale fishery: since narrative thus breaks the continuity of description, the voyage is transferred to the end of the account in the *Compendium*. Such simple rearrangements constantly occur, involving passages of every size.

More difficult problems are found in places where narrative and descriptive details are almost inextricably mingled; yet with great care the related facts are grouped into perfect order. A typical regularization of this sort is effected in the *Compendium's* version of Anson's sojourn at St. Catherine's Island.[13] First, all facts relative to the health of the crew are collected from a great variety of places in the source. The next two paragraphs deal with preparations for sailing: repairs, provisions, and the like; here the compiler brings

11. See above, pp. 25–6.   12. *Comp.*, V, 132.
13. Cf. *Comp.*, VII, 288–93; Walter, pp. 39–56.

in naturally an account of the knavish governor who impeded re-fitting, though Walter gives this information later, in a position which breaks the continuity of the description. The next two para-graphs are filled with details concerning the present state of the island: the first groups facts on produce, water, and climate; the second takes up government. Finally, a page and a half are devoted to description of the newly discovered riches of Brazil. Thus narra-tive and description are completely separated, and both divisions are neatly ordered.

The improvement effected by such rearrangements can be understood only by detailed consideration of such a revision as that performed upon Gemelli's account of his sojourn at Rhodes. Gemelli begins thus:

Thursday the 29th, meeting with the *Rais,* or master, I perceiv'd he had no inclination to leave his house so soon, being detain'd by the embraces of his wife, who was a beautiful *Turkish* woman. The *Rhodian* women out of modesty cover their foreheads with a handkerchief, and their chin up to the nose with another.[14]

Gemelli then devotes a paragraph to a description of Rhodes, be-fore returning to his personal troubles:

My continual instances to the *Rais,* or master, prevail'd with him at length to leave his fair, and set sail on *Saturday* the last day of *October;* but we had scarce sail'd two miles, before he return'd, the thoughts of her perhaps carrying him away.[15]

Smollett, however, plucks forth the intervening description of Rhodes and places it before the personal experiences of the travel-ler. Next he logically introduces the description of Rhodian women, adding a generalization upon their beauty, although Gemelli has mentioned only the beauty of the master's wife. Thus the descrip-tive details are all neatly separated from the personal narrative, and the account of Rhodian women in general forms an introduc-tion to the recital of the master's uxoriousness:

The Rhodian women, who are very fair, cover almost the whole of their faces by means of two handkerchiefs, one of which descends to the nose, and the other rises above the mouth; yet they are counted very beautiful: indeed the rais of the vessel in which Gemelli took his passage was an instance of the truth of this opinion; for, tho' the wind was fair, he could not for several days be persuaded to leave the embraces of his wife, who was a native of this island. At length, however, he was prevailed upon to set sail on Saturday, October 31; but he had not

14. Churchill, IV, 49.   15. *Ibid.*

proceeded above two miles when he returned, either from motives of love or apprehensión; . . . .[16]

The effect of such rearrangements, obviously, does not lie in brilliance of style, but in the cumulative continuity attained by thousands of such neat, competent revisions, scattered throughout the *Compendium*. Thus in the segregation of narrative and descriptive details the process of systematization takes another step forward. But it is still only the beginning: within the portions thus separated the process continues incessantly.

The most extensive rearrangement in purely static passages occurs in the revision of La Peyrère's account of Iceland. Here the entire confused account covering twelve folio pages is reduced to an order similar to that later followed by Smollett in his *Present State of All Nations:* regular sections are devoted to topography, inhabitants, customs, religion, and government, and each section gathers together all the relevant facts scattered at random in the source. Equally effective revision is found in the descriptive sections of Nieuhoff's travels. The opening geographical account is rearranged to give towns in order of importance;[17] then the compiler passes over a long section on natural history to take up the next geographical district; thus the discussion of settlements is made continuous and compact. This omitted section on natural history is transferred to a position nearly a hundred pages later in the *Compendium*, where it is prefixed to another account of natural history which Nieuhoff gives at this later point. The section is not only transferred, but is rearranged to group the various items in order.[18] Such agglomeration of related topics is a constant practice throughout the descriptions of the *Compendium* and includes even the most minute irregularities.

The rearrangement of narrative portions is similar in method and equally extensive: it begins with the separation of mingled stories[19] and penetrates to the structure of individual paragraphs. A striking example is found in the account of Almagro's rebellion in the "Conquest of Peru," where material from Barclay and Campbell is moulded into perfect order. Barclay tells first of the plan

16. *Comp.*, VI, 178.   17. Cf. *Comp.*, IV, 83–6; Churchill, II, 8–12.
18. Cf. *Comp.*, IV, 178–86; Churchill, II, 12–19, 119–27.
19. Thus, after an account of Raleigh's fifth Virginian voyage the compiler explains:
"We ought to have premised some account of an expedition concerted by Sir Walter Raleigh against the Azores, before he gave up all thoughts of Virginia.
"But as it would have broken the thread of our narration, we flatter ourselves, an abstract of it in this place will not be disagreeable." (*Comp.*, III, 132.)

of the loyal Holguin to meet his ally Alvarado, and then shifts the scene to discuss the arrival of the new governor de Castro, his commission, and some of his reinforcements. Then he jumps to the march of the rebel, Almagro, and as abruptly returns to relate Holguin's clever feint which accomplishes a junction with Alvarado. After narrating the ultimate meeting of the combined loyalists with de Castro, Barclay returns once more to Almagro. At the close of the decisive battle, he brings in an offer of aid to de Castro from Gonzalo Pizarro which was made before the combat.

The *Compendium* transposes thus: it gives first Holguin's plan to meet Alvarado and adds the clause, "which he did thus by a feint,"[20] as an introduction to the next paragraph, which relates this ruse and the successful junction of the loyal allies with de Castro. After this comes a long section on the new governor's commission, character, and actions, which consists of mingled details from Campbell and Barclay, greatly revised. Next comes a summary of all the reinforcements for de Castro, including the offer from Gonzalo Pizarro. After thus grouping all details relative to the loyalists, the compiler proceeds to group all the facts concerning Almagro: first, his character, from Campbell, and next, his actions, from Barclay. Then, with the situation of each side neatly summarized, he presents an account of the final battle.[21]

By such condensation and rearrangement the fundamental process of regularization has been completed.[22] The essential material is chosen; description and narrative are deftly separated; descriptive details are so grouped and ordered that the reader may pass from one fact to another with ease and edification; narrative is so arranged that one event follows another in natural succession. Thus, with immense labor, Smollett and his assistants have laid the foundation for achievement of the promise "to polish the stile, strengthen the connexion of incidents, and animate the narration, wherever it seemed to languish."[23] But obviously such revisions cannot by themselves fulfill Smollett's entire aim: order alone may still be stiff and dull, while disorder may be vitally amusing. Smol-

---

20. *Comp.*, II, 239.

21. Cf. *Comp.*, II, 239–43; Barclay, pp. 127–30; Campbell, II, 159–60.

22. The desire for regularity also appears in more technical aspects of the *Compendium*. The division into paragraphs is precise and apt. In all the longer accounts related matters are grouped into distinct chapters, each with a synoptic heading. Outmoded or erroneous spelling is made consistent with the accepted usage of the day.

23. See above, p. 26.

lett, however, aimed at much more than either the simple regularity of a catalogue or the simple sprightliness of an isolated sentence: he aimed to achieve that peculiarly consistent combination of regularity, polish, and power which we call neo-classical, or Johnsonian, prose.

IV

The "Johnsonian" Style

THUS far the study of Smollett's revision has been primarily concerned with the omission, compression, or rearrangement of materials given in the sources. Now it is essential to consider his final steps: the new expressions and details which were added to improve uneven and lifeless passages. Most of these additions, of course, result from the ordinary practices of any compiler. First, there is a small amount of editorial comment, for purposes of clarity or emphasis; but this is negligible: all such additions would scarcely total a dozen pages. More important is the constant use of connective additions, ranging from a word to a long sentence, which impart continuity, and frequently assist in realizing some potential vitality in the source. The use of more graphic and concise phraseology is an equally common tool of this editorial trade. Smollett simply used the last two methods of revision more extensively and skillfully than the average collector of voyages.

It is fair to say, however, that such revisions do not, in the majority of cases, result in a high standard of stylistic excellence. The prose style of the *Compendium* is, for the most part, very competent hack work, better than its sources, far better than the average of such compilations; but, in general, it excels only in comparison with a low standard. On the other hand, many excellent passages occur, passages which may very probably be attributed to the superior hand of Smollett himself. One of these must suffice to show the superiority of the *Compendium* at its best: the account of the Mogul's drinking bout, revised from the journal of Sir Thomas Rowe. That Smollett had a part in the revision of this journal has already been shown;[1] and the quality of this anecdote indicates that it is the work of Smollett's own hand. The original passage in Rowe is very irregular and only slightly amusing:

The good king fell to dispute of the laws of *Moses,* CHRIST and *Mahomet,* and in his drink was so kind, that he turn'd to me, and said, if I am a king you shall be welcome, *Christians, Moors* and *Jews;* he meddled not with their faith, they came all in love, and he would protect them from wrong; they lived under his protection, and none should

1. See above, p. 28.

oppress them. This he often repeated, but being very drunk fell to weeping and into divers passions, and so kept us till midnight.[2]

The revision is a model of the brief anecdote:

After affairs were thus settled, his majesty entered into a familiar dispute with his excellency, concerning the laws of Moses, Christ, and Mahomet, mellowing the argument with old wine; and declaring that his disposition led him to treat with equal mildness Christians, Jews, and Mohammedans, as long as they continued obedient to him, and did not seek to disturb the peace of his dominions. *In short, the good man spoke so feelingly of the spirit of religion, and imbibed so cordially the spirit of the wine, that both conjunctively distilled thro' his eyes;* and he wept to think that so few people, out of the many who professed themselves followers of these great prophets, adhered literally to the excellent rules they had laid down: and at last, his majesty breaking his discourse into short sentences, fell fast asleep, and concluded his sermon with a drunken nap.[3]

The effect of the anecdote depends largely upon its symmetry. The first half presents an objective account of the argument, which gives no hint of the Mogul's maudlin state. Then, in the middle, Smollett emphasizes the dichotomy in the Mogul's activity by a parallel structure which provides the transition to the second, satirical, portion. In the last half the satire gradually emerges as we realize that the Mogul's lament is itself the result of his infringement of one of the laws of the Mohammedan religion, which he sometimes professed; and at last the formality of the whole scene is exploded by the abrupt termination: "concluded his sermon with a drunken nap."

Granting that this is a passage unusual in the *Compendium*, I believe, nevertheless, that it points the way toward the most distinguished and significant aspect of the compilation's style. In the careful structure of this anecdote, particularly in the central parallelism, one begins to glimpse a correlation between the general regularity of the *Compendium* and the specific regularity which distinguishes neo-classical prose. The desire for general continuity and order apparently tends to produce those formal structures in which the Age of Johnson liked to arrange its remarks. One can hardly stress too much the implication that those revisions which aim at continuity, precision, and proportion are manifestations of both a new movement in the compilation of history and a new trend in the quality of English prose.

Certainly much revision for the *Compendium* resulted in a style

2. Churchill, I, 649.   3. *Comp.*, III, 223–4 (my italics).

remarkably similar to that of Samuel Johnson: there is a preference for classical diction and strong rhythm, accompanied by a tendency toward all forms of parallelism. Does this striking similarity mean that Smollett was deliberately striving to imitate the "bow-wow" style so recently presented in the *Rambler* (1750–52)? Possibly some such influence is present; yet this explanation alone is inadequate. Careful study of Smollett's revision shows that this style was the natural outcome of his plan and purpose: if Johnson had never written, the style of the *Compendium* would still be much the same, though perhaps less ponderous in places.

Before considering this conclusion it is essential to explain the sense in which the word "style" is used in this discussion. By "style" I do not mean simply a façade thrown up to cover the rough framework of the sources; I do not conceive of "style" as a rind or shell which can somehow be distinguished from the "matter" and analyzed separately. The meaning of "style" in this study is that given by Buffon: "Le style n'est que l'ordre et le mouvement qu'on met dans ses pensées."[4] In other words, style is a way of thinking, a method of presenting ideas. Accordingly, the nature of style must be examined from the inside, from the standpoint of the author's mentality and aim. As Murry has said,

Style is organic—not the clothes a man wears, but the flesh, bone, and blood of his body. Therefore it is really impossible to consider styles apart from the whole system of perceptions and feelings and thoughts that animate them.[5]

What, then, was the "system of perceptions and feelings and thoughts" which produced the style of the *Compendium?* The preceding pages have already answered the question. The *Compendium* was a product of the movement toward synthesis; hence, Smollett's plan for the work was this: first, the various voyages were to be arranged in chronological order; next, details within these voyages which destroyed order and clarity were to be excluded; and, finally, the materials were to be rearranged and linked into precise, regular, and lucid accounts.

The distinctive qualities of style which result from these aims are aptly illustrated in the following revision:

[Purchas:] . . . [Nunez found Florida] very poorly peopled, and hard travelling, in respect of the troublesome passages, Mountaynes and lakes which are there . . . . exceeding great Lakes are found,

4. Buffon, *Chefs-D'Oeuvre Littéraires* (Paris, 1864), I, 3.
5. J. Middleton Murry, *The Problem of Style* (Oxford, 1922), p. 136.

Mountaynes standing thicke together, and mighty Desarts, and without Inhabitants.[6]

[Smollett:] . . . indeed it promised very indifferently, presenting to the eyes nothing but *inaccessible* mountains, craggy rocks, *impenetrable* forests, *inhospitable* desarts, and *impassable* lakes.[7]

Here, in accordance with Smollett's general plan, an amorphous mass of details is reduced into strict order, and the result is a passage which displays many characteristics of the "Johnsonian" style. Balance and regularity, inherent in any such list of modified nouns, are here emphasized by the similar sounds in the Latin adjectives, three of which are matched in number of syllables. The form is a rigid parallelism; the rhythm is strong and regular; and the effects thus gained are precision, clarity, emphasis.

This is no place to enter into a discussion of that much abused word "rhythm," but it is necessary to notice that I treat prose-rhythm as divisible into two manifestations: one, the periodicity of phrases, clauses, or short sentences, which, by systematic arrangement, produce rhythm on a broad scale; the other, the rhythm within these elements: a marked beat similar to that in traditional verse. In the first sense, then, every parallel structure produces rhythm on a broad scale, while each element of a parallelism may also have rhythm in the second sense. I am aware of the variety of meanings which hover about the term "prose-rhythm"; but since choice is necessary for discussion, I limit myself to these definitions.

Parallelism may be divided into three categories: (1) enumeration: the arrangement of materials into a series of three or more elements; (2) balance of pairs; (3) general parallelism in complex sentences. The quotation already given is an example of enumeration; but this practice extends to much longer elements, which form the same pattern and spring from the same motives as the simpler lists:

[Solís:] *Cortes* was well made, and of an agreeable Countenance; and besides those common natural Endowments, he was of a Temper which render'd him very amiable; for he always spoke well of the Absent, and was pleasant and discreet in his Conversation. His Generosity was such, that his Friends partook of all he had, without being suffer'd by him to publish their Obligations.[8]

[Smollett:] Nor was he less remarkable for other agreeable endowments: his person and address were prepossessing, his disposition was amiable, his conversation entertaining, and his generosity unbounded.[9]

6. Purchas, XVII, 447–8.   7. *Comp.*, II, 268 (my italics).
8. Solís, I, 45–6.   9. *Comp.*, I, 185.

Identical aims frequently motivate the arrangement of simple declarative sentences in a form very close to enumeration: the sentences are piled upon each other in layers. A useful example is found in the revision of the following passage from Solís:

They told him aloud, that he was no longer their King; . . . giving him the opprobrious Names of pusilanimous, effeminate Coward, an abject Prisoner, and Slave to his Enemies: Their injurious Language was drown'd by loud and repeated Shouts; and he endeavoured, by the Motions both of his Head and his Hands, to be heard, when the Multitude began to advance, and let fly their Arrows against him, ...[10]

The spasmodic succession of "Names" is first reduced to a simple triad:

They upbraided this unhappy prince with the epithets of coward, prisoner, and slave, ...

Then the irregular narration of the climax is separated into a distinct succession of parallel sentences:

. . . they cursed him with the most opprobrious invectives;
his motions with the head and hand were disregarded;
his efforts to speak were rendered ineffectual by their repeated shouts;
and, at last, they let fly a shower of arrows against him.[11]

The purpose of this separation seems identical with that which has so often been emphasized in discussing rearrangement throughout the *Compendium:* the classification of all related facts according to categories.

The constant tendency toward balance of pairs appears to spring from similar motives. In such cases the single element of the source is apparently too weak and indistinct for the compiler, and he therefore clarifies and enforces his point by means of two matched elements. This purpose is particularly evident in the frequent employment of antithesis. Thus Gemelli says only:

This city looks more like a wood, because its houses are scatter'd among abundance of palm-trees, ...[12]

Smollett separates and amplifies to produce the simple contrast necessary to enforce the statement:

. . . looks more like a wood than a city, as the houses are *not contiguous, but* built separately amidst plantations of palms, ...[13]

10. Solís, II, 161–2.
11. *Comp.*, II, 87–8 (the typographical arrangement, of course, is mine).
12. Churchill, IV, 168.   13. *Comp.*, VI, 307 (my italics).

In the same way Smollett emphasizes by balance an antithesis which has been indistinctly stated in the source:

[Campbell:] A base and bloody Resolution, which though *Francis Pizarro* at this Time rejected with Horror, yet it was not long before he approved and agreed to it.[14]

[Smollett:] . . . tho' Pizarro at first treated this proposition with the contempt it deserved, yet, in a very short time, *resentment induced him to countenance what honour taught him to abhor.*[15]

Similarly, he sometimes forms an elaborate antithesis which is barely suggested by the original account:

[Barclay:] . . . [Pizarro] was a man of strong natural parts, great abilities both for war and peace, and was endow'd with many qualities which made a great man.[16]

[Smollett:] . . . nature had furnished him with abilities as conspicuous in the busy operations of war, as they were illustrious in the gentler offices of peace; . . . .[17]

In the last two instances the various elements are carefully matched, in order that the ideas may be presented with perfect order and precision.

Identical aims appear to lie behind even the simple balance of single words in pairs, a constant practice throughout the *Compendium.* Thus, it is not enough for soldiers to advance "with incredible Diligence";[18] they must proceed "with equal intrepidity and expedition."[19] A house is not merely "handsomly built";[20] it is "a very elegant and commodious structure."[21] Priests cannot merely repeat "their Bows and Perfumes";[22] they must have "repeated their prostrations and performed their fumigations."[23] The purpose behind the last revision seems particularly clear, since the source commits a solecism: one can repeat or perform "Bows," but not "Perfumes"; hence the latter word is changed to "fumigations"; and then, apparently, "prostrations" is substituted for balance and, consequently, emphasis. The same demand for verbal exactitude and propriety is apparent in the next example, where the balance is enforced by alliteration, frequently used thus throughout the *Compendium:*

[Solís:] . . . the Dispute came to push of Pike and Sword.[24]

14. Campbell, II, 151.
16. Barclay, p. 127.
19. *Comp.*, I, 253.
22. Solís, I, 276.

15. *Comp.*, II, 211 (my italics).
17. *Comp.*, II, 237.
20. Churchill, IV, 79.
23. *Comp.*, I, 259.

18. Solís, I, 257.
21. *Comp.*, VI, 217.
24. Solís, II, 108.

[Smollett:] . . . the dispute soon came to push of pike, and *stroke of sword*; . . . .[25]

Such explicit, balanced pairs occur not only in isolated instances: frequently they are found in clusters, which, of course, produce additional parallelism of pair against pair:

They never engage in war with a view to enlarge their territories, but to maintain their dignity, when they think it is impaired by any *injury or affront:* in such cases they chuse a council of seniors *to estimate and regulate* the *expence and preparations* of the war, and then elect a general, who visits every house, and in set harangues *encourages and animates* the men to deeds of glory.[26]

A particularly striking use of such clustered pairs is found in the revision of a passage in which the parallelism has already been begun, but is not sufficiently regular for Smollett:

[Solís:] From this Place might be seen the greatest Part of the Lake, beautified with various Towns and Causeys; Towers and Pinnacles which seem'd to swim upon the Waters, Trees and Gardens out of their proper Element; . . . .[27]

[Smollett:] From this place might be seen the greatest part of the lake, beautified with towns and causeys, towers and pinnacles, trees and gardens, that seemed to swim upon the water; . . . .[28]

Parallelism, of course, may be manifested in other simple forms: frequently, balance, emphasis, and distinctness are achieved by use of modified pairs:

[Campbell:] . . . when they were upon the Point of reaping the Reward of all their Sufferings: . . . .[29]

[Smollett:] . . . now they were on the eve of reaping a *golden harvest* for their *manifold toils;* . . . .[30]

The same tendency toward parallelism naturally influences the general arrangement of phrases and clauses within longer sections, as in the following revision, which begins with a simple pair of nouns, and then continues the effect by balancing the subsequent clauses in pairs:

[Purchas:] . . . Sirs, I am a Christian, slay mee not, nor these Indians, for they have saved my life.[31]

25. *Comp.,* II, 71 (my italics).
26. *Comp.,* I, 163 (my italics); cf. Osorio, I, 102. The source contains the opening antithesis, but none of the simpler pairs.
27. Solís, I, 365.   28. *Comp.,* I, 285.   29. Campbell, II, 144.
30. *Comp.,* II, 188 (my italics).   31. Purchas, XVII, 527.

[Smollett:] . . . "I am a Christian and a Spaniard; spare me, and recal my scattered friends, to whom I owe my life, and whose intentions are peaceable."[32]

Here the parallelism is rather rough, since the various elements are unequal in length; in the following example, however, the parallelism between the italicized phrases is strongly marked by identical words, similar length, and similar syntactical position:

[Solís:] The Beginning of the Conversation was all Civility and Compliments: But amidst their Mirth, and the Liberties of the Feast, there began soon after some Ralleries to be introduc'd against *Cortes*.[33]

[Smollett:] . . . *in the beginning of the conversation,* he was treated with great civility and compliment: but, *in the midst of their festivity,* some sarcastic animadversions were uttered against Cortes; . . . .[34]

The last two examples lead the way to discussion of the subtlest and most pervasive form of parallelism: the balanced arrangement of elements in a long complex sentence. The effect may be examined in the revision of this passage from Solís.

They endeavoured to invalidate the Authority of the Council, and cast Reflections on *Cortes*, blaming his Ambition, and talking with Contempt of those that were deceived, and did not know it. And as Scandal has its hidden Poison, and an unknown Power over those that hear it, it spread in their Conversations, where there wanted not some who hearken'd to, and endeavoured to foment it. *Hernan Cortes* did all that lay in his Power to remedy this Inconvenience in the Beginning, ... He had already found by Experience how little his Patience avail'd, and that gentle Means produc'd contrary Effects, rendring the Evil worse; and therefore resolv'd to make use of Severity, which generally has the best Effect upon the Insolent.[35]

Smollett first enumerates three expressions of their enmity:

. . . they endeavoured to invalidate the authority of the council,
openly inveighed against the ambition of Cortes,
talked contemptuously of those who adhered to his interest. . . .

Then he concludes with a long section which displays very complex parallelism:

. . . and, *with the breath of slander industriously communicated,*
began to kindle a flame of dissension,
that would have proved of the worst consequences to the expedition,
had not Cortes,

32. *Comp.*, ii, 278.   33. Solís, ii, 90.
34. *Comp.*, ii, 65 (my italics).   35. Solís, i, 169–70.

finding more moderate expedients ineffectual,
extinguished it at once,
by a step that argued his uncommon fortitude and penetration.[36]

This is really a sort of elaborate antithesis: the words, "had not Cortes," divide the passage into two balanced and opposed halves. The italicized passages, all modifiers, match alternately in length; and the second and sixth elements, the central clauses of each half, also balance, boxed as they are between longer elements.

All the foregoing types of parallelism are, of course, combined in various forms, as in the array of parallelisms which comprise the character of Drake, already assigned positively to Smollett himself:

. . . he was naturally eloquent, clear in his expression, and graceful in his delivery: his knowledge in every science requisite to the marine, even in surgery, was extensive; he was feared and respected by his enemies, whom he always treated with tenderness and humanity; beloved and caressed by his owners, to whom he behaved with justice and integrity; and honoured and esteemed by his sovereign, whom he served with courage and fidelity. He was resolute and active; patient in hearing advice; judicious in accepting it; easy of access; fond of the soldiery; liberal of promises; unshaken in his friendship; and irreconcileable in enmity; but open to the grossest adulation. In a word, he was a man who never let private views get the better of his public spirit; and as in life he was generally beloved, in death he was universally regreted.[37]

First comes simple balance of modifiers ("clear . . . delivery") in the opening period; then, ("he was feared . . . fidelity") that perfectly symmetrical combination of alternate main and modifying clauses, buttressed by repetition of "by his" and by the recurrence of simple pairs at the beginning and end of each period. Next, as strict regularity begins to pall, Smollett shifts to rapid enumeration, in which variety is achieved by slight changes of pattern as the series progresses: first, the simple pair of adjectives, then the paired structure of "in" plus gerund, next the triad with "of," and then another pair with "in." Finally, the paragraph closes with the antithetical balance of "private views": "public spirit," "in life": "in death," and the exact parallelism of the last two clauses.

Smollett's fondness for balance is emphasized by the fact that in the first half of the above quotation he has elaborated parallelisms already begun, in much simpler form, by Campbell:

36. *Comp.*, I, 221 (my italics and typographical arrangement).
37. *Comp.*, III, 118–19. See above, p. 27.

. . . He was naturally eloquent, expressing gracefully what he conceived clearly; very knowing, not only in his own Profession, but in all the Sciences relating to it; so that he was able to discharge every Office in a Ship, even to that of a Surgeon; just to his Owners, kind to his Seamen, loyal to his Sovereign, and remarkably merciful to his Enemies.[38]

In Smollett's revision increased parallelism is accompanied by increased precision. Campbell's central passage ("very knowing . . . Surgeon") interrupts the grammatical structure, with the result that the final series of modifiers comes in abruptly, dangling without a subject; but Smollett avoids this defect by condensing the central passage and by giving specific subjects. Though here he has expanded his source, in the next sentence he has returned to the more usual practice of economy, by rearranging this formless, expansive passage from Purchas into succinct enumeration:

. . . Sir Frances beeing of a lively spirit, *resolute, quicke,* and sufficiently valiant: . . . . Sir Francis was *a willing hearer of every mans opinion, but commonly a follower of his owne:* . . . . *did much love the Land-souldier,* . . . . Hee was also affable to all men and *of easie accesse.* . . . *hard in reconciliation, and constancie in friendship;* . . . . He was *infinite in promises,* . . . . He had also other imperfections, as aptnesse to anger, and bitternesse in disgracing, and *too much pleased with open flattery:* . . . .[39]

The details in italics are selected by Smollett from a comparison of the characters of Drake and Hawkins, sent to Purchas by one R. M.

This character of Drake, indubitably drawn by Smollett, strongly suggests that many, if not most, of the preceding examples of parallelism are also the work of Smollett himself. He had read with care the copy prepared by his assistants; he had ordered the insertion of additional matter to remedy defective accounts; he had made editorial references between various voyages and had added medical comments. Certainly, then, it is fair to assume that he frequently evolved parallelisms to produce clarity, emphasis, economy, and precision, when he found the copy seriously at fault.

Even the use of classical diction in these revisions appears to have a connection with the movement which prompted the *Compendium.* Wimsatt, in his study of Johnson's style,[40] has convincingly suggested that Johnson's choice of vocabulary was directed, in large part, by a desire to give his writing the exactitude of sci-

38. Campbell, I, 22.   39. Purchas, XVI, 132–3 (my italics).
40. W. K. Wimsatt, Jr., *The Prose Style of Samuel Johnson* (New Haven, 1941), pp. 59–62.

ence. Words of Latin and Greek derivation dominated the style of the scientific or pseudo-scientific treatises of the day, with which both Johnson and Smollett were familiar—especially the latter, because of his interest in the medical profession. Such diction, used in an essay or history, gave the impression that the author had imbibed the spirit of science, spoke with learned authority, and was presenting his materials with scientific accuracy and discernment.

This effect of Johnson's diction was noticed by Nathan Drake:

> Had our author been writing on abstruse or scientific subjects, the use of Latin derivatives, and recondite philosophical terms, would readily, for the sake of minute precision, have been acceded to; . . . .[41]

And Johnson himself declared in his last *Rambler:*

> When common words were less pleasing to the ear, or less distinct in their signification, I have familiarized the terms of philosophy, by applying them to popular ideas, ...

The "terms of philosophy," one must remember, include (and indeed may primarily refer to) the terms of *natural* philosophy, or science. "For the sake of minute precision" and distinctness of "signification," then, both Johnson and Smollett liked to use a classical vocabulary.

This preference was also guided to some extent by the fact that such diction was sometimes more "pleasing to the ear." "Pleasing" on what grounds? Primarily, I think, because of their emphatic sound: the long roll of syllables pounds home the fact. Moreover, as Tempest has said, "Too frequent use [of monosyllables] produces a jerky and halting style";[42] whereas polysyllabic vocabulary is more effective in producing the rhythm-groups which Fijn van Draat defines as "words logically belonging together welded into a closer union by means of the metrical flow."[43] Thus, such rhythm-groups can assist in achieving the continuity which formed part of Smollett's purpose in revising materials for the *Compendium.*

The use of a classical vocabulary in the *Compendium* therefore plays an integral part in the fulfillment of Smollett's aim, since such words, used properly, help to achieve precision, emphasis, and connection. It cannot be denied, of course, that in many cases the substitution of such diction for the simpler words of the sources is

41. Nathan Drake, *Essays* (London, 1809), I, 256.
42. N. R. Tempest, *The Rhythm of English Prose* (Cambridge [Eng.], 1930), p. 40.
43. P. Fijn van Draat, *Rhythm in English Prose* (Heidelberg, 1910), p. 14. Cited by Tempest, p. 32.

far from successful, and merely results in pretentiousness incongruous with the banality of the matter.

The study of the *Compendium* therefore suggests that the prevalence of "Johnsonian" style may be attributed in large degree to the general movement toward synthesis and scientific exactitude, rather than to the specific influence of any single writer. One should never forget that Johnson himself took an active part in this movement. It is no mere accident that Johnson's *Dictionary* (1755) appeared only one year before Smollett's *Compendium* and two years before Smollett's *History of England*. It is no mere accident that Johnson's Introduction to *The World Displayed* was immediately followed in that compilation by accounts of Columbus and Cortes largely taken from Smollett's *Compendium*.[44] All these compilations had identical aims of order and precision; hence, it is unnecessary to trace "influence" when identical styles appear in them. The same explanation may be applied to the styles of Hume, Robertson, and Gibbon. All these writers played important parts in the movement toward synthesis; inevitably their styles would be similar, since they endeavored, as Buffon would say, to place the same order and movement in their thoughts. One can hardly denounce too severely the habit of discovering specific "influences" in the styles of various authors of this period, as, for instance, Hume upon Gibbon, Johnson upon Robertson, and so forth. It seems essential, rather, to derive the styles of all these men from a common source: the spread of the demand for scientific classification and precision. Probably some empty artificialities in Robertson, for instance, were engrafted from Johnson; but the basically regular style, the orderly, precise balance—all this comes from a deeper source, a scientific mode of thought.

Doubtless other influences were present in the evolution of this peculiar style; but the whole subject clearly lies beyond the scope of the present study. This examination attempts only to stress the fact that the style of the *Compendium* is, in large degree, determined by the deeper intellectual currents of the day; and that it can neither be explained nor appreciated unless it is studied with reference to the compiler's purpose and milieu.

44. See above, p. 18.

PART II

SMOLLETT'S LATER CREATIVE PERIOD

I

Travels through France and Italy

IT HAS frequently been noticed, as a typical tendency, that each of the three great novelists in the third quarter of the eighteenth century turned his hand to a travel-book. Sterne's *Sentimental Journey*, Fielding's *Journal of a Voyage to Lisbon*, and Smollett's *Travels through France and Italy* are constantly cited as examples of genius at work amid that great body of "voyages and travels" which flooded the age. But it is essential to examine with greater care the relationship of these three books to the contemporary trend in travel-literature—the trend toward orderly compilation of historical facts which I have described in the Introduction and illustrated by analysis of the *Compendium of Voyages*.

With this trend it is clear that the travels of Sterne and Fielding have practically no relation. Sterne, indeed, explicitly distinguishes himself from those travellers who "have attempted to swell the catalogues we have of pictures, statues, and churches"; he prides himself upon being instead a delineator of the human "temple," one who gives an account of "the weaknesses" of his own heart.[1] The *Sentimental Journey* can hardly be classed as a travel-book; like *Tristram Shandy*, it is *sui generis*. Fielding's *Journal* is hardly closer to the trend: partially, perhaps, because the author was so closely confined to shipboard that he had little opportunity for historical investigation. But Fielding's choice of materials is, I think, also determined by deeper causes which run counter to the trend of the century. In his Preface to the *Journal* he shows nothing but contempt for "that vast pile" of travel-books which collect concrete facts: a proper traveller, he says, should not record petty details, but should overlook "much of what he hath seen," except for such common matters as may be introduced "for some observations and reflections naturally resulting" therefrom.[2] As Cross has suggested, Fielding's idea of a travel-book, in theory and practice, is that of "a novel without a plot."[3] Accordingly, his *Journal* is largely composed of personal reflections and sketches of the interesting characters whom he met.

1. *A Sentimental Journey* (Everyman ed., London, 1930), pp. 89, 17.
2. *The Journal of a Voyage to Lisbon* (ed. Austin Dobson, London, 1892), pp. 17, 8, 19.
3. Wilbur L. Cross, *The History of Henry Fielding* (New Haven, 1918), III, 62.

Smollett's *Travels,* however, closely accords with the trend of the century, although this accordance has unfortunately been obscured by two unwarranted assumptions in current opinion of the work. The first assumption is found in Thomas Seccombe's declaration that the epistolary form of the *Travels* is not a literary device, such as was adopted by so many travellers of the day, but that, on the contrary, the letters "were actually written (at the places and dates prefixed to each epistle) and sent to personal friends for their private edification and amusement."[4] Smollett, he asserts, had always intended to revise these personal letters, but found himself so loaded with other tasks that the revision "was but very imperfectly carried out."[5] "On his return to England there is little doubt that he hastily collected the letters from his correspondents, and, in order to save time, sent them with scarcely an alteration to press."[6] These statements are based on a few intimate remarks found in only one-third of the letters; yet we are thus led to view the whole work as a hasty assortment of familiar epistles, scribbled off from random personal observations, and hurried to press "expressly for money down."[7] Such conjectures involve the second assumption, expressed by Herbert Read, who praises Smollett's book for "its complete freedom from the secondhand claptrap that almost every traveller repeats from his guidebook."[8] Thus Smollett's work, assumed to be entirely informal and original, is set apart from the trend of the period. But these assumptions need examination.

Smollett himself intimates that the epistolary form of the *Travels* is largely artificial, when, on November 13, 1765, about four months after his return to England, he says, "The observations I made in the course of my travels through France and Italy I have *thrown into* a series of Letters, which will make two volumes in Octavo."[9] This intimation is strongly supported by a personal letter which Smollett wrote to Dr. William Hunter from Nice on February 6, 1764.[10] The letter contains numerous facts and many complete phrases which are repeated in the *Travels;* but these repetitions are scattered through at least four different epistles[11] and combined with a huge amount of other material. Of course, it may

---

4. "Smelfungus Goes South," *Cornhill Magazine,* n.s. xi (1901), 195.
5. Introduction to *Travels* ("World's Classics" ed., Oxford, 1907), p. xiii.
6. *Cornhill Magazine,* n.s. xi (1901), 195.
7. *Travels* ("World's Classics" ed.), p. xvii.
8. Herbert Read, "Tobias Smollett," in *Reason and Romanticism* (London, 1926), p. 193.
9. *Letters,* p. 96 (my italics).   10. *Idem,* pp. 88–94.
11. See *Travels,* Letters xi, xii, xiii, xxi.

seem possible that the letters in the *Travels* which contain these echoes might have been sent to other correspondents; but closer consideration, I think, weakens this possibility. The letter to Hunter is colloquial and disorderly; it is a familiar letter, replete with marks of intimate friendship. But Letter XIII of the *Travels,* which contains most of the echoes of this letter to Hunter, is precise, orderly, and quite devoid of intimate touches; it is distinguished from personal correspondence by the regularity, polish, and succinctness of a practiced historian. These qualities, of course, could have been achieved by careful revision of personal letters; but, since the echoes of the letter to Hunter are so lost in a vast body of additional detail, one must, I think, conclude that Letter XIII is a new composition, not a recension. Certainly the verbal parallels are only such as would normally occur when one author treats the same topic twice.

Other strong evidence of elaborate expansion is found in the summary of the quarrel with Dr. Fizes which Smollett gives in the above letter to Hunter. Here he says, "The correspondence between us [i.e., Smollett and Fizes] was diverting enough—if ever I return to England, you shall see the original Papers."[12] It would appear from this statement that Smollett did not send a copy of the "Papers" to any medical friend in London, or he would have referred Hunter to it, as he later refers him to a letter in the hands of Dr. Macaulay.[13] Yet in Letter XI of the *Travels,* allegedly written to a medical friend of one of the Hunters,[14] Smollett carefully incorporates the whole correspondence with Fizes, extending to more than seven pages. One might argue that the original of this letter could have been sent to a medical friend in Scotland; but this possibility is weakened by a mass of evidence that other letters in the *Travels* are artificial.

Smollett was in Italy during September and October, 1764,[15] yet in his *Travels* we find two letters (XIX, XX) dated from Nice on October 10 and 22, 1764. The first of these contains a reference to sights apparently seen by Smollett at "Genoa, Florence, and Rome,"[16] while the second contains nearly a page of material taken from an Italian guide-book which Smollett did not purchase until after his arrival at Rome.[17] Letter XIX, moreover, is only arbitrarily separated from Letter XVIII, since the two give a consecutive discussion of provisions at Nice. The last letter begins with the

---

12. *Letters,* p. 89.   13. *Ibid.*   14. See *Works,* xi, 117.
15. Smollett says that he left for Italy "in the beginning of September" (*idem,* p. 257) and that the tour lasted "two months" (*idem,* p. 383).
16. *Idem,* p. 207.   17. See below, p. 74.

statement, "I wrote in May to Mr. B——," but is, strangely enough, dated "Nice, May 2, 1764." Smollett later noticed this slip and changed the date to September 2 in his own copy, which contains many manuscript additions and corrections now included in Seccombe's editions of the *Travels*.[18] In Letter XVII, dated "Nice, July 2, 1764," two months before Smollett made his Italian tour, he refers explicitly to a murderer whom he saw in Florence.[19] Thus, it seems certain that these letters are at least partially artificial.

Seccombe's insistence on the authenticity of all these letters leads him into a curious misinterpretation of the section on Nice: "Freed from the necessity of a systematic delineation," he declares, "Smollett rambles about Nice . . . with a stone in his pouch, and wherever a cockshy is available he takes full advantage of it."[20] This description of Smollett's procedure can hold for only two of the eleven letters on Nice: XX and XXI, which do consist largely of rambling observations on a great variety of topics. The nine other letters show little such disorder, and are, in fact, carefully organized to present what Smollett himself calls "a sort of natural History."[21] A thoroughly "systematic delineation" is just what Smollett originally aimed to achieve, for he declares, "I had once thoughts of writing a complete natural history of this town and county."[22] Although lack of health, books, and advice led him to abandon the original project, he did what he could toward this end.

The section on Nice opens formally with Letter XIII: "I am at last settled at Nice, and have leisure to give you some account of this very remarkable place." Then follows an introduction to the county and town of Nice in general, almost equivalent to the opening chapter of a "Natural History." The next letter is confined to description of the past and present state of the neighboring town of Villa Franca, together with reflections on Sardinian naval power which naturally arise from the account of the galleys stationed in this harbor. Letter XV, Smollett's dissertation on duelling, does

18. See *Works*, xi, and "World's Classics" edition. Smollett's copy of the *Travels*, now preserved in the British Museum, also corrects the puzzling introduction to Letter xxxviii, which is directed "To Dr. S—— at *Nice*" and dated from Turin, but opens with the statement, "I am just returned from an excursion to Turin, which is about thirty leagues from hence [i.e., Nice]." This contradiction certainly suggests that the letter is to some extent synthetic. I am greatly indebted to Professor Lewis M. Knapp for allowing me to see his ms. copy of these annotations in the *Travels*.

19. *Works*, xi, 188.   20. *Travels* ("World's Classics" ed.), pp. xliii–xliv.
21. *Letters*, p. 96.   22. *Works*, xi, 228.

not belong to this series, but Letter XVI is wholly concerned with a detailed account of antiquities to be seen in the vicinity of Nice. Letter XVII deals with the city proper: its history, fortifications, ruins, public institutions, government, religion, and nobility. The next two letters contain the orderly account of living conditions and provisions at Nice. After the two rambling letters mentioned above, Smollett returns to formality with a detailed account of the useful arts at Nice which extends through Letter XXII and most of Letter XXIII. The final letter of the group deals with climate and water, from the standpoint of a valetudinarian.

To be sure, the organization of these letters is by no means so rigid as that of a formal history: Smollett digresses and repeats on some occasions, and injects frequent personal reflections. But the letters on Nice are nearly void of intimate comments,[23] and show a marked regularity alien to familiar letters. It is evident, then, that Smollett, in his account of Nice, is by no means "freed from the necessity of a systematic delineation," but that, on the contrary, in spite of his epistolary form, he has taken pains to approximate the systematic presentation of a "Natural History."

Although the dates on these letters from Nice extend from January 15, 1764 to January 4, 1765, Smollett makes no mention in them of the Italian tour which he took during this year, except the inadvertent references already noted. Then, having finished his account of Nice at the end of the first volume of the original edition, he begins the second with an unbroken account of the Italian expedition, which occupies Letters XXV–XXXV, all dated from Nice between January 1 and April 2, 1765. These letters, though much less regular than those on Nice, are similarly almost void of the intimate remarks which one expects in personal correspondence.[24] Moreover, as the later portion of this chapter will show, in at least five of these letters Smollett appears to have supplemented his own observations by reference to certain books which could hardly have been available to him until after his return to England.[25] It therefore seems clear that for publication Smollett organized his remarks on Nice and Italy, which comprise half the book, into two separate and artificial series of letters.

I am not, of course, attempting to prove that actual correspondence had no influence on the *Travels*. Certainly a few of the letters contain allusions to letters received and references to various

23. For slight traces of personal correspondence see *Works*, XI, 164, 193, 210.
24. For traces of personal correspondence see *idem*, pp. 252, 291, 384.
25. See below, p. 87.

friends,[26] which seem to be authentic evidence of actual correspondence. It is quite possible that Smollett kept copies of his personal letters and in some cases (as, for instance, Letter XI, concerning Fizes) simply engrafted additional remarks to produce the published letter. On the other hand, some of these personal remarks may be only artifice, modelled upon memories of what he had written to his friends. It is impossible to be certain. One should remember, at any rate, that the publication of travels in epistolary form was not new to Smollett: in 1754 he prepared for the press Drummond's *Travels*, which appeared "in a series of letters." Since Smollett's revision of this work was clearly very extensive,[27] it seems probable that his task consisted of "throwing" Drummond's notes into the form of letters. Hence there is no need to postulate actual letters to account for the form of Smollett's own *Travels*.

There are, however, indications that some of these letters were composed during Smollett's stay at Nice. In the text of Letter XVIII Smollett says he has never seen swordfish; but in a footnote he adds, "Since I wrote the above letter, I have eaten several times of this fish."[28] Apparently he had the letter already prepared for publication, and did not wish to disturb the finished product. The same observation applies to Letter XXIV, which deals with the climate at Nice. The date of this letter, January 4, 1765, seems to be authentic, since, apparently following his register of the weather, he states, "From the sixteenth of November, 'till the fourth of January, we have had two and twenty days of heavy rain."[29] Then, in Letter XXXVII, dated April 2, 1765, Smollett adds further remarks upon the extraordinary rains "that prevailed from the middle of November, till the twentieth of March."[30]

It seems that Smollett spent much of his time at Nice in working up the copious notes which he must have taken there and during his tour in Italy. In a few cases personal letters may have provided a skeleton for the final product. Perhaps a few of the letters may even have been sent to correspondents largely as they now appear; if so, however, they must have been written with the public in mind rather than the original recipient. But most of the letters were apparently not sent at all in their present form: they seem to represent notes prepared for publication at Nice and after the return to England. This, at least, is certain: the letters in Smollett's

26. See *Works*, XI, 16–19, 27, 54, 56, 83, 117–18, 414.
27. See above, p. 6.   28. *Works*, XI, 197.   29. *Idem*, pp. 245–6.
30. *Idem*, p. 391. See also below, p. 85, for similar treatment of antiquities.

Travels do not represent personal letters sent to press "with scarcely an alteration."

A second misconception is contained in the assumption that the large fund of learning distributed throughout the *Travels* comes straight from Smollett's own knowledge. Smollett, indeed, has taken every care to give us this impression by implication, and, in the midst of his account of Rome, explicitly declares, "I protest the remarks are all my own."[31] Thus the reader is naturally much impressed with the learning displayed in the following passage, in which Smollett corrects a dubious statement made by a popular guide-book:

The Grand Tour says, that within four miles of Rome you see a tomb on the roadside, said to be that of Nero, ... I did see such a thing more like a common grave-stone, than the tomb of an emperor. But we are informed by Suetonius, that the dead body of Nero, who slew himself at the villa of his freedman, was by the care of his two nurses and his concubine Atta, removed to the sepulchre of the Gens Domitia, ... His tomb was even distinguished by an epitaph, which has been preserved by Gruterus. Giacomo Alberici tells us very gravely in his History of the Church, that a great number of devils, who guarded the bones of this wicked emperor, took possession, in the shape of black ravens, of a walnut-tree, which grew upon the spot; from whence they insulted every passenger, until pope Paschal II. in consequence of a solemn fast and a revelation, went thither in procession with his court and cardinals, cut down the tree, burned it to ashes, which, with the bones of Nero, were thrown into the Tyber: . . . .[32]

31. *Works*, xi, 331.
32. *Idem*, pp. 307–8; cf. *Roma Antica*, ii, 129–31:
". . . il Sepolcro de Domizj . . . in cui fù sepolto Nerone, dopo essersi con le proprie mani ucciso nella Villa di Faonte suo Liberto . . . . come Svetonio fà fede, il Cadavere di lui da Egloge, ed Alessandra sue Nutrici, e da Atta sua Concubina fù quì sepolto nel sopraciglio del Colle degl' Ortuli, entro il Sepolcro della Famiglia Domizia, dove anche erano riposte le Ceneri de suoi maggiori; e vi fù posto il seguente Epitaffio, registrato dal Grutero. . . .
"Da tal Collina poi cadendo col tempo in questo piano la Terra, vi si radicò sopra un grand' Albero di Noce, che occupato da Demonj, in forma di tanti neri Corvi, li quali infestavano con insulti diversi chiunque di quà passava; Pasquale II. nel 1099. doppo 3. giorni di digiuno, e doppo ancora molte Orazioni, che fece, avuta rivelazione, che quei maligni Spiriti custodivano le ossa di sì scelerato Imperadore, che ivi sotto erano nascoste, coll' accompagnamento della sua Corte venne processionalmente a questo luogo. Esso stesso fù il primo a percuotere coll' Accetta un tal Albero, che restò in breve dalle Persone a ciò destinate dalle radici tagliato, e dato poi alle fiamme, nel Tevere vicino furono gettate le ceneri, e le ossa dell' empio Nerone alli venti sparse, e dissipate . . . . come racconta diffusamente Giacomo Alberici nel suo Compendio Istorico della Chiesa presente."
For *The Grand Tour*, see below, pp. 86–7.

Smollett, however, has freely translated all this learning, without acknowledgment, from a guide-book entitled *Roma Antica, e Moderna* (3 vols., Rome, 1750), which he tells us he purchased shortly after his arrival in Rome.[33]

In fact, it soon appears upon investigation that a total of about thirteen pages of learned material has thus been plucked from *Roma Antica* and sprinkled throughout Smollett's account of Rome —to say nothing of nearly a page on ancient Roman festivals which he has cleverly copied from the same book into his account of Nice.[34] And these are only facts which can be clearly traced: doubtless many general remarks were also suggested by this guide-book. Since *Roma Antica* thus accounts for most of the learned materials on Rome, it is evident that Smollett's reputation as a scholar has received a serious blow.

But if he loses in one direction, he gains in another, for his use of this guide-book enhances our appreciation of his industry, enthusiasm, and ingenuity. *Roma Antica* consists of over 1,800 octavo pages in small print, crammed with heavy facts; yet, though Smollett's knowledge of Italian seems to have been only recently acquired at Nice,[35] his borrowings indicate that he perused practically every page of the work. Smollett always professed an intense interest in all things ancient: his eagerness to see the Pont du Garde he describes as "the strongest emotions of impatience that I had ever known";[36] and of his Italian tour he declares:

I had a most eager curiosity to see the antiquities of Florence and Rome: I longed impatiently to view those wonderful edifices, statues, and pictures, which I had so often admired in prints and descriptions. I felt an enthusiastic ardor to tread that very classical ground which had been the scene of so many great atchievements; . . . .[37]

Such declarations are borne out by the invincible interest, displayed throughout the *Travels*, in every detail of antiquity which he could crowd into his brain. He scoured this particular guide-book for every fact which might illuminate the remains which he viewed; and he likewise studied its many additional pages dealing with ancient Roman customs. This zeal was by no means motivated only by a plan to publish his observations, for the facts given in

---

33. See *Works*, XI, 313. The only other reference to this guide-book occurs in *Works*, XI, 353, where he calls it by the subtitle, *Descrizione di Roma*. The third volume deals with Roman history and customs, and hence bears the title, *Descrizione Delli Riti, Guerre Piu' Celebri, e Famiglie Piu' Illustri Degl' Antichi Romani.*

34. *Works*, XI, 218–19; cf. *Roma Antica*, III, 103–5. Smollett has derived some details here from another source.

35. See *Letters*, p. 92.   36. *Works*, XI, 105.   37. *Idem*, pp. 252–3.

the *Travels* from *Roma Antica* form only a tiny portion of the pages which he must have read.

Indeed, the freshness of these borrowed details in the *Travels* seems to be due to the fact that they were not read originally for the primary purpose of compilation. To Smollett's credit be it said, we have in his *Travels* no wholesale pilfering in an attempt to give another "compendium" of the curiosities at Rome. We may believe him when he declares, speaking of his account of Rome, "I have described nothing but what actually fell under my own observation,"[38] since the borrowed materials are nearly always merged with descriptions and critical judgments which appear to be entirely original. There also seems to be some truth in Smollett's statement that he is giving his observations on Rome "just as they occur to my remembrance,"[39] for these remarks do not show that careful grouping of related topics which marked the "Natural History" of Nice. That is not to say that the account of Rome is disorderly—it possesses a different, and, I think, a more artistic order, produced by the free flow of association, instead of the arbitrary arrangements of labored compilation. This free flow was possible here because Smollett was not attempting a complete account of external facts, but was primarily interested in presenting personal dissertations, during which the facts observed or read occur *en passant*, as evidence.

Thus, Smollett's observations on the antiquities of Rome are not simply the dull catalogues found in most travel-books—they are often vital and fluent discussions of the ancient way of life. For example, instead of merely describing the circuses and naumachia, he uses facts from *Roma Antica* as proof that "the antient Romans were but indifferently skilled and exercised either in horsemanship or naval armaments":

The Circus Maximus was but three hundred yards in breadth. A good part of this was taken up by the spina, or middle space, adorned with temples, statues, and two great obelisks; as well as by the euripus, or canal, made by order of Julius Caesar, to contain crocodiles, and other aquatic animals, which were killed occasionally. This was so large, that Heliogabalus, having filled it with excellent wine, exhibited naval engagements in it, for the amusement of the people. It surrounded three sides of the square, so that the whole extent of the race did not much exceed an English mile; and when Probus was at the expence of filling the plain of it with fir-trees to form a wood for the chace of wild beasts, I question much if this forest was more extensive than the plantation in St. James's Park, on the south side of the canal: now I leave you to judge

38. *Works,* XI, 362.   39. *Idem,* p. 331.

what ridicule a king of England would incur by converting this part of the park into a chace for any species of animals which are counted game in our country.[40]

All this erudition has been extracted and rearranged from the four-page account of the Circus Maximus in *Roma Antica*. He then goes on to ridicule the naumachia by declaring that the galleys "were not so large as common fishing-smacks," and supports his contention by learned references:

Suetonius in the reign of Domitian, speaking of these naumachia, says, "*Edidit navales pugnas, pene justarum classium, effosso, et circumducto juxta Tyberim Lacu, atque inter maximas imbres prospectavit.*" This artificial lake was not larger than the piece of water in Hyde-Park; and yet the historian says, it was almost large enough for real or intire fleets.[41]

This material from Suetonius, of course, is all taken from the account of Domitian's naumachia in *Roma Antica*.

To work all these facts into a long discussion, Smollett obviously must have had them fairly well in mind; and yet the verbal similarities show that he transcribed some materials from the guidebook. It seems likely that during his tour he kept a commonplace book, in which he entered facts from books or observation according to topics. This hypothesis is strongly supported by the long section in which he attempts to prove, by an astonishing array of facts, that the ancient Romans "were a very frowzy generation."[42] Among other facts in support of this opinion, Smollett collects details from pages 127, 343, 356, and 357 of the third volume of *Roma Antica*. It seems unlikely that he could have thus marshalled these widely separated materials without having previously collected them under one heading in some sort of journal. Such aggregation of details occurs frequently throughout the account of Rome.[43]

40. *Works*, XI, 340–1. Cf. *Roma Antica*, I, 451–4:
"[Il Circo Massimo] . . . si estendeva . . . in larghezza piedi 960. . . . Trà li Portici, ed il vacuo, era da tre lati l'Euripo, cioè un canale d'acqua largo, e profondo, aggiuntovi da Giulio Cesare, allo scrivere di Svetonio, e quì furono uccisi Coccodrilli, ed altri Animali aquatici; leggendosi ancora in Lampridio, che Eliogabalo empì quest' Euripo di buonissimo vino, per celebrarvi Battaglie, e Corsi Navali. . . . Lo spazio, che era tramezzo, chiamato Spina, era talmente diviso, che vi si correva d'intorno; . . . . [Then follows a description, over a page in length, from which, and from the illustration facing p. 451, Smollett derived the passage, "adorned with . . . obelisks"; then, near the end of the description, comes:] Scrive Vopisco, avervi Probo fatta una Caccia singolarissima; talmente che trasportativi moltissimi Abeti verdeggianti, l'aspetto del Circo si vidde tramutato in una Selva, per la quale scorrevano infinite Fiere, perseguitate da Cacciatori, e Mastini."

41. *Works*, XI, 341–2; cf. *Roma Antica*, II, 151.
42. See *Works*, XI, 317–18.   43. See below, p. 80, n. 50.

In many other places, of course, Smollett has simply supplemented his own observations on a particular object by reference to *Roma Antica*, perhaps by use of the index. For example, in speaking of the Mausoleum Augusti, he says:

Part of the walls is standing, and the terraces are converted into garden-ground. In viewing these ruins, I remembered Virgil's pathetic description of Marcellus, who was here intombed.

> *Quantos ille virum, magnum mavortis ad urbem.*
> *Campus aget gemitus, vel que Tyberine, videbis*
> *Funera, cum tumulum preter labere recentem.*

The beautiful poem of Ovid *de Consolatione ad Liviam*, written after the ashes of Augustus and his nephew Marcellus, of Germanicus, Agrippa, and Drusus, were deposited in this mausoleum, concludes with these lines, which are extremely tender:

> *Claudite jam Parcae nimium reserata sepulchra;*
> *Claudite, plus justo, jam domus ista patet!*[44]

The first sentence is Smollett's own, but the origin of the second is suspect: the reason, apparently, for remembering the passage from Vergil is the following sentence in *Roma Antica:* "Il Fulvio, ed il Marliani raccolgono dal sesto libro di Virgilio, che prima di ogni altro, vi fosse stato sepolto Marcello Nipote di Augusto." The rest of the material is taken bodily from a section in *Roma Antica* immediately following this sentence; except that Smollett has chosen to attribute this poem of uncertain authorship to Ovid, instead of following *Roma Antica's* attribution to Albinovanus Pedo.[45]

In his accounts of the various museums of Rome, it seems that Smollett, instead of making his own lists of curiosities, has in some cases merely marked the most important objects and then copied off his list directly from the guide-book. The following notes on sculptures in the Villa Pinciana, for instance, could easily have been taken down by Smollett himself, but the verbal similarities show that most of the passage is simply translated:

. . . I was much struck with a Bacchus, and the death of Meleager, represented on an antient sepulchre. There is also an admirable	. . . un Bacco sopra un antico Sepolcro, dov' è intagliata egregiamente la morte di Meleagro . . . un Sileno bellissimo, che tiene un

44. *Works*, XI, 325–6.

45. *Roma Antica*, II, 116–17: ". . . e Tacito nel 3. degli Annali chiaramente accenna, che vi furono poste anche le ceneri di Germanico. Vi furono parimente collocati (oltre Augusto) Agrippa, Druso, ed altri, menzionati in un Epigramma di Pedone Albinovano *de consolatione ad Liviam,* dove egli conchiude così: [quotation follows, as above]." Smollett goes slightly astray in following this passage; the poem does not conclude with these lines; they occur in the middle.

statue of Silenus, with the infant Bacchus in his arms . . . a curious Moor of black marble, with a shirt of white alabaster; a finely proportioned bull of black marble also, standing upon a table of alabaster; a black gipsey with a head, hands, and feet of brass; . . . and a Daphne changing into laurel at the approach of Apollo. On the base of this figure, are the two following elegant lines, written by pope Urban VIII. in his younger years.

> Quisquis amans sequitur fugi-
> tivae gaudia formae,
> Fronde manus implet, baccas
> vel carpit amaras.

Bacco fanciullo tra le braccia . . . un Moro di pietra negra con camicia di Alabastro . . . un bel Toro di marmo negro sopra una Tavola di Alabastro . . . una Zingara di marmo negro con testa, mani, e piedi di bronzo . . . una Dafne, che cangiasi in Alloro, seguitata da Apollo . . . Leggonsi nella base i seguenti versi, che furono composti dal Pontefice Urbano VIII. ne suoi anni giovanili: [identical quotation follows].[46]

Details from *Roma Antica,* indeed, turn up in every possible form. Sometimes the debt is as general as the following summary, which seems to be gleaned from the nine-page account of the Campus Martius which the guide-book gives from a great variety of sources:

The space between the bridge and Porta del Popolo, on the right-hand, which is now taken up with gardens and villas, was part of the antient Campus Martius, where the comitiae were held; and where the Roman people inured themselves to all manner of exercises: it was adorned with porticos, temples, theatres, baths, circi, basilicae, obelisks, columns, statues, and groves. Authors differ in their opinions about the extent of it; but as they all agree that it contained the Pantheon, the Circus Agonis, now the Piazza Navona, the Bustum and Mausoleum Augusti, great part of the modern city must be built upon the antient Campus Martius.[47]

Finally, in other places, passages are translated almost literally; the longest example of this type of debt is Smollett's three-and-a-half-page dissertation on the baths of ancient Rome,[48] which is the most dazzling display of learning in all the *Travels,* and which is almost entirely a translation from *Roma Antica.* The following page from this section shows the most startling bits of plagiarism:

46. *Works,* xi, 330; *Roma Antica,* ii, 231–3. I have changed the order of the latter list for convenience of comparison.
47. *Works,* xi, 308–9; cf. *Roma Antica,* ii, 89–97.
48. *Works,* xi, 343–6.

True it is, they had baths of cool water for the summer: but in general they used it milk-warm, and often perfumed: they likewise indulged in vapour-baths, in order to enjoy a pleasing relaxation, which they likewise improved with odoriferous ointments. The thermae consisted of a great variety of parts and conveniences; the natationes, or swimming places; the portici, where people amused themselves in walking, conversing, and disputing together, . . . ; the basilicae, where the bathers assembled, before they entered, and after they came out of the bath; the atria, or ample courts, adorned with noble colonnades of Numidian marble and oriental granite; the ephibia, where the young men inured themselves to wrestling and other exercises; the frigidaria, or places kept cool by a constant draught of air, promoted by the disposition and number of the windows; the calidaria, where the water was warmed for the baths; the platanones, or delightful groves of sycamore; the stadia, for the performances of the athletae; the exedrae, or resting-places, provided with seats for those that were weary; the palestrae, where every one chose that exercise which pleased him best; the gymnasia, where poets, orators, and philosophers recited their works, and harangued for diversion; the eleotesia, where the fragrant oils and ointments were kept for the use of the bathers; and the conisteria, where the wrestlers were smeared with sand before they engaged. Of the thermae in Rome, some were mercenary, and some opened

. . . poichè queste erano alcuni luoghi vastissimi, con camere infinite fatte a volta, e destinate ad usi diversi, nelle quali con acque tepide, e spesse volte odorifere, lavansi li Romani, overo con i soli vapori caldi ristoravano deliziosamente i loro corpi ne' tempi jemali, ungendoli con olii, ed unguenti prelibatissimi; e similmente con acque fresche li rinfrescavano negli estivi. . . .

Le loro parti principali erano moltissime . . . : le *Natazioni,* le quali erano amplissimi luoghi destinati per il nuoto . . . li *Portici,* per i quali facevano il passeggio: le *Basiliche,* dove radunavasi il popolo prima d'entrare, o dopo l'uscire dalli bagni . . . li *Atrii,* overo Cortili grandissimi, ornati con nobili colonne di marmo Numidico, e di Granito, dall' uno, e l'altro lato: li *Ephebei,* cioè luoghi assegnati per gli esercizj della Gioventù: li *Frigidarii,* i quali erano certi posti, signoreggiati da' venti, medianti spesse, e larghe fenestre: li *Calidarii,* dove si riscaldavano le acque: li *Platanoni,* cioè amenissime Selve, formate con Platani, ed arbori consimili: li *Stadii,* ne' quali si esercitavano li Atleti: le *Exedre,* luoghi destinati per sedere: le *Palestre,* nelle quali ciascuno attendeva a quell' esercizio, che più li gustava: li *Gymnasii,* dove i Filosofi, Rettorici, e Poeti praticavano, per divertimento, i loro studj: li *Eleotesii,* dove si conservavano olii, ed unguenti diversi, per ungersi: e finalmente li *Conisterii,* ne' quali si aspergevano i Lottatori di arena, prima di combattere. . . .

Furono le Terme di varie sorti, cioè publiche, e private, mercena-

gratis. Marcus Agrippa, when he was edile, opened one hundred and seventy private baths, for the use of the people. In the public baths, where money was taken, each person paid a quadrans, about the value of our halfpenny, as Juvenal observes,
"*Caedere Sylvano porcum, quadrante lavari.*"
But after the hour of bathing was past, it sometimes cost a great deal more, according to Martial,
"*Balnea post decimam, lasso centumque petuntur*
"*Quadrantes—*"

rie, e gratuite. . . . M. Agrippa nel tempo della sua Edilità esibì gratuitamente al Popolo cento settanta Terme, o bagni privati. . . .
Nelle Terme publiche, e venali si pagava dalla Plebe un solo quadrante, che era una moneta di vilissimo prezzo, come asserisce Giovenale nella Setira 6.
Caedere Sylvano Porcum, Quadrante lavari.
Questa moneta nell' ore tarde, cioè dopo l'ora decima, non era sufficiente . . . come accenna Marziale nel 10. libro.
Balnea post decimam, lasso centumque petuntur Quadrantes &c.[49]

Smollett, however, in using *Roma Antica* did not often resort to such wholesale plundering. Whenever the impulse prompted, he included whatever details appealed to his interests or seemed relevant to a given argument. He did not copy off descriptions of things which he had not seen; nor did he even try to include accounts of all that he had seen. Since Smollett exercises much more restraint in his borrowing than most travellers of the time, and since the borrowed details are often lifted from a dead catalogue into vital, pungent discussion, certainly one cannot very severely reprobate his obvious lack of candor.[50]

With eyes opened by Smollett's use of *Roma Antica*, one is not surprised to discover that Smollett likewise used a guide-book to

49. *Works*, xi, 343–4; *Roma Antica*, i, 481–3.

50. Other passages indebted to *Roma Antica*, in addition to those already mentioned, may be found by consulting the following references (all pages in *Travels* [*T*] listed according to *Works*, xi): cf. *T*, 308, lines 13–16, 22–4: *RA*, ii, 128; *T*, 311, lines 3–13: *RA*, ii, 121–4; *T*, 333, lines 21, 24–6: *RA*, i, 57; *T*, 334, lines 27–8: *RA*, i, 71; *T*, 335, line 31–p. 336, line 2, lines 4, 12–32: *RA*, i, 70, 489–98; *T*, 337, lines 16–19: *RA*, i, 49, 336; *T*, 338, lines 1–9, 16–20: *RA*, i, 422–3; *T*, 339, lines 4–5, 9–13: *RA*, i, 399, 428; *T*, 340, lines 7–16: *RA*, i, 424–5; *T*, 343, lines 2–15, line 25–p. 346, line 7: *RA*, ii, 601, i, 284–5, 481–7; *T*, 346, lines 12–19: *RA*, ii, 635–6; *T*, 347, lines 8–15, line 21–p. 348, line 7: *RA*, ii, 640–2, 645–6; *T*, 348, lines 15–25: *RA*, i, 254–5; *T*, 348, line 26–p. 349, line 2, lines 5–19: *RA*, i, 268–9; *T*, 349, line 21–p. 350, line 17: *RA*, ii, 585–6; *T*, 353, lines 3–12: *RA*, i, 83; *T*, 354, lines 1–3, 23–8: *RA*, i, 98; *T*, 355, lines 2–3: *RA*, ii, 339; *T*, 355, lines 6–14: *RA*, i, 344; *T*, 355, lines 30–1: *RA*, i, 353; *T*, 356, lines 3–13: *RA*, i, 355, 360; *T*, 357, lines 11–13: *RA*, i, 347; *T*, 357, line 20–p. 358, line 2, lines 13–16: *RA*, i, 615–17.

supplement his observations on the Uffizi Gallery in Florence. In this description he thrice cites Bianchi, the curator of the museum, as an authority;[51] but he leaves the reader to infer that his knowledge of Bianchi's opinions was picked up during tours of the gallery. The truth is that he has taken a total of about three and a quarter pages, or nearly half this account, from Giuseppe Bianchi's publication, *Ragguaglio Delle Antichità e Rarità che si Conservano Nella Galleria Mediceo-Imperiale di Firenze* (Part I, Florence, 1759), which was probably on sale at the gallery. Another quarter-page of material from this source appears in Smollett's account of Rome.[52]

Here again, despite the little material used in the *Travels,* Smollett's curiosity evidently led him to study all the 234 pages in Bianchi's account. Although the facts from Bianchi are mingled flexibly with original observations, Smollett's use of this source is not so free as his use of *Roma Antica;* for he is giving chiefly a straightforward account of various sculptures in this gallery. The nature of his debt is typically illustrated by the following learned discussion:

. . . what pleased me best of all the statues in the Tribuna was the Arrotino, commonly called the Whetter, and generally supposed to represent a slave, who in the act of whetting a knife, overhears the conspiracy of Cataline. . . . The marquis de Maffei has justly observed that Sallust, in his very circumstantial detail of that conspiracy, makes no mention of any such discovery. Neither does it appear, that the figure is in the act of whetting, the stone which he holds in one hand being rough and unequal, no ways resembling a whetstone. Others alledge it represents Milico, the freedman of Scaevinus, who conspired against the life of Nero, and gave his poignard to be whetted to Milico, who presented it to the emperor, with an account of the conspiracy: . . . . Signore

L'opinione volgarissima di suo significato è, che sia fatta in memoria d'un tal uomo del mestiero di pulire, e arrotare i ferri da taglio, il quale non considerato per sua viltade, ebbe però l'attenzione d'ascoltare chi parlava della congiura di Catilina, e discopersela al Senato, ... Il Cavalier Maffei riflette, che Salustio diligentissimo scrittore di quel fatto, punto non parla di cotale avvenimento, ... E di vero la nostra statua . . . non arruota il ferro, tenendolo anzi fermo collè due dita sopra del marmo, che non ha figura di ruota, nè d'altra pietra da affilare, ma irregolare di forma, e di grossezza, un sasso fatto a caso rassembra. Altri hanno detto, che rappresenti Milico discopritore della gran congiura ordita contro Nerone da' principali uomini di Roma. . . . Lo argu-

---

51. See *Works,* xi, 294, 295, 297.
52. See *idem,* p. 319, line 27–p. 320, line 4; cf. Bianchi, pp. 113, 115.

Bianchi . . . thinks the statue represents the augur Attius Navius, who cut a stone with a knife, at the command of Tarquinius Priscus. This conjecture seems to be confirmed by a medallion of Antoninus Pius, inserted by Vaillant among his Numismata Prestantiora, on which is delineated nearly such a figure as this in question, with the following legend, "Attius Navius genuflexus ante Tarquinium Priscum cotem cultro discidit." He owns indeed that in the statue, the augur is not distinguished either by his habit or emblems; . . . .

mentarono costoro . . . dall' avere letto in Tacito, che Scevino . . . chiese l'onore di uccidere il Tiranno con un famoso pugnale venuto di Toscana, . . . lo diede a Milico, che arrotare lo facesse, e il traditore portollo a Nerone. . . . Notissimo è il fatto, che presso Tito Livio si legge dell' Augure Arzio Navio, il quale alla presenza, e per comandamento di Tarquinio Prisco tagliò una pietra con un coltello. . . . Giovanni Vaillant nell' Indice de' Medaglioni latini da lui veduti, aggiunto nell' ultima impressione di Parigi al suo libro intitolato *Numismata Praestantiora*, porta un medaglione di Antonino Pio del Tesoro Regio coll' iscrizione NAVIVS, e col rovescio rappresentante questa storia, e lo descrive: *Attius Navius genuflexus ante Tarquinium Priscum cotem cultro discidit*, ... Sarà dunque considerato non esser dicevole per un Augure qual era Navio la nudità; non vedersi il lituo; e il ferro, che tiene in mano non essere un rasoio come lo chiama Livio: *Novacula*.[53]

Smollett followed much the same procedure in his account of Nîmes. Here he admits that he "was presented with a pamphlet, containing an account of Nismes and its antiquities, which every stranger buys,"[54] and later he refers to a statue mentioned in the "history of the antiquities of Nismes";[55] but nowhere does he indicate the fact that he has transcribed a total of about four pages from a pamphlet by the Abbé Valette de Travessac, entitled *Abrégé de l'Histoire de la Ville de Nismes* (fourth ed., Avignon, 1760). These apparently original remarks on the Maison Carrée, for instance, are little more than translation:

53. *Works*, XI, 296–7; Bianchi, pp. 199–202. Other passages indebted to Bianchi may be found by consulting the following references: cf. *T*, 293, lines 1–6: *B*, 55, 61; *T*, 293, lines 14–19: *B*, 51–2, 82; *T*, 293, lines 24–32: *B*, 86–7; *T*, 294, lines 7–15: *B*, 134–6; *T*, 294, line 19–p. 295, line 1: *B*, 59–61; *T*, 295, lines 6–8, 13–16, line 26–p. 296, line 9: *B*, 192–6.

54. *Works*, XI, 107.   55. *Idem*, p. 112.

They [the columns] are all of the Corinthian order, fluted and embellished with capitals of the most exquisite sculpture: the frize and cornice are much admired, and the foliage is esteemed inimitable. The proportions of the building are so happily united, as to give it an air of majesty and grandeur, which the most indifferent spectator cannot behold without emotion. . . . Cardinal Alberoni declared, that it was a jewel that deserved a cover of gold to preserve it from external injuries. An Italian painter, perceiving a small part of the roof repaired by modern French masonry, tore his hair, and exclaimed in a rage, "Zounds! what do I see? harlequin's hat on the head of Augustus!"

. . . toutes ces colonnes sont canelées, & enrichies de chapiteaux d'une sculpture très-délicate; la frise & la corniche font aussi l'admiration des connoisseurs; . . . le feuillage est ce qu'il y a de plus inimitable. . . . Il résulte de ses proportions un air de grandeur & de majesté qui vous pénètre l'ame. . . . le Cardinal Alberoni trouvoit qu'il y manquoit une chose, *une boëte d'or pour le défendre des injures de l'air.* Un Peintre pensoit de même en parlant différemment: il considéroit ce monument des fenêtres d'une maison voisine, & ayant apperçu sur la couverture quelque peu de maçonnerie moderne, *ah! ah! s'écria-t'il avec tout le feu de sa profession, je vois le chapeau d'Arlequin sur la tête d'Auguste.*[56]

But notice that Smollett has perfected Alberoni's statement by adding the word "jewel," and that he has injected vigor and personality into the anecdote of the painter.

Since most of the erudition in Smollett's accounts of Rome, Florence, and Nîmes thus proves to be derived from guide-books, one may well suspect that personal investigation and learning did not provide all his facts concerning the antiquities near Nice. The suspicion is correct. Somehow Smollett happened upon an obscure Latin treatise by one Pietro Gioffredo (Petrus Jofredus), entitled *Nicaea Civitas*, first printed at Turin in 1658, and republished by J. G. Graevius in his *Thesaurus Antiquitatum et Historiarum Italiae* (vol. IX, pt. 6, 1723). It appears that he consulted this work at Nice, for in one letter he seems to have copied from it a passage on ancient aqueducts before he personally investigated them.[57] Since it does not appear in the list of books which Smollett shipped to France, he apparently found it somewhere in Nice, despite his

56. *Works*, XI, 112; *Abrégé*, pp. 35–6. For more borrowing from *Abrégé*, see the following references: cf. *T*, 106, lines 19–27, 107, lines 4–7: *A*, 28–9; *T*, 107, lines 8–13: *A*, 22–3; *T*, 107, lines 27–9: *A*, 18–20; *T*, 108, lines 14–18: *A*, 25–7; *T*, 109, lines 5–9: *A*, 66–8; *T*, 109, line 22–p. 110, line 4: *A*, 30–2; *T*, 110, lines 12–29, 111, lines 1–13: *A*, 39–41; *T*, 111, line 19–p. 112, line 4: *A*, 38–9, 33–5; *T*, 112, lines 28–30: *A*, 80–1.
57. See below, p. 85.

complaints that there are no booksellers in the place, and "no public, nor private libraries, that afford any thing worth perusing."[58] At any rate, without the slightest acknowledgment, he has taken from Gioffredo a total of about seven and one half pages, including some of the most impressive erudition in the *Travels*.

Smollett's use of Gioffredo is ingeniously deceptive. Speaking of the ancient city of Cemenelion, near Nice, he declares, "That it was the seat of a Roman praeses, is proved by the two following inscriptions, which are still extant." Then, after giving two inscriptions which the reader is left to assume that Smollett has copied from the originals, he adds, as a bit of gratuitous information from his store:

You know, the praeses of a Roman province had the *jus figendi clavi*, the privilege of wearing the *latus clavus*, the *gladius, infula, praetexta, purpura & annulus aureus:* he had his *vasa, vehicula, apparitores*, Scipio *eburneus, & sella curulis*.[59]

Now Smollett may at some time have seen the original inscriptions, but the whole section in the text is certainly lifted from Gioffredo, who quotes these inscriptions to prove the same point, and follows them, a few lines later, with the same account of presidential insignia.[60]

Similar jugglery is revealed in his long account of the Trophaea Augusti, near Monaco:

There is a description of what it was, in an Italian manuscript, by which it appears to have been a beautiful edifice of two stories, adorned with columns and trophies in alto relievo, with a statue of Augustus Caesar on the top. On one of the sides was an inscription, some words of which are still legible, upon the fragment of a marble found close to the old building: but the whole is preserved in Pliny, who gives it in these words. lib. iii. cap. 20. [an eighteen-line inscription follows].

Pliny, however, is mistaken in placing this inscription on a trophy near the *Augusta praetoria*, now called *Aosta*, in Piedmont: where, indeed, there is a triumphal arch, but no inscription.[61]

This "Italian manuscript" is actually one which is printed by Gioffredo, who also quotes the inscription from Pliny, "*lib. III. cap. xx.*," and gives the correction which Smollett has summarized in

---

58. *Works*, XI, 224; see Eugène Joliat, *Smollett et la France* (Paris, 1935), pp. 251–2.

59. *Works*, XI, 151–2.

60. Gioffredo (Graevius ed.), pp. 18–19:
"Praesidum, qui sedem habuere aliquandò *Cemenelione*, sicut & aliorum per *Romanorum* Provincias, potestas, & insignia varia apud Cassiod. *lib.* vi. *epist.* & alios. Jus scilicèt figendi clavi, lati clavi, gladii gestandi, infularum, praetextae, purpurae, anuli aurei, vasorum, equorum, vehiculorum, apparitorum, scipionis eburnei, sellae curulis, & similium."

61. *Works*, XI, 180–1.

his last sentence.[62] Smollett has likewise compiled from Gioffredo a most erudite discussion of the name and history of Villa Franca, including quotations from Strabo, Ptolemy, and Lucan.[63] Even Smollett's first account of the aqueducts near Nice is largely a translation:

Of the aqueduct that conveyed water to the town, I can say very little, but that it was scooped through a mountain: that this subterranean passage was discovered some years ago, by removing the rubbish which choaked it up: that the people penetrating a considerable way, by the help of lighted torches, found a very plentiful stream of water flowing in an aqueduct, as high as an ordinary man, arched over head, and lined with a sort of cement. They could not, however, trace this stream to its source; and it is again stopped up with earth and rubbish.

Vidimus ipsi nostro aevo, quod multis saeculis, Patribus atque Avis caelarat aggesta humus, per montis interiora longo regionis tractu, foraminato per cuniculos saxo, adeò ut ingressis, praeeuntibus facibus, incolis nondùm primaria apparuerit scaturigo, largè defluentes uberes rivos, ac uberiores futuros, quandò egesto eo, quod eosdem incolas ulteriùs progredi vetuit, limo, purgetur usque ad sui exordium aquaeductus. Id certè opus concameratis fornicibus, atque ad hominis altitudinem, muro hinc indè bitumine interlito, continuum, tale est, ut veterum in aquis vestigandis solertiam admirari nos cogat.[64]

Later, of course, Smollett made an excursion in which he collected two pages of original observations on this aqueduct;[65] but apparently at the time when the above passage was written he had not yet viewed the structure. Aside from this passage, however, Smollett made very little use of the descriptive portions of Gioffredo's work; indeed, the great quantity of original material on other antiquities near Nice proves that Smollett examined them with great exactitude—even going so far as to measure the amphitheater with packthread.[66] Nevertheless, again, most of the erudition in the account of Nice did not really belong to Smollett.[67]

62. See Gioffredo, pp. 44–7. The long and learned footnote in Works, XI, 181, is likewise almost wholly from Gioffredo, p. 49.

63. See Works, XI, 163, lines 8–22, line 29–p. 164, line 15; cf. Gioffredo, pp. 38–42.

64. Works, XI, 154–5; Gioffredo, p. 22.

65. See Works, XI, 176–7.   66. Idem, p. 178.

67. For other passages indebted to Gioffredo, see the following references: cf. T, 140, lines 14–20: G, 27; T, 151, lines 12–13, 19–21: G, 18, 19, 8, 13; T, 153, lines 1–20: G, 19–20, 78–86; T, 153, lines 28–33, 154, lines 5–7: G, 23; T, 154, lines 7–13: G, 26; T, 154, lines 19–21, 24–7: G, 22; T, 155, lines 19–26: G, 35–6; T, 180, line 8–p. 182, line 2: G, 44–9; T, 184, lines 1–13: G, 5–6; T, 184, lines 13–18, 20–1, 185, lines 3–5, 7–9: G, 37–8; T, 186, lines 22–32: G, 38. See also description of Antibes, Works, XI, 405, lines 12–16: cf. G, 9.

These four books, two in Italian, one in French, and one in Latin, thus account for the bulk of the learned materials and a small part of the other observations in Smollett's *Travels*. But there is also evidence that he consulted several additional works available to him in English. In the course of the *Travels* Smollett refers four times to the "Grand Tour," three times to "Addison," twice to "Keysler," twice to "Montfaucon," and once to "Busching."[68] The works concerned here are: Thomas Nugent's *The Grand Tour* (4 vols., London, 1749),[69] a formal guide-book, arranged according to itineraries; Joseph Addison's *Remarks on Several Parts of Italy* (London, 1705); Johann Georg Keysler's *Travels through Germany, Hungary, Bohemia, Switzerland, Italy, and Lorrain* (English trans., 4 vols., London, 1756–57), giving exhaustive accounts which Smollett declares are "so laboriously circumstantial . . . . , that I never could peruse them, without suffering the headach";[70] Bernard de Montfaucon's *The Travels of Father Montfaucon from Paris thro' Italy* (English trans., London, 1712),[71] a huge folio treatise; and Anton Friedrich Büsching's *A New System of Geography* (English trans., 6 vols., London, 1762).

Smollett undoubtedly had read Addison, but I find no very convincing evidence that he actually consulted him while compiling the *Travels*. The other four books, however, seem to have been consulted for a few details. The *Grand Tour*, in particular, was certainly studied carefully by Smollett throughout his trip, since he corrects this guide-book three times, once from his own observation, and twice by comparison with *Roma Antica*.[72] But specific indebtedness to the *Grand Tour* is difficult to establish, since much the same material is given by Keysler, whom Smollett seems also to have used.[73] It appears certain, however, that the last two books provided many of the incidental details which Smollett constantly throws out concerning the towns passed en route. He appears to

68. See *Works*, XI, 140, 305, 307, 336 (*G.T.*); 295, 305, 367 (Add.); 299, 354 (Keys.); 354, 423 (Mont.); 182 (Büsch.).
69. I refer to the second ed. (4 vols., London, 1756), which Smollett probably used.
70. *Works*, XI, 299.
71. I refer to the second ed. of this translation, entitled *The Antiquities of Italy* (London, 1725); this seems to be the better edition, and was perhaps the one used by Smollett.
72. See above, p. 73, and *Works*, XI, 140, 336.
73. For details which almost certainly come from Keysler cf. *T*, 273, lines 9–11: *K*, II, 137; *T*, 306, lines 16–20: *K*, II, 239; *T*, 338, lines 9–13: *K*, III, 217–18; *T*, 353, lines 29–31: *K*, III, 97. Details which might come from either Keysler or the *Grand Tour* may be found by consulting the following references: cf. *T*, 302, lines 10–21: *K*, II, 229, 232, 236, *G.T.*, III, 347–9; *T*, 299, lines 4–5, 8–10: *K*, II, 199–200, *G.T.*, III, 329.

have referred to Büsching for a few facts concerning towns passed during the journey by sea from Nice to Genoa, for neither Nugent nor Keysler includes a description of the Riviera.[74] Finally, he seems to have looked up Montfaucon's remarks on the Laocoön for a few learned details not contained in *Roma Antica* or Keysler; and, strangely enough, close verbal similarities show that he also took his account of the Templum Pacis at Rome from Montfaucon, although *Roma Antica* gives an ample account of this ruin. But Montfaucon seems to have supplied nothing else except a few remarks on a ruin at Vienne.[75]

Smollett's use of these works in English furnishes the best evidence of his curiosity for antiquarian details and his exacting demand for accuracy. The total amount of material taken from these books could hardly amount to much more than a dozen pages; yet Smollett has laboriously compared them with each other and with *Roma Antica* in an effort to discover the best possible information. It is important to notice also that his use of Keysler, Büsching, and Montfaucon provides additional evidence that Smollett revised his observations extensively after his return to London. These three authors are not included in the list of books which Smollett shipped abroad;[76] it is hardly conceivable that he would have carried with him the heavy volumes of Büsching and Montfaucon; and, if he had with him Keysler's small volumes on Italy, it is hard to believe that he would not have taken them along to Rome, as he did the *Grand Tour*, which he says is "the only directory" he took to Italy.[77] Smollett's complaint about the lack of books at Nice makes it highly improbable that he could have procured these works in that city. Accordingly, it seems that he consulted them in London while preparing his observations for the press.

All the foregoing conclusions thus combine to demand a thorough revision in current opinion of Smollett's *Travels*. The author's reputation as a scholar of antiquity must suffer considerably, for of thirty-four quotations from classical authors scattered through the *Travels*, half prove to be lifted from the above secondary sources; all the nine inscriptions which he gives are likewise secondary; and most of the authorities cited, together with nearly all the erudite details, are similarly offered at second hand. Smollett therefore appears as a zealous general reader, with an intense en-

74. Cf., for example, *T*, 182, lines 9–10: Büsching, III, 35; *T*, 261, lines 26–8: *B*, III, 106; *T*, 275, lines 4–6: *B*, III, 104.

75. Cf. *T*, 354, lines 4–12, p. 320, line 27–p. 321, line 4, p. 423, lines 19–24: Montfaucon, 90, 128, 2.

76. See Joliat, *loc. cit.*

77. *Works*, XI, 305.

thusiasm for things ancient and a generous acquaintance with classical authors; but he can by no means be called a scholar.

The theory that the letters in the *Travels* represent actual correspondence can no longer be used, as it is by Seccombe,[78] to palliate
Smollett's fits of temper, preoccupation with medical matters, discussion of unsavory topics, and dogmatic pronouncements on art,
which from the first have alienated many readers. It is clear that
such remarks were not simply thrown out in the heat of impulse
and left to stand through faulty revision. At Nice and at London,
composing from books and his own notes, Smollett had ample time
to expunge any comments which he might have wished to retract.
Accordingly, the book, as it stands, invites no apologies: these
comments were included by Smollett because they assisted in the
illusion of the epistolary form, represented his firm opinions, concerned his earnest interests, or provided opportunities to display
his knowledge.

Indeed, it is dangerous to insist upon the "personal" nature of
these letters, for the reader who begins them with this preconcep-
tion is likely to be disappointed or disgusted. He will soon find
that nearly half the book consists of descriptions or disquisitions
which might with slight alterations be printed in a "Natural History" or a "Present State of All Nations." One should not forget
that much of the *Travels* represents compilation, embodying the
desire for accuracy, the eclectic use of books, the demand for regularity and precision, which are revealed in the *Compendium of
Voyages.*

In fact, it may well be said that without the preceding thirteen
years of compilation, Smollett's *Travels* would never have appeared. He had travelled on the Continent in 1749 and 1750; yet
despite his grievous need of money he published no "Travels" dealing with these experiences. He drew upon them while composing
Peregrine Pickle; but here, as I have said in the Introduction,
Smollett is not concerned with historical description, but with the
adventures of his hero. Then, as his picaresque period ended, he
turned to his arduous work with materials related to the literature
of travel: Drummond's *Travels*, the *Compendium of Voyages*, *The
Modern Part of the Universal History*, *The Present State of All Nations*, to say nothing of the numerous works of travel which he must
have reviewed for the *Critical*. By such labors Smollett's interests
were deflected from his earlier preoccupation with Le Sage, Cervantes, and the "romance" of roving adventure; he turned instead
to spend many years in compilation of historical details. After such

78. See *Cornhill Magazine*, n.s. XI (1901), 194–5.

work it was inevitable that, on his arrival at this practically unknown town of Nice, he should at once have "thoughts of writing a complete natural history of this town and county," and that he should, like Drummond, begin to keep a "register of the weather." It was natural that, as he again turned to creative literature, his travels should produce, not a portion of a picaresque novel, but a compilation containing accurate, historical facts.

Thus, Smollett has not, like Sterne and Fielding, produced a creative work by avoiding the characteristics of the usual travel-book: he has instead transmuted the typical matter of the traveller by the power of his satiric wit, narrative verve, shrewd observation, and intellectual independence. He cannot be set apart from the trend of the century on the grounds that his letters are authentic, for, like so many other travellers of the time, he has adopted an epistolary form which is largely artificial. Nor can Smollett's book be distinguished on the score of complete originality, for at least forty pages, and probably a good many more, have been compiled from the usual guide-books and antiquarian treatises. Neither can it be distinguished simply on the basis of its subject-matter, since this, too, is largely typical of the age: it must be remembered that half his *Travels*—a half which Smollett was particularly proud of[79]—contains concrete descriptions.

Accordingly, accounts such as those of Boulogne and Nice should not be regarded merely as unfortunate interruptions in the midst of amusing personal opinions and experiences; they should be taken as they were intended—as neat and accurate history. The erudition shown in the descriptions of Rome, Florence, Nîmes, and Nice should not be regarded as Smollett's own, but rather as skillful adaptation from other books. Finally, one should not esteem only the careful personal observation contained in the descriptions, but also the care with which Smollett has compared facts seen with facts written, and has even verified one printed source against another.

When such adjustments have been made, Smollett's *Travels* will at last receive its due as the careful composition of one who was not only a vigorous narrator and satirist, but also an accurate historian and an expert man of letters.

79. See *Letters*, p. 96, and the title-page of the original edition.

II

The History and Adventures of an Atom

SMOLLETT'S *History and Adventures of an Atom*[1] has for long suffered the neglect which inevitably overtakes works so largely dependent upon topical allusions and contemporary passions. When Pitt, Newcastle, Bute, Wilkes, and their colleagues were still fresh topics of argument, factional animosity gave zest to the discovery of English politicians under transparent Japanese names; with the result that Smollett's diatribe seems to have run through a dozen editions within seventeen years after its appearance.[2] But to-day the labor of historical reconstruction robs the satire of its wit; little vitality remains to excuse the noisome indecencies and pedantic digressions; the abuse so common in the political quarrels of Smollett's day seems now the work of an unbalanced brain. Thus, it is clearly impossible for modern readers to enjoy the *Adventures of an Atom* as they do Smollett's novels; but by patient study of the work in its original setting one may learn, in spite of the satire's obvious faults, to appreciate and respect its ingenious form, its trenchant language, its withering caricature.

The present chapter is concerned primarily with the form of the work: an atom, which has existed for many years in Japan, after numerous transmigrations enters the brain of one Nathaniel Peacock, "of the parish of St. Giles,"[3] and here it relates aloud to the astonished Englishman its memories of a certain "Japanese" era, which represents the period 1754–68 in Great Britain. This complicated scheme has produced what is generally regarded as "a peculiar type of political satire,"[4] or even as a work which "accommodates itself to none of the known rules of any school of satiric writing."[5] But investigation shows that in this work Smollett did not create a new method of satire: he simply combined a number of well-established, popular devices.

1. Published on April 1, 1769, apparently as an All-Fools' Day present to the English people (see the *London Chronicle*, March 25–28, 1769). This chapter is frequently indebted to Miss Martha P. Conant's useful work, *The Oriental Tale in England in the Eighteenth Century*, New York, 1908.
2. Lowndes lists a tenth edition in 1778, and two more, in 1784 and 1786.
3. *Works*, XII, 227.   4. Seccombe's "Note," *idem*, p. xii.
5. Oliphant Smeaton, *Tobias Smollett* (Edinburgh and London, 1897), p. 117.

The doctrine of transmigration, in various adaptations, had long been used as a vehicle for satire: by Addison, for instance, in the *Spectator* (no. 343, 1712), by Fielding, in his *Journey from this World to the Next* (1743), and, most significantly, by Hawkesworth in the *Adventurer* (no. 5, 1752). The last work, indeed, seems to provide a direct model for Smollett's transmigratory atom: here Hawkesworth relates how, after long meditating unsuccessfully in search of a theme for his article, he gave up and went to bed; and there, in a dream, he says, "I imagined myself to be still sitting in my study, pensive and dispirited, and that I suddenly heard a small shrill voice pronounce these words, 'Take your pen, I will dictate an *Adventurer.*'" The voice, which ultimately proves to be that of a flea, then relates its various transmigrations in satirical vein. This device is almost identical with Smollett's, even down to phraseology: Peacock similarly declares, "Sitting alone in my study, . . . meditating upon the uncertainty of sublunary enjoyment, I heard a shrill, small voice," which commanded, "Take up the pen, . . . and write what I shall unfold."[6] Then, before relating the history of Japan, the atom narrates briefly his various transmigrations. Such close similarity, it seems, could hardly be accidental.

Hawkesworth, however, was not Smollett's only predecessor in the use of this particular method: the *Adventures of an Atom* also bears great similarity to another work, Charles Johnstone's *Chrysal; or, the Adventures of a Guinea*, the first part of which appeared in 1760, went through three editions by 1762, and achieved such popularity that a continuation was published in 1765. In Johnstone's work "Chrysal," the spirit of gold, astonishes an alchemist by appearing and speaking to him from amidst his crucibles; the spirit then tells of its travels from hand to hand in the form of gold and relates the characters and experiences of its various possessors. Most of the work consists of satire on the very period of English history treated in the *Adventures of an Atom*. The date, the form, and the materials are all so close to Smollett's satire that his indebtedness to Johnstone can hardly be doubted.[7]

Still another specific source for the contrivance of the atom may be traced: as Sir Walter Scott long ago noticed,[8] there is a close similarity between the plan of *Chrysal* and that of Le Sage's *The Devil upon Crutches*. Le Sage's Asmodeus, of course, does not

6. *Works*, XII, 227, 229.
7. I have not been able to see the unpublished dissertation written at Halle by E. Muhlberg, entitled "Tobias Smollet's 'History and Adventures of an Atom,' und Charles Johnstone's 'Chrysal or the Adventures of a Guinea'"; but the existence of the study indicates the validity of my conjecture concerning Johnstone's influence.
8. See *Ballantyne's Novelist's Library* (London, 1821–24), IV, XXX.

transmigrate; but each work introduces a supernatural spirit who sees through the pretences of the world and reveals to a mortal the true thoughts and feelings of mankind. Knapp has discovered that Smollett performed some work of correction upon an edition of *The Devil upon Crutches* which appeared in 1759; he conjectures that Smollett may even have been responsible for the original edition of this translation, which appeared in 1750—a conjecture substantiated by Putney.[9] It is reasonable to assume, then, that Le Sage also contributed to the creation of Smollett's omniscient atom.

Whence, however, came the idea of substituting a speaking atom for a flea, a guinea, or a devil? It came, I think, from Voltaire's *Micromegas*, which, according to Ralph Griffiths,[10] Smollett himself translated for an edition published in 1752.[11] Since Smollett wrote articles for Griffiths in the *Monthly Review* during 1751 and 1752,[12] Griffiths may well have had Smollett's own authority for assigning this translation to him. At any rate, it is certain that Smollett in 1762 included this very translation of *Micromegas* in his edition of Voltaire's *Works*, and here added copious notes which prove that he had read the satire with considerable care.[13] It is thus significant that in this translation Voltaire's giants frequently refer to the inhabitants of earth as "atoms" and are, like Nathaniel Peacock, amazed to find that these relatively tiny "atoms" think and speak.

From these various suggestions, then, Smollett seems to have moulded his conception of the "atom," which constitutes one part of the dual form in which his satire is couched. The other part, of course, is the Oriental disguise under which Smollett presents his caricature of English history. Here again Smollett was by no means creating a new satirical method. As Miss Conant has amply shown, the Oriental disguise for satire, in various manifestations, had long been popular in England. Marana's *Turkish Spy* (translated 1687–93), Thomas Brown's *Amusements Serious and Comical* (1700),[14] Montesquieu's *Persian Letters* (translated 1730), Lyttelton's *Per-*

---

9. L. M. Knapp, "Smollett and Le Sage's *The Devil upon Crutches*," *MLN*, XLVII (1932), 91–3. R. D. S. Putney, "Lesage and Smollett" (unpublished Yale dissertation, 1936), Chap. IV.

10. See B. C. Nangle, *The Monthly Review, First Series, 1749–1789* (Oxford, 1934), p. 55.

11. *Micromegas:* . . . . *Together with A Detail of the Crusades: And a new Plan for the History of the Human Mind. Translated from the French of M. de Voltaire*, London, 1753. This translation was actually published in November, 1752 (see *Gentleman's Magazine*, XXII, 539).

12. See Nangle, *op. cit.*, p. 42.

13. See Voltaire's *Works* (London, 1761–69), XI (1762).

14. An adaptation of Dufresny's *Amusemens Serieux et Comiques* (1699).

sian Letters (1735), Horace Walpole's *Letter from Xo-Ho* (1757), are only a few important manifestations of a vogue which, in England, culminated in Goldsmith's *Citizen of the World* (1760–61). These works, to be sure, differ from Smollett's method, for they relate European matters as seen by an Oriental visiting Europe; Smollett relates European events as if they were actually Oriental history. But Goldsmith's "Citizen" shows how closely the two methods are related: in his Letter XXV the Chinese philosopher warns England against placing faith in colonies by relating "The Natural Rise and Decline of Kingdoms, Exemplified in the History of the Kingdom of Lao" in China.

More specific influence may be traced to Smollett's edition of Voltaire, since here he edited, with abundant notes, *Zadig* and *The World as it Goes*, which satirize European matters under Oriental disguise.[15] But his immediate model was probably a French work of uncertain authorship, entitled *Memoires Secrets pour Servir a l'Histoire de Perse*, or, in the translation, *The Perseis; or, Secret Memoirs for a History of Persia*. The work first appeared in 1745 and went through at least four continental editions by 1763; the English translation went through two editions in 1745 and was still popular enough in 1765 to warrant a reprint in Dublin. *Perseis* satirizes the reign of Louis XV under the pretence of relating a history of Persia, in which European characters and places are represented by real or pretended Oriental names, while numerous allusions to Oriental customs are introduced. Except for the representation of England by Japan, these names do not correspond specifically to Smollett's usage; but the general method is identical with that of his Oriental framework. Certainly, then, there is a strong probability that Smollett had this popular satire in mind while he was composing his *Adventures of an Atom*.

Other suggestions might be advanced *ad taedium*: the general influence of *Gulliver's Travels* and its progeny is obvious, and, apparently, Smollett's digressions were suggested by Swift's similar practice in his *Tale of a Tub*. But it is sufficiently clear that the form of the *Adventures of an Atom* is an amalgam of popular devices derived from Smollett's hack work and general reading. From Hawkesworth, Johnstone, Le Sage, and Voltaire he apparently de-

15. See Voltaire's *Works* (London, 1761–69), xi (1762). One bit of farce in the *Adventures of an Atom* seems to have been derived from the spurious second part of *Candide*, which Smollett included and annotated in his edition of Voltaire: the "Japanese" emperor's peculiar mark of favor, the kick, is remarkably similar to the bastinadoes, punches, and "kicks on the posteriors" with which the Sophi of Persia honors his favorites in this pseudo-Voltairean work (see Voltaire's *Works*, xxiii [1762], 155–7).

veloped his omniscient atom; from Voltaire, *Perseis*, and the general use of the Oriental disguise he apparently derived suggestions for his Oriental framework.

With all these influences fermenting in his mind, Smollett then evolved the final vehicle for his political satire from one primary source which he himself suggests, under the guise of S. Etherington, publisher, in his prefatory "Advertisement" to the *Adventures of an Atom:*

> As to the MS, before I would treat for it, I read it over attentively, and found it contained divers curious particulars of a foreign history, without any allusion to, or resemblance with, the transactions of these times. I likewise turned over to Kempfer and the Universal History, and found in their several accounts of Japan, many of the names and much of the matter specified in the following sheets.[16]

The obvious irony of the first sentence here has obscured the truth contained in the second: Engelbrecht Kaempfer's *History of Japan*[17] and the account of Japan in *The Modern Part of the Universal History*[18] really do contain "many of the names" and some of the matter in the *Adventures of an Atom*. Indeed, the essential inspiration for the Japanese framework may be found in Smollett's connection with the *Universal History*.

Smollett, as we have seen,[19] was apparently concerned with the editing and compilation of nearly a third of this vast project; accordingly, it is no accident that the *Critical Review* published thirty-seven sizeable articles dealing with the various volumes of the work, generally with favorable comment, and often with enthusiastic praise. At least a dozen of these reviews appear to have been written by Smollett himself,[20] who obviously felt that his reputation was seriously bound up with the fate of the compilation.[21] To this personal interest in the project, then, one may attribute the fact that in September, 1759, he appears to have reviewed the account of Japan in the *Universal History*. This review constitutes the germ of the Japanese setting for the *Adventures of an Atom*.[22]

16. *Works*, XII, 225–6.   17. Two vols., London, 1727–28.
18. IV, 1–77.   19. See above, pp. 7–8.
20. See my article, "Tobias Smollett and the *Universal History*," *MLN*, LVI (1941), 12–14.
21. See *Letters*, p. 193–4.
22. *Critical Review*, VIII, 189–99. The attribution of this review to Smollett depends on the following internal evidence: (1) the later use of certain ideas in the *Adventures of an Atom*, as explained below; (2) the style of the first two pages, with its array of parallelisms; (3) the satirical thrusts (p. 190); (4) the choice, as

In the beginning of this review Smollett, for nearly two pages, develops a comparison between Great Britain and Japan which has been suggested to him by the following comment in the *Universal History:*

Were *South* and *North Britain* divided by an arm of the sea, *Japan* might be most aptly compared to *England, Scotland,* and *Ireland,* with all its attendants of other smaller islands, peninsula's, bays, chanels, *&c.* and all under the same monarch.[23]

Citing this passage of "our author," Smollett remarks, "He might have pursued the comparison in divers other particulars," and then goes on to complete the comparison himself, by considering similarities in coasts, climate, produce, resources, and, above all, in "the genius and disposition of the people." After listing the similar virtues of the Japanese and the English, he continues with a passage which is almost an epitome of the *Adventures of an Atom:*

The resemblance will likewise hold in their vices, follies, and foibles. The Japanese are proud, supercilious, passionate, humourous, and addicted to suicide; split into a multitude of religious sects, and so distracted by political factions, that the nation is at last divided between two separate governments.

Then, noting the analogy between the geographical situation of Japan and China, and that of Great Britain and France, he proceeds to develop a detailed contrast between the Japanese and the Chinese which emphasizes the analogous contrast between the British and the French.

It seems, then, that unconsciously the Oriental framework of Smollett's satire had already been germinated as far back as September, 1759, nearly three years before the *Briton* embroiled Smollett in the vicious political controversy which sent him into France a bitter man, who regarded himself as "traduced by malice, persecuted by faction, abandoned by false patrons."[24] In a savage mood, sometime after this disastrous political excursion of 1762–63, he evidently cast about for some device by which he could express his indignation at the folly and corruption of English politics. Naturally, one of his first inspirations was to adopt the Oriental disguise already so popular in France and England. With this idea in

one of three extracts from the history, of a long quotation dealing with a surgical operation, with introductory comments in medical jargon (pp. 191–3; for evidence that Smollett was very familiar with this passage, see below, p. 100); (5) Smollett's obvious familiarity with this history of Japan, as shown in the present chapter, and in a long note to his edition of Voltaire's *Works*, VI, 153–4 (cf. *Univ. Hist.,* IV, 8, 12–13, 16–17, 64–5).

23. *Univ. Hist.,* IV, 1–2.   24. *Works,* XI, 1 (*Travels*).

mind, Smollett apparently remembered the surprising similarity between Great Britain and Japan which he had described at such length in his review of the *Universal History* several years before. It was this memory which enabled Smollett to give an original twist to his satire, despite the fact that neither his atomic nor his Oriental device was new.

As Miss Conant points out, authors who used the "Oriental Tale" for philosophic, moralistic, or satiric purposes tended to neglect the creation of an authentic Oriental atmosphere:

> . . . the amount of local colour, the richness of detail, and the truth to oriental manners and places are greater as the stories approximate genuine Eastern fiction like the *Arabian Nights*. At the other end of the scale, in thoroughly Anglicized oriental tales, such as *Rasselas* and *Nourjahad*, the background is pale and shadowy, details are sparse, and references to Eastern places and customs are rare.[25]

Although in the later part of his satire Smollett does thus neglect the Oriental setting, in the earlier part he has taken extraordinary pains to inject a "richness of detail" which makes his Japanese background bright and precise, instead of "pale and shadowy." Moreover, most of these details are not imaginary, nor are they tossed in at random: he has chosen them with great regard for their accuracy and for their actual similarity to their European application. England, Scotland, and Ireland are aptly represented by the three chief islands of Japan, Niphon, Ximo, and Xicoco; France is represented by China, Spain by Corea, Germany by Tartary, and so on. But such geographical parallels are simple: the real ingenuity of Smollett's Oriental setting lies in the fact that he sought to give a flavor of authenticity by gleaning detailed parallels and much superficial coloring from the account of Japan in the *Universal History*. There is no evidence that he consulted Kaempfer on this occasion; for the *Universal History's* account is largely derived from Kaempfer, as Smollett could easily have seen from scores of references.

If the introduction and the digressions of the atom are set aside, it is clear that Smollett's account of "Japan" mimics, in general, the order followed in this, and other accounts in the *Universal History*, some of which we know he compiled or edited.[26] First comes an introductory section on "Japan" in general, in which Smollett discusses geography, inhabitants, commerce, government, and reli-

25. Conant, *op. cit.*, p. 227.
26. There is no evidence to suggest that Smollett was in any way responsible for this history of Japan; in fact, the above reference to what "our author" might have done indicates that Smollett had no connection with the history.

gion; then follows the political history of the country. The "character" of the people is an account of the caprices of the English temperament without any overt attempt to copy the characteristics of the Japanese; but, as we have seen from his review, he was fully aware of the similar contradiction between vices and virtues which was stressed in the account of Japan in the *Universal History;* and therefore to some extent this similarity may have determined the specific direction of the satire in this description of the English.

Specific indebtedness to the *Universal History* is obvious in Smollett's account of government and religion:

Japan was originally governed by monarchs who possessed an absolute power, and succeeded by hereditary right, under the title of Dairo. But in the beginning of the period Foggien, this emperor became a cypher, and the whole administration devolved into the hands of the prime minister, or Cuboy, who now exercises all the power and authority, leaving the trappings of royalty to the inactive Dairo. The prince, who held the reins of government in the short period which I intend to record, was not a lineal descendant of the antient Dairos, the immediate succession having failed, but sprung from a collateral branch which was invited from a foreign country in the person of *Bupo,* in honour of whom the Japonese erected Fakkubasi,* or the temple of the white horse.

* Vid. Kempfer, Lib. i.[27]

In the first sentence here, which introduces Smollett's method of treating the English government throughout the work, he has ingeniously represented the evolution of the limited monarchy by using the actual development of the Japanese government, as described in the following passage from the *Universal History:*

Antiently the emperors were likewise sovereign pontiffs, under the title of *dairo's;* at which time, their persons and dignity were held so

27. *Works,* XII, 234–5. Smollett, several pages earlier (*idem,* p. 230), adds a footnote: "The history of Japan is divided into three different aeras, of which Foggien is the most considerable." The *Universal History* (IV, 49) does describe the "three aeras or epochs" of Japanese history, but "Foggien" is not one of these: it is one of the many short eras instituted by the emperors (see *idem,* p. 57). This may be only a slip, but Smollett seems to have copied directly from the very paragraph of the *Universal History* in which the "aeras" are described (see below, p. 101), and therefore should have known enough to avoid this confusion. Probably the change was deliberate, for, according to the *Universal History* (IV, 57), during the period Foggien occurred "a bloody and destructive war, which, from the time of its beginning, was called *Foggienno Midarri,* or *The desolation of the* Foggien *aera."* Since a great part of Smollett's attack is directed against the desolation and slaughter wrought by the Seven Years' War (1756–63), it seems that the repeated use of "Foggien" is another example of Smollett's ingenious adaptation of actual Japanese history—to say nothing of the pun involved!

sacred, that not only every rebellion against them, but even every con-
travention to their decrees, whether in civil or religious matters, were
detested as crimes against the Deity itself. . . . And as they lived thus
in the grandest splendor, luxury, and effeminacy, they committed the
chief care of the civil, and all the military, affairs to their prime minister,
who was styled *cubo*,[28] . . . and it was by one of these cubo's that the
dairo's were stripped of their whole civil authority, . . . and from that
time have been only at the head of all religious matters, whilst the cubo,
or emperor, bears an absolute sway over all civil and military affairs
throughout the empire. The former is still permitted to live in the same
state and grandeur as his ancestors did, and the latter is still obliged to
pay him a kind of homage, as if he acted only as his deputy, or viceroy:
but all that is mere ceremony, ...[29]

Since Smollett notes this similarity to English politics in his review,
there can be no doubt that the above passage, and subsequent remarks on the same subject in the *Universal History*, were directly
responsible for this part of his disguise.

In the last part of the above quotation from the *Adventures of
an Atom* Smollett has adapted Japanese history more freely. According to the *Universal History*,

. . . *Bupo*, otherwise called *Kobot*, landed in *Japan*, from the *Indies*,
and brought with him, on a white horse, a book, called *Kio*, containing
the mysteries of his religion; not long after which, a temple was erected
to him, which is still called *Fakkubasi*, or the temple of the white horse.[30]

Obviously Bupo had nothing to do with the dynasty of Dairos, but
was the founder of a religious sect; Smollett, however, has cleverly
utilized Bupo's foreign origin and the worship of Bupo's beliefs
as a vehicle for satire against the Hanoverian policy, which he constantly ridicules as "the religion of Fakkubasi" or "the worship of
the White Horse." Smollett's learned allusion to Kaempfer is, as
we might expect, a fake, apparently suggested by similar references in the *Universal History*.

Equal care and cleverness are shown in the representation of
Pitt under the name, "Taycho," for, as Pitt dominated England
during the period treated by Smollett, so the historical Taycho
dominated his era in Japan. According to the *Universal History*,
Taycho was a man of common birth who, "no less dreaded for his
courage than his wisdom," suppressed "the pirates at sea," waged
a Corean war, subdued the factions of petty lords, restrained "the
insolence and unruliness of the common people," and, in thus bring-

28. On the next page the *Universal History* notes the alternative form, "cuboy,"
which is used throughout the *Adventures of an Atom*.
29. *Univ. Hist.*, IV, 12–13.   30. *Idem*, p. 51.

THE HISTORY AND ADVENTURES OF AN ATOM 99

ing order to a chaotic empire, raised himself to noble rank and the position of absolute ruler.[31] As Pitt's career is distorted for Smollett's satirical purposes, the parallel is so obvious that no reader of Kaempfer or the Universal History could have missed it. The parallel seems particularly strong in the portion of the Adventures of an Atom in which "Taycho" succeeds in padlocking the lips of "the council of Twenty-eight"[32] and blindfolding the "Dairo" (George II);[33] for the historical Taycho also "stripped the emperors of the last remains of their secular authority, and made himself absolutely independent of them in all secular affairs."[34] Certainly, then, the rôle of "Taycho" is another tribute to Smollett's adroitness in integrating his Oriental coloring with his satire.

Sometimes Smollett even descends to puns in his use of actual Japanese terms. Thus, for example, in introducing the Duke of Cumberland, "who had bore the supreme command in the army," Smollett declares that he "was stiled Fatzman, . . . by way of eminence," and adds a learned reference, "Vid. Kempfer. Amaenitat. Japan,"[35] to prove the authenticity of the title. Since Smollett at once emphasizes the fact that this general had "more flesh" than any other Japanese and constantly refers to him as "the Fatzman," the word-play appears to be intentional; but the real ingenuity of the name arises from the fact that, according to the Universal History, this actually was an honorary Japanese title, equivalent to "Mars," and awarded for eminence in "martial exploits."[36] Smollett's solemn reference to Kaempfer is apparently suggested by similar references in the Universal History.[37]

Such passages, supported by a dozen more instances of similar cleverness,[38] clearly indicate that Smollett's Oriental setting was

31. Univ. Hist., IV, 64–5.
32. According to the Universal History (IV, 13), a council of twenty-eight nobles in Japan performed functions analogous to those of the English privy council.
33. Works, XII, 341 f.   34. Univ. Hist., IV, 61.
35. Works, XII, 255.   36. Univ. Hist., IV, 51, 57.
37. The work referred to here is Kaempfer's Amoenitatum Exoticarum (Lemgo, 1712); the Universal History (IV, 44–5) refers to it as "Amoenit. Japan."
38. Equally ingenious allusions are found in the following passage, in which Smollett describes the adulation of Newcastle: "But, by none was he more cultivated than by the Bonzas or clergy, especially those of the university Frenoxena." (Works, XII, 242.) Here, too, he adds a learned reference, "Vid. Hist. Eccles. Japan. Vol. I." All this has been suggested by the Universal History's long description (IV, 17) of the Japanese university of Frenoxama, directed by the bonzas, or priests and monks of Japan; in this case, however, Smollett's footnote is accurate; he seems to have taken it from the similar reference which the Universal History gives for its account of the above university. London is called "Meaco," a city described by the Universal History (IV, 33–5) as "the antient metropolis of the whole empire," the "grand storehouse of all the manufactures" and the "principal seat of their commerce." The navy is properly called "Fune" (see Univ. Hist., IV, 58), while an

not merely a random camouflage, but was, to a large extent, a carefully wrought párallel between English and Japanese affairs.

All these examples naturally suggest the problem: did Smollett refer to the *Universal History* for the specific purpose of gaining material for the *Adventures of an Atom,* or did he depend upon recollections? The answer, I think, is that he did both. The following passage, for instance, is garbled from memory: "These blisters were raised by burning the moxa upon his scalp. The powder of *menoki* was also injected in a glyster; and the operation of acupuncture, called *Senkei,* performed without effect."[39] The *Universal History* is the source of all this unsavory medical information;[40] but it gives the spelling, "Senki," not "Senkei," and applies this name to the disease which the acupuncture cures, not to the operation. It is significant that the section on Senki and moxa is one of the three extracts from the account of Japan which are included in Smollett's review;[41] this extract, then, explains why Smollett thought he could depend upon his memory in the above passage.

In the following section, however, Smollett seems to have referred to his source, for the materials are taken from the *Universal History* with very little alteration:

He was in magnificence extolled above the first Meckaddo, or line of emperors, to whom divine honours had been paid; equal in wisdom to Tensio-dai-sin, *the first founder of the Japanese monarchy;* braver than Whey-vang, of the dynasty of Chew; more learned than Jacko, the chief pontiff of Japan; more liberal than Shi-wang-ti, who was possessed of the universal medicine; and more religious than Bupo, alias Kobot, who, from a foreign country, *brought with him, on a white horse, a book called Kio, containing the mysteries of his religion.*[42]

admiral is signified by "Sey-seo-gun," actually the title given by the Japanese to the "grand general of the crown" (see *ibid.*). "Quanbuku" (Duke) is properly defined as "the first hereditary dignity in the empire" (see *Works,* XII, 240; cf. *Univ. Hist.,* IV, 61). "Day" is also used accurately in referring to a "high lord" (see *Univ. Hist.,* IV, 58). Astonishing industry is shown in Smollett's reference to Jews as "the sect of Nem-buds-ju," which was "few in number" (*Works,* XII, 242); this allusion has been extracted from a detailed footnote in the *Universal History* (IV, 34), which lists the names and numbers of all sects in Meaco, the smallest being that of "Dai-nembudsiu." The worship of "Fo" (Catholicism) is actually a Japanese religion (see *Univ. Hist.,* IV, 6, 7). "Syko" (Anne) is also the name of an actual Japanese empress (see *Univ. Hist.,* IV, 53). The atom's discussion (*Works,* XII, 274–5) of the theories of Linschoten and Kaempfer about the origin of the Japanese is probably based on the long account of such theories given in the *Universal History* (IV, 47–8).

39. *Works,* XII, 370.   40. *Univ. Hist.,* IV, 18–19.   41. See above, p. 94, n. 22.
42. *Works,* XII, 241–2 (my italics). To avoid confusion I have deleted the original italics of "Bupo" and "Kobot."

The italicized parts follow the source verbatim; the spelling of the proper nouns is exactly the same, except that the source gives "Mikaddo" and "Shi-whang-ti"; every statement is an adaptation of facts presented in the *Universal History*.[43] It is impossible to believe that Smollett could have carried the facts, spelling, and phraseology so exactly in his memory; he must have compiled most of this passage by actual reference to the *Universal History* during the process of composition. On the other hand it is hard to believe that Smollett read through the whole history again to provide an accurate framework for his satire; if he had, one might think, the Oriental allusions would be more numerous, and slips such as "Sen-kei" would not occur. Probably he looked up the accurate versions of some facts which he vaguely remembered, flipped through the pages in search of Japanese names, and left the rest to his memory.

In the last two quotations it is important to notice that the materials, except for the part on Bupo, are not integrated with the satire. About a third of the Japanese matter taken from the *Universal History* is of this external, decorative kind, without any real parallel in English history.[44]

A final use of Oriental coloring is found in the parody of the style of the "Oriental Tale" which Smollett ingeniously introduces to satirize the oratory of Pitt. As Miss Conant points out, " 'pompous language' was one essential in the eighteenth-century concept of the oriental tale";[45] in particular, this concept required elaborate figures of speech in profusion. It is this view of "Oriental" style which Goldsmith ridicules in his *Citizen of the World* (Letter XXXIII), where an author gives a description of how he has written in the true Eastern manner:

I have compared a lady's chin to the snow upon the mountains of Bomek; a soldier's sword to the clouds that obscure the face of heaven. If riches are mentioned, I compared them to the flocks that graze the verdant Tefflis; if poverty, to the mists that veil the brow of Mount Baku.

43. See *Univ. Hist.*, IV, 49, 17, 47, 51, and see above, p. 98.

44. See, for example: his accurate reference to "the fourteen sects of religion that are permitted in Japan," which is taken from a detailed footnote in the source (cf. *Works*, XII, 240: *Univ. Hist.*, IV, 34); his note, undoubtedly the result of direct reference to the source, which explains the meaning of "Copan" (cf. *Works*, XII, 232: *Univ. Hist.*, IV, 26); his references to punishments (cf. *Works*, XII, 251, 257: *Univ. Hist.*, IV, 16); his references to the festivals of Cambadoxi and Matsuri (cf. *Works*, XII, 239, 276: *Univ. Hist.*, IV, 7, 11, 54); and a few proper nouns taken from the Japanese without any particular suitability to their English application: "Gotto-Mio" (62), "Kowkin" (50), "Quambacundono" (65), "Fide-tada" (61), "Soo-Son-Sinno" (64), "Koan" (50), "Fatsissio" (15). I give the forms and page-references here according to *Univ. Hist.*, IV. For their application see Seccombe's key, *Works*, XII, 434–5.

45. Conant, *op. cit.*, pp. 91–2.

It is significant, then, that in his great oration of solace[46] for the loss of "Yesso" (Hanover), "Taycho" extravagantly declares that the "filial tenderness" of the people and the "parental care" of the emperor "may be compared to the rivers Jodo and Jodo-gava, which derive their common origin from the vast lake of Ami." Thus begins the ludicrous simile, thirteen lines long, which carries the rivers through their respective landscapes, and seems to be based on actual Japanese topography:[47]

"The one winds its silent course, calm, clear, and majestic, . . . : the other gushes impetuous through a rugged channel . . . : at length, they join their streams below the imperial city of Meaco, and form a mighty flood devolving to the bay of Osaca, bearing on its spacious bosom, the riches of Japan."

Here the "Cuboy" (Newcastle) is so delighted that he cries, "O charming simile! Another such will sink the Dairo's grief to the bottom of the sea; and his heart will float like a blown bladder upon the waves of Kugava." Thus encouraged, "Taycho" again opens "the sluices of his elocution," and pours forth a dazzling shower of figures:

". . . yes, that jewel hath been snatched by the savage hand of a Chinese freebooter:—but, dry your tears, my prince; that jewel shall detect his theft, and light us to revenge. It shall become a rock to crush him in his retreat;—a net of iron to entangle his steps; a fallen trunk over which his feet shall stumble. It shall hang like a weight about his neck, and sink him to the lowest gulph of perdition."

Smollett's contemporaries, I think, would at once have recognized this as a burlesque of the popular idea of an "Oriental" style; and, at the same time, the literary satire is cleverly designed to ridicule the oratorical prowess of Pitt.

All these Japanese details, of course, form only a small proportion of the words in the *Adventures of an Atom:* as I have said, in

46. *Works*, XII, 306–9.

47. According to the map of Japan in the *Complete System of Geography* (the work which Smollett took with him to France: see below, p. 105) there actually were two large rivers springing from a lake called Omi; one, the Kamogava, takes a short, direct route to the sea; the other, the Jodogava, takes a winding, roundabout course; these two rivers meet below Meaco and their combined waters fall into the bay of Osaca. According to the same map, a town named Jodo is situated at the junction of these rivers: apparently Smollett mistook this name for that of the Kamogava. Smollett's later reference to "Kugava" may allude to the Dsusu Kugava, a river which this map shows near the Jodogava. It seems quite possible that Smollett actually went to the above map (or a similar one) to construct this simile; certainly his desire for accuracy elsewhere is astonishing enough to warrant the conjecture. The *Universal History* does not make this topography clear, but it may have suggested some ideas (see *Univ. Hist.*, IV, 3, 38).

the later part Smollett casts aside nearly all pretence of disguise and gives nothing Oriental except the usual proper nouns. And, indeed, of the hundred-odd proper nouns to be found in "Keys" to the satire, only a third are actual Oriental names, although most of the remainder, puns, anagrams, and nonsense, are either clever imitations or contain parts of actual Japanese names, and thus help to create an Eastern atmosphere. Nevertheless, such was the practice of the day: as Miss Conant has shown, a very little coloring could produce what passed for an "Oriental Tale." But Smollett frequently gives much more than a little, and what he gives is generally selected with the same exactitude which he showed when he measured the amphitheater at Cemenelion with pack-thread. Other Orientalists might depend upon fantasy—might satisfy Goldsmith's lady with "a history of Aboulfaouris, the grand voyager, of genii, magicians, rocks, bags of bullets, giants, and enchanters, where all is great, obscure, magnificent, and unintelligible!"[48]—but not Smollett. Even in writing an "Oriental Tale" the habits of mind manifested and developed during Smollett's years of labor for booksellers could not be overthrown. Authenticity was constantly demanded in his compilations and Travels: accordingly, the peculiar merit of his Oriental framework is found, not in exuberant fancies, but in its ingeniously exact parallels, its ridiculously accurate details.

Thus it appears that the Adventures of an Atom is in large part the result of Smollett's activities during his "fallow" period: his connections with Le Sage, Voltaire, the Critical Review, and the Universal History all combined to produce essential elements. And one should not forget that work upon two other projects also contributed much to the satire. Smollett's political pamphleteering in the Briton (1762–63) naturally concentrated his attention upon many matters treated in the Atom; and, indeed, the violent tone of the satire may be attributed, in large degree, to his bitter experiences with this periodical. Furthermore, Smollett's Continuation (1760–65) to his History of England, dealing with the years 1748–65, undoubtedly fixed in his mind the events which he later satirized; and the precipitation of these materials in his memory made possible an easy fusion with Oriental details and a fluent adaptation to his satirical ends.

Hence one may say of the Adventures of an Atom what I have already said of the Travels: that without Smollett's years of drudgery this work would probably never have appeared, and certainly would never have assumed its present character.

48. *Citizen of the World,* Letter xxxiii.

III

The Present State of All Nations: *Its Accounts of Scotland and England*

SMOLLETT'S *Present State of All Nations* (8 vols., 1768–69) has sunk into such obscurity that biographies of Smollett either neglect to mention it or acknowledge its existence only by an erroneous date. Indeed, the compilation seems to have been neglected from the start, since the alleged second edition of 1768–69 apparently extended no farther than the first volume: at least, I have found no set of the work which bears the imprint, "Second Edition," on the title-pages of the last seven volumes. Apparently the first volume of the first edition sold out quickly under the promise of Smollett's name, but readers soon discovered the disappointing quality of the work.

Robert Anderson seems to be responsible for the wrong date generally assigned to this publication: evidently misled by the "second edition," he stated in his enlarged biography of 1800 that *Present State* was first issued "about" 1763.[1] Apparently following this lead, John P. Anderson listed the date of the first edition as 1764 in his bibliography of Smollett's works.[2] These mistaken guesses have been generally propagated,[3] despite obvious evidence to the contrary. A copy of the first edition, dated 1768–69, is in the British Museum; Dr. John Armstrong, in a letter written to Smollett on March 28, 1769, refers to the work among "recent publications";[4] proposals for the work are advertised in the *London Chronicle* for May 14–17, 1768; and, finally, the announcement of its initial publication is made in the *Public Advertiser* for June 25, 1768.[5] The long acceptance of this error furnishes ample evidence of the neglect which Smollett's last compilation has suffered—a neglect well deserved, for, as a whole, *Present State* is a perfunctory job.

Nevertheless, buried under a weight of dullness, lie about three hundred and fifty pages worthy of careful examination. These pages

1. See *Miscellaneous Works of Tobias Smollett* (Edinburgh, 1800), I, lxxii.
2. Appended to Hannay's *Life of Tobias George Smollett*, London, 1887.
3. Noyes (*Letters*, p. 207) correctly lists the date of the first appearance of the compilation as 1768.
4. See below, p. 130.
5. My attention was called to these advertisements by Professor Lewis M. Knapp.

comprise the description of Scotland and the introductory section on England, which are often readable and often provide valuable material for the historian. The chief significance of these sections, however, lies in the fact that they provided an essential part of the inspiration for *Humphry Clinker*.

But, as usual with Smollett's hack work, the question arises: how much of *Present State* was the product of his own hand? Some suggestion as to the answer may be found in the list of his works which Smollett sent to Richard Smith on May 8, 1763. Here the earlier compilations, *A Compendium of Voyages* and *The Modern Part of the Universal History*, are dismissed with the brief comments, "very small part" and "small part,"[6] despite the great amount of labor which we now know he performed upon these projects.[7] In mentioning *The Present State of All Nations*, however, he speaks at length in a manner which gives the impression that he is compiling the work himself:

I had engaged with Mr. Rivington and made some Progress in a work, exhibiting the present state of the world: which work I shall finish if I recover my health.[8]

This impression is substantiated by the fact that *Present State* is the only one of these three compilations to bear Smollett's name on the title-page of the first edition. Additional evidence lies in the probability that Smollett worked, or intended to work, on this compilation during his trip to the Continent in 1763–65, when, presumably, no understrappers were available. Among the books which Smollett shipped abroad were fifty-eight octavo volumes of the *Universal History* and at least one of the two great folio volumes of the *Complete System of Geography* (1744–47).[9] Random study of the sources of *Present State* indicates that these two works were used in making this compilation; accordingly, it appears that Smollett carried these works with him in order to continue his labors abroad.[10]

It seems, then, that Smollett performed a considerable amount

---

6. See *Letters*, pp. 81–2.   7. See above, pp. 7–8 and Part I.
8. *Letters*, p. 82.

9. See Eugène Joliat, *Smollett et la France* (Paris, 1935), pp. 251–2. The "Ancient Part" of the *Universal History* had been published in 20 octavo volumes, 1747–49. Smollett could take with him only 38 volumes of *The Modern Part*, for he departed in June, 1763, and the 39th volume did not appear until July of that year (see the *London Chronicle*, July 5–7, 1763).

10. It was, of course, unnecessary to convey abroad all these volumes of the *Universal History* for this purpose only. Probably he also planned to work upon another edition of the *Universal History*, as he did during his last years in Italy (see above, p. 8). An abridgment of this work had been projected as early as October 12, 1760 (see *Letters*, p. 68).

of work for *Present State,* but it is highly improbable that he compiled all of it. The account of Italy, for instance, was evidently composed after Smollett's trip to the Continent;[11] yet it bears such slight resemblance to corresponding portions of Smollett's *Travels* that it could hardly have been composed by the same hand. But the exact extent of Smollett's work upon such an inferior project is of little importance: the chief significance of *Present State* lies in the above-mentioned account of Scotland and introductory section on England. In addition to striking evidence of style and opinion, Smollett's authorship of these portions is proved by the numerous close parallels with *Humphry Clinker* which will be considered in the remainder of this study; by about sixty pages in the account of Scotland which contain original remarks by one intimately acquainted with the country; and by numerous details of political history, particularly in regard to the Scottish rebellions, which suggest the author of the *Complete History of England.*

Before a discussion of these parts of *Present State* and their influence upon *Humphry Clinker,* it is essential to show that the accounts of Scotland and England in the compilation were projected and composed before the novel. It has sometimes been suggested that Smollett may have begun *Humphry Clinker* as early as 1766–68; hence, there would appear to be a slight possibility that the novel preceded the compilation in describing Scotland and England.

The history of the composition of *Present State,* however, reveals a protracted delay unusual even for Smollett. In his letter to Richard Smith, Smollett states that he "had engaged with Mr. Rivington" to produce *Present State;* but James Rivington, to whom he here refers,[12] had moved to Philadelphia by 1760.[13] Obviously, Smollett's contract for the compilation must have been made before that date. The account of Scotland is found at the end of the first and beginning of the second volumes of *Present State,* and the introductory section on England immediately follows; hence, it seems highly probable that these parts were included in the "progress" on the compilation which Smollett mentions in this letter to Smith.

11. See *Pres. St.,* VI, 372, where the account of Genoa mentions the treaty with France concerning Corsica, signed in 1768.

12. It is certain that James Rivington is the publisher mentioned, for Smollett's letter is an answer to various queries from Smith prompted by the latter's acquaintance with James Rivington in America. See *Notes and Queries,* CLXIV (1933), 316.

13. See *Dictionary of National Biography,* "James Rivington," in article "Rivington, Charles."

This conjecture is strengthened by evidence that, in compiling the description of Scotland, Smollett used the fifth edition of Daniel Defoe's *Tour Thro' the Whole Island of Great Britain*, published in 1753, and not the sixth edition of 1761–62.[14]

More specific evidence of an early date of composition is found in footnotes added to correct the text of *Present State*. The most significant of these concerns "the noble family of Douglas, whose chief, the duke of Douglas, resides in an ancient castle, situated near the banks of [the Clyde]." Here a footnote states: "The late duke dying without issue, the title is extinct."[15] Archibald Douglas, third Marquis and first Duke of Douglas, died in Edinburgh on July 21, 1761, and the celebrated litigation over his estate, known as "the Douglas Cause," began in 1762.[16] This portion of the text was evidently composed before 1761–62, since such notorious events could not long have escaped the notice of Smollett.

In another place Smollett gives the following description of Duff House, taken from Defoe's *Tour:*

On the banks of the river Deveron, and in the neighbourhood of the town of Bamff, stands the shell of a princely edifice, of modern architecture, built by Duff lord Braco, *lately created earl of Fife in Ireland:* but the work was suspended, in consequence of a difference between his lordship and the architect; and the former leaving this noble pile unfinished, in a most delightful situation, resides among the wild mountains of Strathbogy.

A footnote, however, states: "This house is now finished, and the present lord lives in it."[17] An approximate date for the composition of the above passage in the text is suggested by the italicized phrase, which Smollett has added to Defoe's account: William Duff was created Earl Fife on April 26, 1759.[18] The mansion was ready for habitation by 1760, when Richard Pococke found James Duff, the earl's eldest son, living there.[19] James, "the present lord" of the above footnote, succeeded to the property and titles on September 30, 1763, while Smollett was in France.[20] Apparently, then, the description in the text was composed shortly after April, 1759, and

14. See below, p. 117, n. 49.   15. *Pres. St.*, II, 103.
16. See *Dictionary of National Biography*, articles "Douglas, Archibald" (1694–1761), and "Douglas, Archibald James Edward" (1748–1827).
17. *Pres. St.*, II, 62 (my italics); cf. Defoe, *Tour* (fifth ed.), IV, 212.
18. See Cokayne's *Complete Peerage*, ed. Gibbs and Doubleday, V, 376–7.
19. See Richard Pococke, *Tours in Scotland*, ed. D. W. Kemp (Edinburgh, 1887, *Publications of the Scottish History Society*, vol. 1), p. 195; cf. Alistair and Henrietta Tayler, *The Book of the Duffs* (Edinburgh, 1914), I, 171.
20. *Complete Peerage*, V, 377.

the footnote added after Smollett's return to England, probably from information received during his Scottish visit of 1766.

Similarly, Smollett extracts from Defoe's *Tour* a half-page devoted to description of the palace at Leslie belonging to the Earl of Rothes; but he adds a curious footnote: "This elegant seat was entirely consumed by fire in the year 1755."[21] The palace of Rothes, however, was burned to the ground in December, 1763,[22] while Smollett was abroad. The date, 1755, may be a printer's error; at any rate, this portion of the text was apparently composed before the end of 1763.

From all the above evidence,[23] then, it appears that the description of Scotland in *Present State* was projected before 1760, was at least partially compiled by 1761, and, at the very latest, was completed before Smollett left England in June, 1763; for the books which he shipped to France include only one of the seven works used in compiling this account of Scotland. Since *Humphry Clinker* is clearly influenced by Smollett's tour through Great Britain in 1766 and residence at Bath in 1765–68, there can be no reasonable doubt that the description of Scotland in *Present State* was both projected and composed before the novel; and, from its early place in the compilation, one may reasonably assume that the account of England in *Present State* also preceded the novel.

In order to understand the influence which these accounts exerted upon *Humphry Clinker,* it is necessary to examine Smollett's purpose and methods in compiling these neglected descriptions. His purpose is elucidated by considering the other descriptions of England and Scotland available in his day.

Smollett was hardly exaggerating when he declared in *Humphry Clinker:*

What, between want of curiosity, and traditional sarcasms, the effect of ancient animosity, the people at the other end of the island know as little of Scotland as of Japan.[24]

Truly, while English presses were flooded with descriptions of practically every other region in the known world, the land beyond the Tweed remained in outer darkness. The Union brought only a slight increase of English interest in information on Scotland, while,

21. *Pres. St.,* II, 87; cf. Defoe, *Tour* (fifth ed.), IV, 160–1.
22. See Colonel Leslie, K.H. of Balquhain, *Historical Records of the Family of Leslie* (Edinburgh, 1869), II, 130–4.
23. For another footnote to *Present State* which indicates composition before 1764 see below, p. 156, n. 31.
24. *Works,* IV, 60.

on the other hand, English vilification of Scotland increased until, during Bute's administration (1761–63), it reached a climax in the abuse of John Wilkes's *North Briton*. English knowledge of Scotland had actually progressed so little that Wilkes could still suggest to Englishmen an account of present conditions by reprinting in his *North Briton* (no. 13) the contemptuous description of Scotland written by James Howell in 1649. The Scots themselves, however, must bear part of the blame, for they made little effort to combat this ignorance with adequate descriptions: thus, Richard Gough, in his great treatise, *British Topography* (1780), introduces his scant section on descriptions of Scotland with the significant complaint:

Whether through want of materials or application, the nationality of our northern neighbours long suffered the natural and artificial face of their country to lie as undescribed as their poverty left it unimproved and unadorned.[25]

The English, on the other hand, had no lack of curiosity about their own part of the island. From the beginning of the eighteenth century the county histories poured in from every part of England; travellers were eager to add their testimony to the growing pile of topographical tributes to English prosperity. Consequently, as early as 1720 Thomas Cox could begin the compilation of his "complete Historical Geography"[26] of England, originally entitled *Magna Britannia et Hibernia, Antiqua & Nova. or, a New Survey of Great Britain* (6 vols., 4to, 1720–31). Cox obviously intended to include accounts of Scotland and Ireland; but, perhaps because of English contempt for these countries, the work includes only England and Wales. The early popularity of descriptions of England is evident from the fact that all Cox's information was apparently collected from printed material.[27]

Excluding all reports of individual journeys and all specialized histories, in the period from the turn of the century until the appearance of *Humphry Clinker* in 1771, no less than twenty-two separate, comprehensive descriptions of England were in print. Of these works at least fourteen are divided into accounts of all the various shires; three are single folio volumes; four are in two volumes; two, in three volumes; one, in six volumes; and one, in ten volumes.

Descriptions of Scotland for the same period present a sorry contrast. The only comprehensive separate account is Thomas

25. *British Topography*, II, 553.
26. *Magna Britannia*, I, 1.
27. See *idem*, p. [i].

Pennant's *Tour in Scotland,* published at the very end of the period, in 1771. This represents the first adequate inquiry into both the natural history and antiquities of Scotland, and contains the first extensive drafts of various interesting objects in the land. English knowledge of Scotland before the appearance of *Present State* therefore depended almost entirely on two different sources of information, which were both consulted by Smollett.

The first source consists of static descriptions annexed to much larger accounts of England or contained in general compilations. The two best accounts of this type up to 1722 are found in the second edition of Edmund Gibson's revision of Camden's *Britannia* (2 vols., folio, 1722), and in the *New General Atlas* (folio, 1721), attributed to J. Senex. But these accounts are composed largely of antiquated materials from Camden, and from the "Theatrum Scotiae" of Joannes Blaeu, contained in his great Latin atlas, *Theatrum Orbis Terrarum* (vol. V, 1654); and the supplementary matter is very imperfect.

About this time, however, the rapid improvement in commerce and transportation resulted in a fresh form of description which soon infused new life into such compilations. It consisted in the presentation of description in the form of a tour through the island of Great Britain—the form of *Humphry Clinker.* The first extensive attempt of this type appears to have been James Brome's *Travels over England, Scotland, and Wales,* published in 1700.[28] Brome's section on Scotland, however, is negligible, for it amounts to only forty pages and is the outmoded record of a visit in 1669. A more important attempt was John Macky's work, *A Journey through England. In Familiar Letters from a Gentleman Here, to his Friend Abroad,* of which the first volume appeared in 1714, the second in 1722, and the third, entitled *A Journey through Scotland,* in 1723.[29] Macky, a native of Scotland, devoted most of his "journey" through his homeland to a lavish account of its noble seats and detailed histories of its noble families, in an obvious effort to impress the English. As a result, Macky's work added little to English knowledge of the vital facts of Scottish topography, customs, and commerce. The importance of his *Journey* lies in the fact that it set a vogue for description of Great Britain in the form of familiar letters—a vogue which culminated in *Humphry Clinker.*

Daniel Defoe, the journalistic opportunist, lost no time in capitalizing upon the popularity of Macky's idea: he at once proceeded

28. The work was republished in 1707 and 1726.
29. At least the first volume of Macky's work had gone into a fourth edition by 1724.

to compose, in the form of familiar letters, his well-known work, *A Tour Thro' the Whole Island of Great Britain*. The first volume of this work appeared in 1724, the second in 1725, and the third, containing an account of Scotland, in 1727. The first edition gives an accurate, modern description of Scotland, of which a large part undoubtedly comes from personal observation. In 1738, however, Defoe's *Tour* was extensively revised in accordance with the growing demand for the "compendium" of information. While retaining the form of letters, the editor omitted many personal touches which lent vitality to Defoe's account, and foisted in a mass of facts gleaned from other works. This process of excision and accretion was continued in Samuel Richardson's revision of 1742 and subsequent editions, with the result that the fifth edition of the *Tour* (4 vols., 1753), which Smollett used in compiling *Present State*, presented a full duodecimo volume of dry facts on Scotland. Defoe's *Tour* thus became an imperfectly regularized compilation, in which the letter-form interrupted order without enlivening the facts. Nevertheless, the revised work enjoyed a surprising popularity, which resulted in the publication of nine editions by 1779.

The fresh information added in these tours thus tended to merge with the earlier material in static compilations. The two sources were more comprehensively mingled in that huge work, *A Complete System of Geography* (2 vols., folio, 1744–47), upon which Smollett based his description of Scotland in *Present State*. The *Complete System* grouped materials from Gibson's edition of Camden's *Britannia*, the *New General Atlas*, Defoe's *Tour*, Macky's *Journey*, and numerous minor works, to present the most comprehensive account of Scotland which had thus far appeared. But the account is badly confused and wretchedly written; the compiler assembled much of the best information, but scarcely attempted to digest his unwieldy materials. A description of about half this size also appeared in a similar work, the *New System of Geography*, published by Fenning and Collier in 1764–65.

Meanwhile, the vogue of the epistolary tour continued in 1747 with *A Journey through Part of England and Scotland Along with the Army. . . . By a Volunteer. Comprised in Several Letters to a Friend in London*, which contained descriptions largely pilfered from Defoe's *Tour*, together with an account of the rebellion of 1745. The work met with great popularity, for three editions appeared within the single year of 1747.

The scant descriptions of the Highlands in this last work were soon superseded by a work to which Smollett is indebted: Captain Edward Burt's *Letters from a Gentleman in the North of Scotland to his Friend in London,* in two volumes, written about 1730, but not published until 1754. The author reveals that the form of his description was directly suggested by Macky's *Journey;*[30] but his material is utterly different, for the *Letters* present, in rough, but humorous style, the first adequate description of the Scottish Highlands. Burt's opening remarks give an ample account of the ignorance which he desires to combat:

. . . to the People of England, excepting some few, and those chiefly the Soldiery, the Highlands are hardly known at all: for there has been less, that I know of, written upon the Subject, than of either of the Indies; and even that little which has been said, conveys no Idea of what a Traveller almost continually sees and meets with in passing among the Mountains; nor does it communicate any Notion of the Temper of the Natives, while they remain in their own Country.[31]

This ignorance had not been enlightened by 1754, for the *Gentleman's Magazine* emphasizes the unique value of the *Letters* with a long notice of over a column, in which the reviewer declares:

They contain an account of many customs with which the inhabitants of *South Britain* are as little acquainted as with those of the wild barbarians in the heart of *Africa.* . . .[32]

Accordingly, extracts from the *Letters* appeared in three subsequent issues of the *Gentleman's Magazine,* and new editions of the work were quickly called for in 1757 and 1759.

Such, then, was the comparative extent of descriptions of England and Scotland before the appearance of Smollett's *Present State of All Nations.* Only five accounts of Scotland existed which were worthy of comparison with the corresponding descriptions of England: and these five, in Gibson's edition of Camden's *Britannia,* the *New General Atlas,* the *Complete System,* the *New System,* and Defoe's *Tour,* were dwarfed by being appended to huge accounts of England; they were, moreover, frequently archaic, incomplete, and irregular. At the same time, in addition to "journeys," and long accounts of England contained in general compilations, no less than twenty-two separate, comprehensive descriptions of England were available. Clearly, in compiling his account of Scotland for *Present State,* Smollett was faced with an opportunity to disseminate new information; whereas, in compiling his account of England, he

30. See Burt, I, 6. All references to Burt are to the reprint published in Edinburgh in 1876.
31. Burt, I, 5.   32. *Gentleman's Magazine,* xxiv (1754), 342.

needed only to rearrange the vast fund of materials already prepared.

Smollett therefore approached the description of Scotland in
Present State with the dual desire to fill a gap in knowledge and to
perform an important service for his native land. Consequently,
this description as a whole excels the descriptions of other countries
in *Present State* and presents the most comprehensive, lucid, and
orderly account of Scotland which had thus far appeared; and I
have no doubt that it was generally the most accurate. One cannot,
of course, deny that many parts of the description are tedious for
the modern reader, since much of it naturally consists of heavy
facts; nevertheless, even its dullest parts glitter in comparison with
the wretched execution of the other accounts extant in Smollett's
day.

The description of Scotland in *Present State* is divided into three
general sections. First comes "The Islands of Shetland and Orkney," twenty-five pages in length; and next, "The Hebrides, or
Western Isles of Scotland," eighty pages in length. These two sections close the first volume of *Present State*. The second volume
begins with the account of Scotland proper, one hundred and fifty
pages in length.

At the close of the first volume of *Present State* Smollett gives a
list of alleged authorities for his account of the Hebrides; but no
such list appears for the account of Scotland proper. The authorities cited are these:

(Authors.)—Buchan.—Sibbald.—Martin.—Tindal.—Complete System of Geography.—Hist. Gen. de Lambert.—Salmon's Geographical
Grammar.[33]

The list is chiefly sham: for the account of the Western Islands
Smollett has used only the two famous works by Martin Martin:
A Late Voyage to St. Kilda (1698), and *A Description of the Western Islands of Scotland* (1703).[34] The first reference alludes to *A
Description of St. Kilda* (1727), attributed to Alexander Buchan;
it is a short account, consisting chiefly of patent transcripts from
Martin. Since Smollett made no use of the few original remarks
in the volume, and clearly used a great deal of material from Martin which it does not include, there is no reason to suppose that
he consulted this trifling pamphlet. The case is the same with

33. *Pres. St.*, i, 510.
34. The first work was available in the fourth edition of 1753; the latter, in
the second edition of 1716. I have used the first editions for subsequent references.

the reference to the *Complete System of Geography*, which drastically condenses Martin's accounts.

Smollett gives equally specious references in citing the *Histoire Générale, Civile, Naturelle, Politique et Religieuse de tous le Peuples du Monde*, by Claude François Lambert,[35] and *A New Geographical and Historical Grammar*, by Thomas Salmon.[36] Lambert devotes to this subject only ten tiny pages containing general comments which Smollett must have known from mere gossip; while Salmon gives only a page of bare details, of which Smollett could have used nothing but degrees of latitude and longitude. The situation appears to be much the same with the reference to Sir Robert Sibbald. Smollett's antiquarian interests undoubtedly led him to read some of Sibbald's works, and perhaps slight memories of this reading may have crept into Smollett's account; but there is no evidence that he actually consulted any of Sibbald's works in compiling the description.

The allusion to "Tindal" presents an amusing puzzle from which it appears that Smollett outwitted himself. No work by anyone named Tindal seems to have been written on the subject of Scottish topography; and there is no reason to believe that Smollett used any sources except the accounts of Martin. Accordingly, the name appears, like the rest, to be a vague reference to some work on Scotland which Smollett remembered and tossed in to swell the list. Smollett probably meant to cite *A Specimen of the Critical History of the Celtic Religion and Learning*,[37] by John Toland, the Deist, which contains some remarks on the Western Islands, including acknowledged transcripts from Martin. But, by association with Matthew Tindal, of the Deist controversy, the names of Tindal and Toland were apparently confused in Smollett's mind.

This haphazard manner of citing "authorities" is emphasized by the fact that Smollett appears to have forgotten to include one source which he really used. At the close of the section on Shetland and Orkney he does not add a list of authorities; probably he intended to include them in the list at the end of the volume. When he came to fabricate this list, however, he evidently forgot his previous intention, and thought only of books on the Hebrides. At any rate, about six pages[38] in the account of Orkney are derived from James Wallace's work, *An Account of the Islands of Orkney*

35. Fourteen vols., Paris, 1750.
36. First ed., London, 1749; tenth ed., London, 1766.
37. First published in *A Collection of Several Pieces of Mr. John Toland*, 2 vols., London, 1726.
38. Cf. *Pres. St.*, 1, 416, line 19–p. 417, line 27: Wallace, pp. 71–4, 77–8, 66–8; *PS*, 420–3: W, 51–61; *PS*, 426, line 9–p. 427, line 21: W, 78–80.

(enlarged edition, 1700), which is not mentioned in the above list. Most of the remainder of this section on Shetland and Orkney is taken from the *Complete System of Geography;*[39] the entry of this work in the above list may thus be considered as truthful, although Smollett was evidently not thinking of works on the northern islands. These two descriptions appear to have been compared with Martin's brief accounts of Shetland and Orkney appended to the *Description of the Western Islands;*[40] but since the *Complete System* condensed Martin, and Martin condensed Wallace, it is in many cases impossible to tell exactly which source Smollett used for a particular statement.[41]

The section on Shetland and Orkney, however, is of slight importance: it had little direct influence upon *Humphry Clinker;* and Smollett added nothing except a few general observations. Nevertheless, it is significant to notice Smollett's typical thoroughness in consulting three good sources in order to collect all the best information relative to the subject. Furthermore, the material is regularized to an extent never even attempted in any previous work on these islands. The account of each of the two groups begins with systematized general sections on "Number and Situation," "Climate," "People," "Soil," "Animals," etc., and closes with detailed, orderly descriptions of the "Particular Islands." The rewriting and rearrangement are performed in the manner already discussed in connection with the *Compendium of Voyages,* although the product, being crammed with details, is even more regular and precise, and contains less neo-classical diction.

The succeeding account of the Hebrides is much more valuable: some of the description directly influenced parts of *Humphry Clinker;* and a total of nearly ten pages in the opening general section consists of original observations by Smollett. Moreover, the description of the particular islands presents the most comprehensive, regular, and lucid condensation of Martin's accounts which had thus far been made. Smollett's almost complete dependence on Martin, of course, needs no defence, for Martin's two descriptions were the best, and indeed the only reputable, accounts of the Western Islands available at the time.

The reader of Johnson and Boswell will recall that Martin's *Description of the Western Islands* was the book which had aroused Johnson's interest in the region: naturally, when at last the pair made their famous tour of the Hebrides, the *Description* was car-

39. I, 278–384.   40. Pp. 350–92.
41. One detail, at least, is certainly from Martin: cf. *Pres. St.*, I, 423, line 34– p. 424, line 2; *Descrip. of W. Is.*, p. 367.

ried along as a Baedeker. But, despite the great fascination of the work, Johnson could not help contrasting the rough style of Martin with the polish of neo-classical prose. "There is now an elegance of style universally diffused," he declared. "No man now writes so ill as Martin's Account of the Hebrides is written."[42] The stricture is justified, for Martin knew not the meaning of order. The various islands are described at random; the general account of the inhabitants is placed, Shandy-like, in the middle of the *Description;* subheadings are used to introduce single paragraphs, while long dissertations remain undistinguished; reports of superstitions, humorous incidents, personal anecdotes, medical observations are interspersed anywhere and everywhere at the whim of the author; topics of all sorts are intermingled with "Gothic" abandon.

Smollett, being possessed of a Johnsonian love for regularity, naturally strove to remove the disorders which annoyed the "great Cham." Martin's misplaced general remarks on inhabitants are incorporated with Smollett's own observations to form a long introductory section on "People."[43] Martin's plea for exploitation of the resources of these islands is likewise removed from a position at the very end of his account of the Hebrides and placed in Smollett's introductory section on "Trade and Manufacture."[44] In accordance with the general plan of *Present State*, which moves southward from the Pole, Smollett begins his particular description with the outermost island, St. Kilda, and then takes up the various islands in a regular progress from north to south.[45] The long account of St. Kilda represents a careful conflation of facts from Martin's earlier *Voyage to St. Kilda* and his later brief account in the *Description of the Western Islands*. Within the account of each island related topics are carefully grouped and condensed, sentence structure is regularized, diction is polished, and the narrative is animated, in the manner already described in connection with the *Compendium*.

This account, however, does not achieve the vigor and fluidity of the historical narratives of the *Compendium*. Because it consists

42. Boswell's *Life* (Powell's revision of Hill's ed., Oxford, 1934), III, 243.

43. *Pres. St.*, I, 431–9. All this section seems to be original with Smollett except the following portions: cf. *Pres. St.*, I, 432, line 37–p. 433, line 15: *Descrip. of W. Is.*, pp. 208–9; *PS*, 435, line 11–p. 436, line 13: *DWI*, 101–4, 108; *PS*, 436, line 37–p. 438, line 6: *DWI*, 108–9, 114–16, 119–20, 209–10.

44. Cf. *Pres. St.*, I, 442–3: *Descrip. of W. Is.*, pp. 336–49.

45. The one serious irregularity of the description occurs when Smollett follows Martin in placing a general account of the "second sight" after the description of St. Kilda.

largely of solid, orderly facts, the account loses vitality and becomes at time perfunctory. Flashes of "elegant" style appear in the revision, and the few anecdotes which Smollett retains are effectively invigorated, but in general one can only admire the industry displayed in regularization. One should except from this statement the general section on "People," largely original with Smollett; here, in eight pages, Smollett presents the most succinct and vivid description of the Scottish Highlander and his life which had thus far appeared. Indeed, it is doubtful whether a better account has ever been packed into so little compass.

For the description of Scotland proper no list of authorities is given, and only two incidental references for specific facts are found in the whole account. Nevertheless, many verbatim echoes prove that Smollett compiled this elaborate description from the best sources available in his day.

As the basis for his particular description of the various shires, one hundred and twenty-five pages in length, he used the account of the *Complete System of Geography* (1744–47),[46] which provided material for about eighty pages. The great disorder in this "System" is regularized with the diligence already displayed in the revision of Martin.

Smollett then perused Captain Edward Burt's *Letters from a Gentleman in the North of Scotland* (1754), and from widely scattered portions in both volumes of this later source he collected a total of about five pages of material, which he added to the account of Inverness-shire.[47] Possibly a few scattered remarks elsewhere are also derived from Burt.[48]

With the same industry Smollett took from the fifth edition of Defoe's *Tour Thro' the Whole Island of Great Britain* (1753) a total of about four and a half pages of material scattered throughout the accounts of the various shires.[49] A few of these additions ex-

46. I, 250–94.

47. The great labor of selection and aggregation which Smollett performed to add these few facts may be appreciated by a glance at the following references (pages from Burt are given in the order of their appearance in *Present State*): cf. *PS*, II, 35, lines 20–30: *B*, I, 268–9; *PS*, 36, lines 30–5: *B*, II, 131, 132; *PS*, 37, lines 11–37: *B*, I, 35, 36, 52, 54–6, 53, 36–7; *PS*, 38, line 26–p. 39, line 6: *B*, I, 113, 45–6; *PS*, 39, line 14–p. 40, line 11: *B*, I, 235–6, II, 315–16, I, 247, 46, II, 319–20, I, 249–50, [256]–7; *PS*, 40, line 32–p. 41, line 23: *B*, II, 285–7, 292, 330–1. In addition to these references numerous statements in the account of Inverness-shire represent generalizations from Burt, *passim*.

48. See below, pp. 150, 158 n. 39 a, 160 n. 44, 166 n. 15.

49. The evidence that Smollett used the fifth edition (1753) and not the sixth (1761–62) rests upon one sentence in *Present State* (II, 58, lines 24–7); the passage

tend to a quarter- or half-page, but most of them are tiny details which would have been added only by a remarkably conscientious compiler. Smollett must have realized that most of the materials in this edition of the *Tour* had already been covered by the *Complete System;* nevertheless, he evidently read through most of the account of Scotland in the *Tour* in order to note any significant facts which might have been omitted.

Smollett's personal interests led him to give special attention to antiquities: he appears to have been the first compiler of a general description of Scotland to include accounts from Alexander Gordon's excellent antiquarian treatise: *Itinerarium Septentrionale: or, a Journey Thro' most of the Counties of Scotland, and those in the North of England* (folio, 1726). Additions from this source, however, amount to only four pages and a quarter.[50] It is inconceivable that Smollett read through the whole of this huge treatise to glean these few facts: he had evidently read the whole work previously (probably while preparing his *History of England*), and by using the index made the few additions as they were suggested in the course of compiling from other sources.

Finally, although the *Complete System* contained almost everything in Gibson's second edition of Camden, Smollett added a few facts, amounting to about one page, from the *Britannia* itself.[51] The small amount of the additions indicates that he remembered the specific facts from a previous perusal of the work (probably in connection with his *History of England*), and merely looked them up to complete his account.

in Defoe on which this sentence is based (see second reference below) is removed in the sixth edition. The thoroughness of Smollett's procedure may be ascertained by consideration of the following references: cf. *Pres. St.*, II, 45, lines 21–5: Defoe, IV, 217; *PS*, 58, lines 15–27: D, 180; *PS*, 62, lines 25–34: D, 212; *PS*, 87, lines 14–31: D, 160–1; *PS*, 137, lines 12–21: D, 114; *PS*, 139, lines 20–34: D, 148, 146; *PS*, 142, lines 28–32: D, 147–8. The minor additions are too numerous and insignificant to list.

50. The additions, as usual, are scattered throughout the accounts of the various shires: cf. *Pres. St.*, II, 56, line 20–p. 57, line 27: Gordon, pp. 164–5; *PS*, 71, line 16–p. [72] (mispr. 27), line 8: G, 162–4; *PS*, 75, lines 20–9: G, 150–2; *PS*, 91, line 33–p. 93, line 10: G, 50, 63–4, 23–32; *PS*, 127, line 38–p. 128, line 9: G, 116–17; *PS*, 139, lines 12–18: G, 114–15. Gordon's work receives one of the two specific citations in Smollett's account (see *Pres. St.*, II, 92).

51. Smollett probably used the third edition of Gibson's revision of the *Britannia*, published in 1753; this is a reprint of the second edition, with identical pagination. I have used the second edition in this study. Specific indebtedness to Camden may be found by consulting the following references: cf. *Pres. St.*, II, 96, lines 16–25: Camden, II, 1224; *PS*, 99, lines 29–38: C, 1214; *PS*, 137, lines 3–12: C, 1206. Smollett notes (*Pres. St.*, II, 96) that Camden has described the castle of Dumbarton, and undoubtedly the account of this town in *Present State* (II, 96–8) owes much to Camden (II, 1218), although specific indebtedness cannot be traced.

With these five sources[52] to provide a solid basis of detail, the accounts of the various shires were then amplified and invigorated by the addition of a total of about thirty pages from Smollett's personal knowledge. A small part of this consists of scattered facts which Smollett probably learned in compiling his *History of England;* in particular, he is careful to note the location of all important events in the Jacobite rebellions. But throughout his accounts of the northern shires, Smollett could do little more than rearrange the material from his sources into concise order and add a few general observations. The proportion of original material is only a little larger in the accounts of the extreme southern shires. The extensive additions are found in the descriptions of the south-central portion upon which Smollett concentrates in *Humphry Clinker.* The account of Smollett's native Dumbartonshire is almost entirely original, and much original material is found in the accounts of the neighboring regions, which Smollett had visited in boyhood or later years: Argyleshire, Perthshire, Stirlingshire, Lanarkshire, Renfrewshire, and the Lothians.

These original additions do not usually occur in long, continuous passages: they are intermingled almost inextricably with material from the printed sources. Smollett obviously added his bits of personal information as they were suggested in the course of compilation from books. In many places personal observations have so transmuted the underlying source that it is no longer traceable; nevertheless, verbatim borrowings in proximate parts show that Smollett must have been writing the account with the printed source as his pattern. Because of Smollett's personal interest the accounts of the south-central shires are much more vigorous than those of the other shires, which often become perfunctory.

To complete the entire description Smollett added, chiefly from his own knowledge,[53] a general introduction to the account of Scotland proper, twenty-five pages in length, which constitutes the best summary view of the Scottish land and life available in

52. An additional source may have been used for several brief lists of fine seats which do not appear in *Complete System* (*Pres. St.,* II, 40, 100–1, 109, 111). These could have been found in Chamberlayne's *Magnae Britanniae Notitia* (38th ed., 1755).

53. In composing this introduction Smollett undoubtedly consulted the similar sections on Scotland in the *Complete System* and Defoe's *Tour,* and he may have consulted other works such as Chamberlayne's *Magnae Britanniae Notitia* and Miege's *Present State of Great-Britain* for material on government and commerce. This account in *Present State* is so amplified and generalized that it is difficult to trace definite sources; but, including extremely dubious indebtedness, the total amount of this section taken directly from books cannot be much more than five pages.

Smollett's day. Again, the best section is the keen analysis of "People, their Character and Peculiarities";[54] but the true Smollettian touch may be found in other parts: in the eloquent description of Highland scenery, in the ridicule of Scottish clergy, even in the account of commerce.[55] The amount of original material in the whole description of Scotland proper is thus swelled to fifty pages, or about one-third of the account.

Throughout the whole description material from the sources is rearranged and integrated with the original observations. The heavy facts naturally will not allow many flights of neo-classical prose, but at least the sentence structure is always precise, and the diction is polished wherever possible. Thus, by a combination of industry and originality Smollett composed the most comprehensive, clear, orderly, and probably the most accurate description of Scotland proper which had thus far appeared.

In performing this service for his native land, Smollett did not adopt the tone of a brash patriot. He strove only to win respect for the virtues of Scotland which the prejudiced Englishman unjustly scorned; he never attempted to screen obvious faults. Thus, although his accounts of Scottish resources are obviously advertisements designed to attract English capital, his statements undoubtedly present a true picture of the potential wealth of the land. Similarly, his favorable accounts of Scottish landscapes, towns, and seats strive only to correct the misconceptions of prejudice by means of accurate information. And he is never loath to admit that sloth and indigence form too great a part of the Scottish national economy: while he adopts Martin's attractive prospectus for settlers in the Hebrides, he also includes Burt's descriptions of the filth and poverty of Inverness-shire. Smollett thus achieves such a judicious estimate of both vices and virtues that the modern reader can detect little evidence of the national prejudice rampant in Smollett's day.

In compiling the description of England for *Present State*[56] Smollett must have been faced with many temptations to return the harsh treatment which he and his fellow-Scots received in England. But he was writing a history, not a pamphlet or a periodical essay; he therefore allowed himself no more than guarded, judicious censure, and candidly admitted the flourishing, powerful state of England.

54. *Pres. St.*, II, 9–16. 55. *Idem*, pp. 2, 17–18; see below, p. 174.
56. *Pres. St.*, II, [151]–III, 349.

The tone of impartial analysis is particularly evident in the introductory section, one hundred and ten pages in length, which Smollett prefixed to this description. Despite the constant abuse of Scotland which came from the English, Smollett gives England enthusiastic praise:

England, except in a very few places, exhibits to the view an inchanting variety of gently swelling hills, level plains, corn fields, meadow grounds, wood and water, intermingled in the most agreeable manner. . . . The uncultivated part of the ground is cloathed with a perpetual verdure; and the lands, in general, display the perfection of agriculture. The seats of noblemen and gentlemen rise like inchanted castles on every hand: populous villages, thriving towns, and flourishing cities, abound in every part of the kingdom, which excels all the states of Europe in beauty, opulence, and cultivation.[57]

But the praise is qualified: Smollett shows equal force in denouncing the mutable English climate:

These sudden transitions must disorder and obstruct the perspiration. The matter, which ought to have been thrown off by this out-let, being detained in the circulation, will excite feverish frays in the animal oeconomy, will be thrown upon the lungs, the arms, the joints, or the membranes of the brain, producing catarrhs, gravel, gout, rheumatism, scurvy, dejection, and madness.[58]

His description of the inhabitants is equally judicious: they are the most comely and clean people in Europe, but they are "variable in their tempers, whimsical, capricious, and inconstant":

An Englishman, unrefined by travel and communication, numbers among his privileges the right of speaking his sentiments on all occasions without reserve, even when inconsistent with the universal rules of good breeding and humanity: hence those shocking reflections and reproaches, national and personal, which have often been productive of quarrels and homicide. An Englishman, however, is not naturally cruel, but rather mild and compassionate, and though extremely irascible, easily appeased by submission. He is neither tenacious of resentment, nor addicted to revenge; but compromises differences, and forgets injuries, easier and sooner than the natives of some other countries could well imagine.[59]

Indeed, it is regrettable that this introduction, providing a survey of the contemporary state of England, has escaped the attention of scholars of Smollett and the eighteenth century. It contains a crystallization of Smollett's opinions on every aspect of the age. Interspersed among the necessary facts of government and trade

57. *Pres. St.*, II, 152.   58. *Idem*, pp. 156–7.   59. *Idem*, p. 214.

are incisive comments which reveal the experience of many years passed in political controversy. Some sections, such as those headed "State of Learning" and "Liberal Arts,"[60] provide an epitome of Smollett's views on the scientific and cultural life from which he had gleaned a livelihood. Other sections, particularly those headed "People, their Persons, Attire, Disposition, and Manners," "Amusements and Diversions," and "Habitations, and Manner of Living,"[61] epitomize the candid observations scattered throughout Smollett's novels: it is questionable whether one could find a more acute estimate of the English character than that presented here in less than four pages.[62]

The style, to be sure, is more compact than "elegant"; but it represents the notably precise and lucid expression achieved by years of practice in compilation. Furthermore, one needs only to read such a passage as the amusing history of the Quakers which Smollett here presents, to recognize the neat, concise style which distinguishes *Humphry Clinker*.[63] On the whole, these one hundred and ten pages by one of the canniest observers of the age afford a better introduction to eighteenth-century life than many longer and more famous accounts.

Unfortunately, as much cannot be said for the subsequent particular descriptions of English shires, which consist of little more than lists of towns, buildings, products, and antiquities, overwhelmingly perfunctory and dull. It is impossible to say how much of this part was done by Smollett himself. A few parallels with *Humphry Clinker* suggest that his hand is present; but the most one can fairly assume is that the account had his editorial approval. Although he gives an adequate and favorable account of the shires, he is apparently bored with the whole tedious task: after all, England had already been copiously described. According to his contract, Smollett gave the required facts in concise order, but without the vitality produced by belief in the necessity for another description.

The contrast between the accounts of London and Edinburgh is typical of the difference between the particular accounts of England and Scotland. Beginning the section on London, Smollett says:

London . . . has been so fully and so often described, that it would be altogether superfluous to enter into a minute account of it: we shall therefore content ourselves with a very brief and general description.[64]

60. *Pres. St.*, II, [223]–31 (misprinted 221).   61. *Idem*, pp. 212–22.
62. *Idem*, pp. 213–16.   63. See *idem*, pp. 189–93, and below, Chapter VIII.
64. *Pres. St.*, III, 160.

Accordingly, he presents practically nothing but a perfunctory account of its government and a barren catalogue of notable places. In sharp contrast, Smollett approaches Edinburgh as a practically unknown city, and includes many illuminating remarks on the customs and manners of its inhabitants, with the result that the description is usually fluent, and often vigorous. But this superior vitality is not simply the result of prejudice, for the most vigorous portion is devoted to condemnation of the Scottish custom of dumping filth in the streets. In the particular account of Scotland Smollett was inspired by a real opportunity to correct ignorance; in the corresponding account of England he was merely repeating the facts already available in dozens of other compilations. As a result, he evaluated the particular qualities of each country with almost equal objectivity, but not with equal energy.

IV

The Genesis of Humphry Clinker

I N THE Introduction[1] I have already discussed at length the differences between the products of Smollett's earlier and later creative periods. The three earlier novels were concerned primarily with rambling adventures; the heroes travelled a great deal, but the emphasis fell upon amusing incidents, not upon historical details. Thus, in Roderick Random's trip to Carthagena the author was interested primarily in the experiences of his hero, not in actual naval or military events; while in Peregrine Pickle's tour of the Continent the spots visited are barely mentioned, not historically described. But in his later creative period Smollett's focus has changed: half his *Travels* presents minute and exact historical material; the *Adventures of an Atom* is almost wholly concerned with historical details, both Japanese and English; and half his last novel, *Humphry Clinker*, deals with historical matter, topographical, social, and political.

Without this final novel the other two works might be explained as merely the products of temporary conditions: the desire to make money from his travels, in the absence of any better inspiration; or, in the case of the *Atom*, an almost psychopathic urge to flog the land and the politicians who had treated him (as he thought) so scurvily. But, in the presence of *Humphry Clinker*, such explanations will not suffice: the political satire of the *Atom* turns up again in Melford's accounts of the levees held by the King and Newcastle, and in Bramble's excoriations of the London mob; while the historical interests of the *Travels* find their counterpart in the detailed descriptions of England and Scotland. The *Travels* and the *Atom*, then, stand as legitimate products of a new-found inspiration in Smollett—the inspiration of historical facts, as opposed to the fictitious adventures of a picaresque hero; and *Humphry Clinker*, far from being merely a happy anomaly, becomes, like the immediately preceding works, a natural result of all the historical materials with which Smollett had been concerned since 1753.

A more particular influence of Smollett's hack work upon *Humphry Clinker* is suggested in the headings which the *Whitehall Evening-Post* in 1771 gave to a series of extracts from this novel:

1. See above, pp. 12–16.

part of Bramble's letter of April 23 is reprinted under the title, "The Present State of Bath," while part of his letter of May 29 is similarly headed, "The Present State of London."[2] Clearly the writer of these headings recognized in Smollett's descriptions an essential kinship with Smollett's *Present State* and its many predecessors under that title. The influence of Smollett's last compilation is not limited to its general effect upon Smollett's interests—its warping of Smollett toward historical matter; it appears to have supplied specific inspiration for the tone and content of a large part of the novel. To understand this inspiration it is necessary first to examine some significant features of *Humphry Clinker*.

The reader who turns from *Present State* to *Humphry Clinker* will notice at once that in the novel's descriptions of England and Scotland Smollett has discarded the impartiality of the compilation. As Austin Dobson has observed, "Mr. Bramble's heart shows signs of softening as he nears Smollett's native land."[3] Bramble ceases the diatribes which marked his accounts of Bath and London and becomes an astonished admirer of the neglected virtues of Scotland. In England scarcely anything could please him: his first letter from London, for example, metes out eight lines of praise and follows them with five pages of slashing denunciation; and this proportion is fairly indicative of his temper throughout the tour from Gloucester to Berwick. But Scotland reverses his outlook: although, as a South Briton, he naturally allows himself some adverse criticism of the North, his strictures on Scotland occur in only a little larger proportion than did his grudging praise of England. Moreover, while his censure of England is violent and virulent, his censure of Scotland is judicious and mild—at times even apologetic: "If I may be allowed to mingle censure with my remarks upon a people I revere. . . ."[4] —a courtesy never accorded the English!

Melford, too, in his remarks on England, is almost as derogatory as his uncle; true, he speaks in a different tone, for, as he says, "Those follies, that move my uncle's spleen, excite my laughter";[5] but it is generally the laughter of the Comic Spirit. His account of Bath, though written in a healthier mood, supports his uncle's jaundiced view; while his letters from London are mainly concerned with satirical accounts of the levees and entertainments of politicians and authors. On the other hand, he is so "caressed and

2. See the *Whitehall Evening-Post*, June 15–18, 18–20, 1771. For this information I am indebted to Professor Lewis M. Knapp.

3. Austin Dobson, *Eighteenth Century Vignettes* (second series, New York, 1894), p. 159.

4. *Works*, IV, 94–5.   5. *Idem*, III, 75.

feasted in the *good town of Edinburgh*" that he declares he is almost converted "into a downright Caledonian";[6] and he and his uncle soon vie with each other in declaring their "raptures" over this New Found Land. Lydia, to be sure, is in ecstasies over Bath and London, just as she is over Scotland; but her feminine flutterings weigh light against the virile satire of her brother and uncle; in fact, it seems quite clear that Smollett is enjoying Liddy's girlish enthusiasm with tongue in cheek.

Furthermore, the novel's accounts of the two countries contain many incidents and descriptions which contrast so specifically that they enforce a duality of tone. The account of Paunceford's ingratitude to Serle, related at Bath, forms a patent contrast to the generosity of Captain Brown in the nameless Scottish borough:[7] both were men who, from low origins, had made fortunes abroad; but on returning home they put their gains to utterly different uses; hence, Paunceford is treated with bitter contempt, Brown with extravagant commendation. It is no accident that these anecdotes conform to the mood of the descriptions amid which they occur.

Similarly, one cannot miss the even more pointed contrast between the satirical treatment of Squire Burdock's "*old English hospitality*" in the North of England and the constant eulogies of Scottish hospitality which shortly after flow from both Bramble and Melford. The long account of Burdock, moreover, is introduced by a paragraph scorning the general English pretension to hospitality, and is immediately followed by the contemptuous shorter account of the company's reception by Mr. Pimpernel, in comparison with whom Bramble declares that even Burdock appears a prince.[8] But in Scotland not an inhospitable host appears: everyone, Highlander, Lowlander, lawyer, duke, is so gracious and generous that Bramble, soon after his arrival, declares he has "met with more kindness, hospitality, and rational entertainment, in a few weeks, than ever I received in any other country during the whole course of my life";[9] and later he adds that the party has been entertained "not barely with hospitality, but with such marks of cordial affection, as one would wish to find among near relations, after an absence of many years."[10] With all these encomiums in mind, one must feel with double force the shock of their rude reception by Lord Oxmington, as soon as they return to England.[11] It seems that Scotland was a refuge not only from the noise, unhealthfulness, folly, and corruption of Bath and London, but also from English churlishness and selfishness. Later, of course, Smollett makes

6. *Works*, IV, 73.   7. *Idem*, III, 106–11, IV, 144–8.   8. *Idem*, III, 268–82.
9. *Idem*, IV, 89.   10. *Idem*, p. 125.   11. *Idem*, pp. 176–81.

amends to England by including the hospitality of Dennison; but the earlier effect is too strong to be eradicated: the visit to Scotland has been prefaced by all manner of annoyances in England; and, in particular, has been framed by the irritations of English inhospitality.

Less obvious contrasts are numerous: the nauseous "London dainties" and the excellent provisions in Edinburgh;[12] the corruption of Justice Buzzard and the integrity of the Scottish "college of justice";[13] the two famous English authors whose arrogance and rancor make them "not fit for conversation" and the many Scottish authors who are "as agreeable in conversation as they are instructive and entertaining in their writings";[14] the satire on clergy at Bath and the praise of clergy in Edinburgh;[15] Bramble's disgust with English wealth and his pride in the beginnings of Scottish prosperity.

The duality, as I have said, is not absolute. "The public inns of Edinburgh, are still worse than those of London";[16] and the comparison of England to Scotland, Bramble admits, "is unfavourable to Scotland in all its exteriors, such as the face of the country in respect to cultivation, the appearance of the bulk of the people, and the language of conversation in general."[17] Underneath the whole novel lies the assumption that England is richer in all material goods; but she is not allowed much credit for these, since she has, according to Bramble and Melford, put them to either abominable or ridiculous misuse. Scotland, though less opulent, wins the palm by the superior virtue of its inhabitants, who have not yet been seduced by excessive prosperity. Thus, after all allowances have been made for praise of England and censure of Scotland, the plain fact remains that the tone of the novel changes at the Tweed.

In place of the judicious description of England in *Present State* Smollett has given in *Humphry Clinker* an account which is dominated by displays of satirical virtuosity—almost as if he were deliberately retracting most of the compliments he had previously paid to England. Whereas *Present State* declares, "Nothing can be more pure and salutary than the air of these downs,"[18] the irate Bramble cries, "It makes me sick to hear people talk of the fine air upon Clifton-Downs."[19] Similarly, *Present State* declares, "Bath

12. *Works*, III, 194–8, IV, 66.
14. *Idem*, III, 169–72, IV, 92–3.
16. *Idem*, IV, 69.
18. *Pres. St.*, III, 114.

13. *Idem*, III, 249, IV, 91.
15. *Idem*, III, 115, IV, 92.
17. *Idem*, p. 90.
19. *Works*, III, 11.

is the general hospital of the nation, and a great number of invalids find benefit from the waters,"[20] while Bramble snorts, "A national hospital it may be; but one would imagine, that none but lunatics are admitted."[21]

Indeed, Bramble's whole account of Bath contradicts the pages in *Present State* devoted to modest praise of the resort. Thus, *Present State* says:

A cemicircular range of buildings is just begun near the Circus, to be called from its form the Crescent. . . . In a word, new houses appear in every corner, and Bath is continually extending itself through all its different avenues. If this rage for building continues, and people persist in flocking thither from all quarters, Bath will soon become one of the largest and most populous cities in England. Their advantages for building here are very great, having excellent free-stone, limestone, and slate in the neighbourhood.[22]

Bramble adapts these materials to satire, which grows in intensity until he brazenly contradicts the facts in regard to building-stone:

The same artist, who planned the Circus, has likewise projected a Crescent; when that is finished, we shall probably have a Star; and those who are living thirty years hence, may, perhaps, see all the signs of the Zodiac exhibited in architecture at Bath. These, however fantastical, are still designs that denote some ingenuity and knowledge in the architect; but the rage of building has laid hold on such a number of adventurers, that one sees new houses starting up in every out-let and every corner of Bath; contrived without judgment, executed without solidity, and stuck together, with so little regard to plan and propriety, that the different lines of the new rows and buildings interfere with, and intersect one another in every different angle of conjunction. . . . What sort of a monster Bath will become in a few years, with those growing excrescences, may be easily conceived: but the want of beauty and proportion is not the worst effect of these new mansions; they are built so slight, with the soft crumbling stone found in this neighbourhood, that I should never sleep quietly in one of them, when it blowed (as the sailors say) a cap-full of wind; . . . .[23]

The same distortion is found in Bramble's account of London food. *Present State* praises the quality of English food in general:

Their butter, it must be owned, is delicate, their cheese rich and palatable, their bread light, white, sweet, and easy of digestion, except in the metropolis, where the flour is adulterated by knavish bakers.[24]

20. *Pres. St.*, III, 120.   21. *Works*, III, 49.   22. *Pres. St.*, III, 119.
23. *Works*, III, 52–3.   24. *Pres. St.*, II, 220.

In sharp contrast Bramble retches at "the tallowy rancid mass, called butter, manufactured with candle-grease and kitchen-stuff,"[25] and transfers the blame for poor bread from the baker to the degenerate public:

The bread I eat in London, is a deleterious paste, mixed up with chalk, alum, and bone-ashes, insipid to the taste, and destructive to the constitution. The good people are not ignorant of this adulteration; but they prefer it to wholsome bread, because it is whiter than the meal of corn: thus they sacrifice their taste and their health, and the lives of their tender infants, to a most absurd gratification of a mis-judging eye; and the miller, or the baker, is obliged to poison them and their families, in order to live by his profession.[26]

Merely to attribute such remarks to Bramble's eccentricity is to evade the issue. Why is Bramble made eccentric? His eccentricity, of course, admirably assists in producing those ludicrous incidents which are Smollett's delight; but the desire to provide a vehicle for denunciation of England, I believe, constitutes another essential reason for the emphasis, in the first part of the novel, upon Bramble's "morbid excess of sensation,"[27] his peevishness, hypochondria, and misanthropy. Bramble's eccentricity serves to guard Smollett from the charge of taking sides, and makes the diatribes more acceptable for an English audience: to the average Englishman such abuse of England could come only from an acknowledged eccentric! Then, as he moves northward, Bramble's characteristics change: his hypochondria disappears with the bracing air and healthful diet of Scotland; his misanthropy is turned to fervent admiration for the excellence of Scotsmen; his "excess of sensation" ceases to produce "morbid" effects, and becomes instead the channel for enthusiastic enjoyment of everything from food to scenery. This transformation is not simply the result of "characterization" in the ordinary sense: it is prompted, in large part, by Smollett's desire to lash England and praise Scotland.

In this deliberate contrast between England and Scotland lies an essential inspiration for Humphry Clinker—an inspiration which, I believe, may be traced in part to the dispassionate attitude which Smollett adopted in describing both Scotland and England in Present State. For, as usual, the impartial observer was accused of unfairness by those whose views were distorted by prejudice. Smollett's Scottish friends were irritated equally by his condemnation of Scottish faults and by his praise of English

25. Works, III, 198.   26. Idem, p. 195.   27. Idem, p. 20.

virtues. This effect is evident from a letter which Dr. John Armstrong wrote to Smollett on March 28, 1769:

But, talking of some recent publications, puts me in mind of something I had almost forgot to tell you— That several people, who have a particular regard and esteem for the reputed author of the Present State of all Nations, are sorry to find that he has too much exposed the posteriors of our brothers in the north; and made some undeserved compliments to their neighbours in the south, who have already a comfortable enough share of self-conceit; and that, amongst other perfections, he allows them to be the handsomest people in Europe, which they think a very disputable opinion.[28]

One motivation for the novel may be found in a desire to answer such objections with a description of Great Britain in which the purpose could not be misunderstood. The satire of England and encomium of Scotland may well represent Smollett's attempt to reconcile himself with those of his countrymen who were offended by *Present State*.

A further, related motivation must also be considered. Since the description of England occurs in the second and third volumes of *Present State*, it is quite possible that it was compiled before 1763,[29] at a time when Smollett still apparently believed that unbiased facts could make their way; accordingly, although the conceit which marked descriptions of England undoubtedly annoyed him, he contented himself with combating this conceit by judicious evaluation. In 1761–63, however, English bumptiousness and prejudice against Scotland were inflamed to new heights by Bute's administration, in defence of which Smollett engaged in the fiercest controversy of his life and exposed himself to the devilish mockery of John Wilkes. After 1763 Smollett's attitude toward England was bitterly resentful, as one can see from the well-known opening remarks in his *Travels* and from the notoriously vicious *Adventures of an Atom*. It is difficult to see how the account of England in *Present State* could have contained so little rancor and so much compliment, if it had been compiled after this date. The most plausible explanation is that Smollett had the account already prepared before this controversy and had neither the time nor the energy to revise it in accordance with his later feeling. When, however, the objectivity of this description annoyed his Scottish friends, surely their feelings would have combined with his own to produce a desire to counteract this favorable account of his hereditary enemies.

28. *Miscellaneous Works of Tobias Smollett* (Edinburgh, 1820), I, [188]–9 (first page misprinted 198).
29. See above, pp. 106–8.

Accordingly, in *Humphry Clinker*, Smollett by implication ridicules the complimentary attitude which marked previous descriptions of England, including his own; while the aim of the account of Scotland in *Present State* is revealed by the presentation of characters who declare their "conversion from illiberal prejudices"[30] in the very act of repeating parts of this previous description. In the novel Smollett can retain to some extent the judicious tone of the previous description of Scotland, because it is obviously appropriate to South Britons who are being converted.

Another motivation arising from *Present State* may also have contributed. *Present State* was, apparently, a failure:[31] the advertisement of Scotland upon which Smollett had lavished such care was evidently lost beneath the weight of the whole work. Smollett was not one to accept the loss of anything with which he had been so intimately concerned: witness his plea to the publishers for completion of the *Universal History,* or at least for publication of parts upon which he had worked.[32] Since, as the subsequent study will show, about twenty-six pages of *Humphry Clinker* echo the description of Scotland in *Present State,* it seems probable that the novel may to some extent have been inspired by a desire to salvage some part of this previous description; or, at least, by a desire to give Scotland the recognition which the earlier description had failed to achieve.

It thus appears that essential inspiration for *Humphry Clinker* may be found in a three-fold influence emanating from *The Present State of All Nations:* (1) Smollett may have desired to placate his countrymen who accused him of betraying Scotland in *Present State;* (2) his embroilment in political controversy during Bute's administration may have induced a desire to retract the complimentary account of England given in *Present State;* (3) he may have desired to salvage some part of the neglected but valuable description of Scotland which he had compiled for *Present State,* or to achieve its aim in a more acceptable form. What could better accomplish all these purposes than the presentation of descriptions in the popular form of a tour through Great Britain, in which satire on England would serve as a foil for a favorable account of Scotland?

All the above suggestions will go far toward explaining the remarkable change in Smollett's interests and methods as a novelist

30. *Works*, IV, 89.   31. See above, p. 104.
32. See *Works* (Edinburgh, 1820), I, 179, and my article, "Tobias Smollett and the *Universal History*," *MLN*, LVI (1941), 6–7, 10.

which is manifested in *Humphry Clinker*. Even the choice of an epistolary form may be partially explained by Smollett's work on *Present State*. In compiling his earlier account of Scotland, Smollett had carefully perused Burt's *Letters from a Gentleman in the North of Scotland*, as well as Defoe's *Tour*,[33] which, like *Humphry Clinker*, relates in the form of letters the observations of a traveller through Great Britain. Since, as we shall see, Smollett evidently composed *Humphry Clinker* with the description of Scotland in *Present State* clearly in his mind, there can be little doubt that he also associated the novel with the books consulted in making this earlier description.

But the decision to imitate a travel-book and the choice of the specific form of the travel-letter were, of course, influenced by many other forces. First among these was the fact that Smollett's tour through Great Britain in the summer of 1766 came at exactly the time when he was learning of the success of his own travel-letters on France and Italy, which appeared in May, 1766. The suggestion that he capitalize upon his domestic travels in the same way must have been inevitable. Supporting this particular motivation lay the contemporary demand for travels of all kinds, and the vogue for relating these travels in the epistolary form already familiar to Smollett from his work upon his own and Drummond's *Travels*.[34] Smollett himself notes the importance of these general influences in a letter prefatory to the novel:

Then there have been so many letters upon travels lately published— What between Smollett's, Sharp's, Derrick's, Thickness's, Baltimore's, and Baretti's, together with Shandy's Sentimental Travels, the public seems to be cloyed with that kind of entertainment—[35]

Since all these books appeared between 1766 and 1770, it is evident that Smollett was consciously following a contemporary

---

33. See above, pp. 117–18.   34. See above, pp. 6, 72.
35. *Humphry Clinker* (first ed.), I, xi–xii. Smollett refers to the following works:
  (a) His own *Travels* (1766).
  (b) Samuel Sharp, *Letters from Italy*, London, 1766.
  (c) Samuel Derrick's *Letters;* see below, p. 134.
  .(d) Philip Thicknesse, *Observations on the Customs and Manners of the French Nation, in a Series of Letters*, London, 1766; and *Useful Hints to those who make the Tour of France, in a Series of Letters*, London, 1768.
  (e) Frederick Lord Baltimore, *A Tour to the East*, London, 1767. This work is not written in the form of letters.
  (f) Joseph Baretti, *An Account of the Manners and Customs of Italy*, 2 vols., London, 1768. This work is not written in the form of letters. Also, *A Journey from London to Genoa*, 4 vols., London, 1770. This work is written in the form of letters.
  (g) Laurence Sterne, *A Sentimental Journey*, London, 1768. This work, of course, is not written in the form of letters.

fashion. The extraordinary popularity of travel-books in general and of travel-letters in particular was undoubtedly emphasized in his mind by Thicknesse's and Sterne's attacks upon his own *Travels*, and by the notorious controversy between Sharp and Baretti, in which Smollett was evidently asked to engage.[36]

The choice of an epistolary form may also have been partially directed by Smollett's familiarity with this form in works other than travel-books. One should remember that he was already well versed in the composition of fictitious letters from his work on the unfortunate *Briton*, which frequently gives Smollett's views through the device of epistles allegedly received from readers. One of these, as Whitridge has noted, forms a prototype for Winifred Jenkins's inspired epistles: it is a letter, replete with malapropisms, signed "Winifred Bullcalf."[37] In another of these letters in the *Briton*, as I shall show subsequently, lies the prototype of Bramble's letters about Lismahago.[38]

Moreover, residing frequently at Bath in the years 1766–68, Smollett undoubtedly became familiar with the work which is sometimes said to have supplied the primary motivation for *Humphry Clinker:* Christopher Anstey's popular *New Bath Guide: or, Memoirs of the B—r—d Family. In a Series of Poetical Epistles*, first published in 1766 and issued in a fifth edition by 1767. Certainly Anstey's general idea bears a marked similarity to the plan of *Humphry Clinker*, for he introduces epistles by different members of a family (the ward, the son, and the daughter of Lady B—n—r—d) which reveal different aspects of life at Bath. In particular, Jenny, the ward of her aunt and uncle, in her sentimental, romantic epistles to a girl-friend, suggests Lydia, the young ward of her aunt and uncle, Tabitha and Matthew Bramble. A maid named Tabitha, or Tabby, is mentioned, who undoubtedly suggested the name for Tabitha, or Tabby, Bramble. This maid and Prue, the daughter, are both afflicted with the new enthusiastic religion and obtain relief by mysterious communication with two ministers of the gospel; perhaps these remarks suggested the Methodism of Tabitha Bramble, Winifred Jenkins, and Hum-

36. In a letter (April 1, 1768) to one Antonio, an Italian who had been attacked by Baretti along with Sharp, and who was evidently planning an answer, Sharp says: "Dr. Smollett is too ill, and too much engaged, to revise your pamphlet; and besides, he would have answered him himself, had Baretti been worthy of his pen." (*Private Correspondence of David Garrick* [London, 1831–32], I, 297.) For this information I am indebted to Dr. Donald C. Gallup.

37. See *Briton*, Aug. 7, 1762, and Arnold Whitridge, *Tobias Smollett* (Brooklyn, 1925), pp. 71–2.

38. See below, pp. 171–3.

phry Clinker in Smollett's novel. But the only specific incident which is echoed by the novel is that in which the son, practicing dances to the music of the "city-musicians," irritates by his stomping the irascible Lord Ringbone, who, incapacitated by the gout, is confined to the floor below. This seems to have suggested the incident at Bath in which Bramble, suffering from the gout, is infuriated by the music of the "town-waits" and by the stomping overhead of Sir Ulic Mackilligut, who is practicing his steps for the ball.[39]

Here, however, the similarities end. Anstey's satire consists merely of general comments on the manners and customs of the day, the charlatanry of physicians, and the folly of individual characters—all composed in a burlesque of neo-classical poetry which avoids particularity. Smollett, on the other hand, presents a detailed description of the town and a particular account of its inhabitants. Anstey, then, is only one of many influences at work in the novel.

An additional influence upon the account of Bath may be found in one of the works cited by Smollett in the above quotation from the remarks prefatory to *Humphry Clinker:* Samuel Derrick's *Letters Written from Leverpoole, Chester, Corke, the Lake of Killarney, Dublin, Tunbridge-Wells, Bath,* published in 1767. Derrick, being Master of Ceremonies at Bath, devotes four of his letters to a particular description of the town and its inhabitants, in an effort to attract visitors to the scene of his activities; accordingly, it seems that the work must have enjoyed at least a moderate popularity at Bath, along with Anstey's epistles, as Smollett was spending part of his last years at the resort. Furthermore, Derrick was one of Smollett's acquaintances, and is described in *Humphry Clinker* in his official capacity at Bath. Thus, although Derrick's letters display no striking similarities to *Humphry Clinker,* it seems highly probable that Smollett was well acquainted with them, and that they exerted some influence in suggesting the particularity of Smollett's letters on Bath, in contrast to the vague and general nature of Anstey's remarks. Perhaps, too, the complimentary tone of Derrick was in Smollett's mind when he wrote his denunciations of the resort.

Which of all these influences really came first in the genesis of *Humphry Clinker?* Which exerted the largest force in creating the novel as it now stands? In determining the epistolary form, Smollett's own *Travels* and Anstey's *Guide* were probably the most

39. Cf. *Bath Guide* (fifth ed., London, 1767), pp. 35-7; *Works,* III, 41-3.

direct and significant influences; in determining the matter, Smol-lett's tour of 1766 and his *Present State* would appear to have been the leading forces. But the importance of the other influences suggested above cannot be denied, nor should one omit to mention other forces which I have not discussed: such as the nostalgia of the final exile enforced by Smollett's health, and the change in attitude and temper which comes to one who suspects that his death may be imminent. In the absence of any statement from Smollett, the questions of priority and scope must really be left uncertain in any discussion of the forces which inspired and moulded *Humphry Clinker*. Hence I do not wish to claim too much for the influence of *Present State;* one can only suggest and conjecture; and one can say with certainty only that the influence of *Present State* provided essential ingredients for the novel as it now appears.

V

The Description of Scotland in Humphry Clinker

IT HAS long been accepted that the description of Scotland in *Humphry Clinker* represents Smollett's observations during his final visit to his homeland in 1766. Robert Chambers, for instance, declares that "Smollett's last novel . . . was regarded by his relations as only a history, fictitiously coloured, of his northern tour in search of health, and his residence successively in Edinburgh and Glasgow."[1] Thomas Seccombe goes so far as to state that Smollett "made notes . . . during his journeys through England and Scotland, in 1766–7, and these notes . . . formed the nucleus of his greatest work, the inimitable *Humphrey Clinker*."[2]

It now appears, however, that this traditional explanation must be radically altered, for comparison with *Present State* proves that Smollett was well acquainted with nearly half this material on Scotland several years before he made the tour of 1766. In Henley's edition of *Humphry Clinker* passages equivalent to about seventy pages consist of direct description or discussion of Scotland and its inhabitants;[3] specific, detailed parallels with *Present State* can be found for at least eleven of these pages in the novel; general similarities with *Present State* are found in at least fifteen more pages; and undoubtedly much more material in *Humphry Clinker*, consisting of comment or elaboration upon the facts of *Present State*, owes its inspiration to the earlier account of Scotland. Most of these similarities occur in portions of *Present State* which appear to be original with Smollett; not more than six pages can be safely paralleled with parts of *Present State* taken from printed sources. About five additional pages of the novel appear to have been suggested by material which Smollett read in the course of preparing the earlier account, but which does not appear in any recognizable form in *Present State*.

Although many verbal echoes of *Present State* are found in these

1. Robert Chambers, *Smollett: His Life and a Selection from his Writings* (London and Edinburgh, 1867), p. 130.
2. Thomas Seccombe, "Bibliographical Note on Smollett's Travels," *Works*, XI, xii–xiii.
3. This figure, of course, excludes all anecdotes which are primarily for entertainment, not instruction, and all mention of individual characters, fictitious or actual, who cannot be said to illustrate Scotland in general.

parallel passages, they are only such occasional similarities as occur in the repetition of materials from memory: there is no evidence that Smollett copied any part of the novel directly from *Present State* or its printed sources. It is therefore impossible to ascertain exactly the influence of the sources of *Present State* upon *Humphry Clinker*. This much, however, may be said: Smollett had apparently perused these books with the assiduous attention necessary for the labor of compilation; thus, although he had probably seen most of the places described in the novel, his personal observations must have been fused with memories of the descriptions he had read.

In many portions of the novel where original passages of *Present State* appear to be repeated, the similarity is often so general that it seems scarcely worthy of notice. But before discarding such parallels, it is important to ascertain just when Smollett might have gathered these original observations which appear in *Present State*.

It has long been known that Smollett visited Scotland in 1755 and 1766, and it has recently been discovered that he also returned there in 1760.[4] The early date now established for the inception of *Present State* and the composition of its description of Scotland[5] makes it barely conceivable that Smollett may have projected the compilation before his visit of 1755; certainly he had planned, and possibly he had begun, the description of Scotland before his similar visit of 1760. It thus seems highly probable that during one or both of these two earlier tours Smollett took careful observations for the specific purpose of making his description of Scotland in *Present State* as accurate and comprehensive as possible. Such a procedure would easily account for the detailed nature of some of these original additions in the compilation, which otherwise could be explained only by attributing to Smollett an incredibly accurate memory.

Some of these original remarks, of course, may have been remembered from boyhood, or from conversation and correspondence with his many Scottish friends. But, however the materials were gathered, it is important to recall the old pedagogical adage that facts are best remembered and opinions best expounded after they have been fixed in memory by application to some specific purpose. All these materials were precipitated in Smollett's mind during the arduous process of compilation: their reappearance in

---

4. The evidence for this visit is in the possession of Professor George M. Kahrl, who has kindly allowed me to make use of his discovery.

5. See above, pp. 106–8.

Humphry Clinker may thus be regarded as a probable result of the earlier account, even though the repetition may consist only of a personal opinion or general description.

It is thus clear that the influence of Smollett's tour of 1766 is not so essential to the description of Scotland in *Humphry Clinker* as it has been traditionally represented; but this last visit must not be neglected. When Smollett visited Scotland in 1766, he naturally viewed with fresh interest the scenes already described in *Present State;* he may even have written down additions and corrections, as he did for his *Travels through France and Italy* during his last years on the Continent.[6] A bit of this new material may appear in footnotes to the text of *Present State,* but apparently he did not wish to disrupt the finished description. During this last tour, at any rate, the facts learned from the printed sources of *Present State* and from his own earlier tours must, it seems, have been enlivened and more deeply impressed upon Smollett's memory; while new facts were probably fixed more firmly in his mind by conscious or unconscious association with the description already prepared.

With all these considerations in mind, one may now turn to examine specific examples of the influence of *Present State* upon *Humphry Clinker.* The present chapter will simply illustrate the various ways in which echoes of the compilation occur; later chapters will discuss the aesthetic consequences of these echoes, providing by the way numerous additional illustrations.

One manifestation of the influence of *Present State* is found in the transfer of facts from printed sources through *Present State* to *Humphry Clinker.* The *Complete System of Geography,* for example, is the ultimate source for the following passage in the novel:

The castle of this place [Stirling] is such another as that of Edinburgh, and affords a surprising *prospect of the windings of the river Forth,* which are so extraordinary, that *the distance from hence to Alloa by land, is but four miles, and by water it is twenty-four.* Alloa is a neat thriving town, that depends in a great measure on the commerce of Glasgow, the merchants of which send hither tobacco and other articles, to be deposited in warehouses for exportation from the Frith of Forth.[7]

6. See above, p. 70.

7. *Works,* IV, 111–12 (my italics). The opening portion may have been influenced by this description of Stirling in *Present State:* "The town is nobly situated, well built, upon the declivity of a hill, which commands a *prospect of the charming windings of the Forth,* as well as of Edinburgh castle, the town of Alloway, a great number of fine seats, and distant views of other counties." (II, 90.) This, in turn,

This is directly influenced by the following description of Alloa in *Present State*, although the details in the novel are linked with Stirling:

But the most flourishing place of this shire is the village of Aloa or Aloway, situated on the Forth, where this river falls into the Frith, ... Here the merchants of Glasgow had a settled [*sic*] a factory, and erected warehouses for tobacco, surgar [*sic*], and other American commodities, for the conveniency of re-exporting them to Holland, Hamburgh, and the Baltic; . . . . One of these views [from Alloa Castle] terminates in the castle of Stirling, which, *though no more than four miles distant by land, is about four-and-twenty by water*, tracing the Forth in its beautiful meanders.[8]

Present State, in turn, takes its materials from *Complete System:*

. . . a Factory was lately settled at this Place [Alloa] for the Merchants of *Glasgow*, who not being very far distant by Land-carriage, have erected Warehouses for stowing their Tobacco, Sugar, and other Goods of their importing from the *British* Colonies in *America*, to be ready for Re-exportation to *Holland, Hamburgh, Bremen*, the *Baltick, London*, or wherever else they are wanted; . . . .[9]

Of three different views from Alloa Castle described by *Complete System*, Smollett chooses to include only this:

One of them shews *Stirling-Castle;* which tho' but four Miles from hence by Land, is 24 by Water; . . . .[10]

Smollett probably had visited Stirling, but the clear, precise nature of the description in the novel is obviously the result of the information learned in the process of compilation. The details have been fixed in his mind and emerge easily in the new form of the fictional tour.

Similarly, two sentences on the island of Iona[11] are certainly transmitted through *Present State* from Martin, although the only specific indication of indebtedness is found in these few words:

[Martin:] This *Isle* was anciently a Seminary of Learning, Famous for the severe Discipline and Sanctity of *Columbus*. He built two Churches, and two Monasteries in it, ...[12]

appears to be derived from *Complete System*, I, 291, which here repeats the figures on distance given above in *Humphry Clinker*, though *Present State* does not give them again.
  8. *Pres. St.*, II, 76–7 (my italics).
  9. *Complete System*, I, 258.   10. *Ibid.*
  11. *Works*, IV, 133, lines 12–17; cf. *Pres. St.*, I, 499, 501; *Descrip. of W. Is.*, pp. 256–61. The remainder of the paragraph in the novel, giving a general description of the inhabitants, is no doubt inspired by the reading of Martin's account.
  12. *Descrip. of W. Is.*, p. 257.

[*Present State:*] . . . he erected two churches and two monasteries, and instituted a seminary that soon became famous for learning and sanctity.[13]

[*Humphry Clinker:*] It was respected for its sanctity, and college or seminary of ecclesiastics—[14]

In other cases, though a printed source may be suspected, the description is too general to reveal definite indebtedness. Thus, for instance, *Humphry Clinker* mentions the fact that Fife "exhibits a surprising number of fine seats, elegantly built, and magnificently furnished."[15] Smollett, of course, probably knew this without consulting books; nevertheless, the actual appearance of the statement in the novel may be traced to the fact that Smollett had previously compiled for *Present State* a special section on fine seats of Fife from three separate places in *Complete System* and two in Defoe's *Tour*.[16]

The most interesting instance of such general indebtedness to source-material is found, I think, in the conversation on Scottish superstitions which occurs in *Humphry Clinker* at the Duke of Queensberry's table. Here a gentleman relates a tale of the "second sight": "a supernatural faculty of seeing visions of events before they happen."[17] He tells that he and four companions, taking provisions with them, paid an unexpected visit to an old friend who had lived sequestered for twenty years. But behold, when they arrived at their destination, the old friend met them with open arms and led them to a table already set for six! "He told me, very gravely," says the narrator, "he had seen me in a vision of the second sight."[18]

It seems that the inspiration for this particular incident may have come from various anecdotes on the second sight related by Martin. At the close of the description of St. Kilda in *Present State* Smollett introduces a special section, "Of the Second Sight," in which he presents selected remarks from Martin's long chapter on the subject.[19] Among various manifestations of the power which Smollett here cites, this significant one appears:

13. *Pres. St.*, I, 499.
14. *Works*, IV, 133. The sentence on Islay on the preceding page of the novel (*idem*, p. 132, lines 23–5) is apparently derived from Martin in the same manner. Cf. *Pres. St.*, I, 504; *Descrip. of W. Is.*, pp. 240–1.
15. *Works*, IV, 94.
16. Cf. *Pres. St.*, II, 87–8; *Complete System*, I, 268–9; Defoe, IV, 160–1, 176.
17. *Pres. St.*, I, 460.
18. *Works*, IV, 157. See *idem*, pp. 156–8 for the whole incident.
19. Cf. *Pres. St.*, I, 460–3; *Descrip. of W. Is.*, pp. 300–35.

. . . the vision of a stranger is seen before his arrival, and accurately described by the seer, though he had never heard of his name, and was quite ignorant of his coming. Martin declares, that he himself had been frequently seen at the distance of an hundred miles, by seers of both sexes, with whom he had no personal acquaintance.[20]

A little later in *Present State* Smollett revises Martin's account of the arrival of a new minister in the island of Rona, who was received with fully prepared hospitality, because the inhabitants had foreseen his coming by means of the second sight.[21] Smollett certainly knew of this superstition before reading Martin, but the specific form in which it is presented in *Humphry Clinker* may be traced back to these materials which he had compiled for *Present State*.

After this anecdote in *Humphry Clinker* Smollett, in order to emphasize the absurdity of such superstitions, adds another anecdote which relates the scourging of a gentleman by the ghost of his grandfather. This, of course, proves to have no other foundation than Lismahago's chastisement of that "degenerate rascal,"[22] his nephew. By such a tenuous trail the dull process of compilation may lead to brilliant fictional incidents.

Generally such echoes of source-material in the novel are combined with echoes of additions made in *Present State* from Smollett's personal knowledge. This description of Paisley is typical:

[*Humphry Clinker:*] . . . one of the most flourishing places of the kingdom, enriched by the linen, cambrick, flowered lawn, and silk manufactures. [It was formerly noted for a rich monastery of the monks of Clugny, who wrote the famous *Scoti-Chronicon,* called *The Black Book of Paisley.*] The old abbey still remains, converted into a dwelling-house, belonging to the earl of Dundonald.[23]

[*Present State:*] . . . flourishing by means of the linen manufacture. . . . [famous for its abbey, founded in the twelfth century by Alexander II. high steward of Scotland. It was instituted for monks of the order of Cluny, who for many ages continued a chronicon of the nation, known by the name of the Black Book of Paisley, which agreed in every material fact with the Scoti-Chronicon of Fordun, and is by some people supposed to be the same performance.] At the Reformation, the abbey, with all its dependencies, was given to the family of Hamilton, who converted it into a lodging house; and it afterwards became the property of the earl of Dundonald, ...[24]

20. *Pres. St.,* I, 461.
21. *Idem,* pp. 469–70; cf. *Descrip. of W. Is.,* pp. 19–21.
22. *Works,* IV, 160. See *idem,* pp. 158–61 for the whole incident.
23. *Idem,* p. 118 (my brackets).   24. *Pres. St.,* II, 99 (my brackets).

Only the passages in brackets appear to have been derived from *Complete System:*

Here are still to be seen the Remains of an Abbey, founded by *Alexander* II. High Steward of *Scotland, Anno* 1160, whose Monks of the Order of *Cluny* wrote a History of this Nation, about 1451, which is commonly called the *Black Book* of *Pasley*. . . . It seems to agree with *Fordon's Scot's* Chronicon, if it be not the same.[25]

In many places *Humphry Clinker* retains only the personal comments. Thus, for example, in the novel Melford denounces the pictures at Holyroodhouse:

. . . and as for the pictures of the Scottish kings, from Fergus I. to king William, they are paultry daubings, mostly by the same hand, painted either from the imagination, [or porters hired to sit for the purpose].[26]

All this, except the satirical suggestion in brackets, had already appeared in *Present State:*

In one gallery we see the portraits of the Scottish kings from the first Fergus, who is said to have reigned three hundred and twenty years before Christ, to William III. prince of Orange: but they are, for the most part, paultry pieces, drawn from the imagination of the painter; and indeed one may perceive that the majority have been painted by one hand.[27]

As usual, Smollett has here enlivened and elaborated upon the facts given by *Complete System:*

. . . there is a long Gallery adorned with the Pictures of all the Kings of *Scotland*, from *Fergus* their first King, 320 Years before the Birth of *Christ*, to the Revolution; . . . .[28]

Of all such original additions, one of the most striking in its effect upon the novel is this passage in the account of Smollett's native Dumbartonshire in *Present State:*

The river Leven is a *pure transparent pastoral stream, that warbles o'er a bed of pebbles,* through a *delightful* vale adorned with its farms, seats, woods, and plantations. It derives origin from the great lake called Loch-Lomond, of which indeed it is the overflowing, and, after a *delightful meandring course* of five or six miles, disembogues itself into the Clyde at the castle of Dumbarton.[29]

25. *Complete System*, I, 289.   26. *Works*, IV, 77 (my brackets).
27. *Pres. St.*, II, 120.   28. *Complete System*, I, 263.
29. *Pres. St.*, II, 94 (my italics).

This first reappears in part of Bramble's enthusiastic description of Smollett's boyhood haunts:

We now crossed the water of Leven, which, though nothing near so considerable as the Clyde, is much more *transparent, pastoral,* and *delightful.* This charming stream is the outlet of Lough-Lomond, and through a tract of four miles pursues its *winding course, murmuring over a bed of pebbles,* till it joins the Frith at Dunbritton.[30]

Two pages later some of the same materials are repeated in Smollett's *Ode to Leven Water:*

> *Pure stream!* in whose *transparent* wave
> My youthful limbs I wont to lave;
> No torrents stain thy limpid source;
> No rocks impede thy dimpling course,
> That sweetly *warbles o'er its bed,*
> With white, round, polish'd *pebbles* spread; . . . .[31]

Since no record of this poem is found before its appearance in *Humphry Clinker,* it is possible that the description of Dumbarton-shire in *Present State* led to the composition of the *Ode;* though, naturally, one cannot be certain that the poem did not come first.

In other cases, while treating the same topic, *Humphry Clinker* gives original matter, and *Present State* follows the printed source almost exactly. It seems that the previous description had excited Smollett's interest to such an extent that he made personal inquiries on the topic during his last visit to Scotland and then added supplementary facts in the novel.

This procedure may be traced in a passage of *Humphry Clinker* which relates to one of Smollett's forbears:

Mull affords several bays, where there is safe anchorage; in one of which, the Florida, a ship of the Spanish armada, was blown up by one of Mr. [Commissary] Smollett's ancestors— About forty years ago, John duke of Argyle is said to have consulted the Spanish registers, by which it appeared, that this ship had the military chest on board— He employed experienced divers to examine the wreck; and they found the hull of the vessel still entire, but so covered with sand, that they could not make their way between decks; however, they picked up several pieces of plate, that were scattered about in the bay, and a couple of fine brass cannon.[32]

Smollett's interest in this subject was probably aroused by an account by Martin which he transferred bodily to *Present State:*

30. *Works,* IV, 118–19 (my italics).   31. *Idem,* p. 121 (my italics).
32. *Idem,* pp. 132–3.

[Martin:] Near to the North East end of *Mull*, lies the Isle *Calve*, it is above two Miles in compass, ... Between this Isle, and the Isle of *Mull*, there is a capacious and excellent Bay, called *Tonbir Mory*, ...

One of the Ships of the *Spanish Armada*, called the *Florida*, perished in this Bay, having been blown up by one *Smallet* of *Dunbarton*, in the year 1688 [*sic*]. There was a great Sum of Gold and Money on board the Ship, which disposed the Earl of *Argyle*, and some Englishmen to attempt the recovery of it; but how far the latter succeeded in this Enterprize, is not generally well known; only that some pieces of Gold, and Money, and a golden Chain was taken out of her. I have seen some fine brass Cannon, some Pieces of Eight, Teeth, Beads and Pins that had been taken out of that Ship.[33]

[*Present State:*] Near the north-east end of Mull, lies the island Calve, above two miles in compass, and forming with the other a capacious bay, called Tonber-mory, in which the Florida, one of the largest ships of the Spanish armada, was blown up by one Smollet of Dumbarton. It was supposed that she had on board a large sum of money; a circumstance which has induced several adventurers to dive upon the wreck, with the permission of the duke of Argyle. Pieces of gold and silver, beads, pins, toys, and some fine brass cannon have been recovered; but not enough to defray the expence of diving.[34]

Smollett has evidently searched out additional facts since the compilation of *Present State*, and in *Humphry Clinker* has combined these new facts with those given by Martin.

Finally, *Humphry Clinker* appears to include source-material which Smollett had read, but had not included in his earlier description. Thus, *Present State* says only, "One Gilouir Mackirain attained to the age of one hundred and fourscore,"[35] whereas *Humphry Clinker* tells of "one Mackcrain, who lived one hundred and eighty years in one house, and died in the reign of Charles the Second."[36] The additions may have been made from Smollett's remembrance of the passage in Martin from which he took the statement in *Present State*:

Several of the Natives have lived to a great Age, I was told that one of them called *Gillouir Mack Crain* lived to have kept one hundred and eighty *Christmasses* in his own house; he died about fifty years ago, and there are several of his acquaintance living to this day, from whom I had this account.[37]

The same explanation may apply to this passage in which Melford relates the sleeping-accommodations of the Highlanders:

33. *Descrip. of W. Is.*, pp. 253–4.   34. *Pres. St.*, I, 498.   35. *Idem*, p. 503.
36. *Works*, IV, 132.   37. *Descrip. of W. Is.*, p. 234.

At night, half a dozen occasional beds are ranged on each side along the wall. These are made of fresh heath, pulled up by the roots, and disposed in such a manner as to make a very agreeable couch, where they lie, without any other covering than the plaid— My uncle and I were indulged with separate chambers and down beds, which we begged to exchange for a layer of heath; and indeed I never slept so much to my satisfaction. It was not only soft and elastic, but the plant, being in flower, diffused an agreeable fragrance, which is wonderfully refreshing and restorative.[38]

Present State, condensing Martin, gives only the terse statement:

. . . they lie on beds of straw or heath, which last is an excellent restorative: . . . .[39]

Smollett may have remembered the original account by Martin, perhaps because his memory had recently been refreshed by personal experience in 1766:

They lie for the most part on Beds of Straw, and some on Beds of Heath; which latter being made after their way, with the tops uppermost, are almost as soft as a Feather-bed, it yields a pleasant scent after lying on it once. The Natives by experience have found it to be effectual for drying superfluous Humours, and strengthning the Nerves. It is very refreshing after a Fatigue of any kind.[40]

In these two instances the evidence of indebtedness depends largely on the brief mention of the facts in *Present State.* Various other portions of the novel appear also to have been influenced by source-material, although no such definite link can be found in the compilation. The similarities, of course, might easily have been the result of separate observation, but since Smollett had evidently read through all the descriptions in Defoe, Burt, and the *Complete System,* one can hardly doubt that he picked up much miscellaneous information which eventually found its way into *Humphry Clinker.* One instance of such a direct transfer from source to novel may be found in Bramble's initial observations on entering Scotland:

. . . this plain, to the extent of several miles, was covered with as fine wheat as ever I saw in the most fertile parts of South Britain— This plentiful crop is raised in the open field, without any inclosure, or other manure than the *alga marina,* or sea-weed, which abounds on this coast; a circumstance which shews that the soil and climate are favourable; but that agriculture in this country is not yet brought to that perfection which it has attained in England.[41]

38. *Works,* IV, 108.   39. *Pres. St.,* I, 489.
40. *Descrip. of W. Is.,* p. 196. 41. *Works,* IV, 63.

Since such favorable descriptions of Scotland were rare, it is probable that these remarks were suggested by the observations made by Defoe, as he entered East Lothian:

> But here we began to see, that *Scotland* is not naturally so barren, as some People represent it; but might be made equal even to the richest, most fruitful, most pleasant, and best improved Part of *England,* if the *Scots* had the same Methods of doing it, and were as good Husbandmen, as the *English;* and this might easily be brought to pass, would the Gentry set about it, ...
> The Truth is, the Soil hereabouts is very good, and the Sea-ware, as they call the Weeds which the Sea casts up, abundantly supplies the Defect of Marl, Chalk, or Lime-stone; for by laying this continually on the Land, they plow every Year, without letting it lie fallow, as we do; and I found they had as much Corn, as our Ploughmen express it, as could stand upon the Ground.[42]

Such general influences, however, are too vague to warrant much consideration: the probability may be stated, but specific proof cannot be found.

Thus, the influence of *Present State* upon the description of Scotland in *Humphry Clinker* may be divided into four manifestations: first, the repetition of derivative portions of *Present State;* second, the repetition of original portions of *Present State;* third, the addition of new material to the novel through the interest aroused by facts presented in *Present State;* fourth, the direct influence of the printed sources of *Present State.* Remembering these types of indebtedness, one must next turn to a discussion of broader, aesthetic issues involved in the influence of *Present State* upon the novel.[43]

42. Defoe, IV, 51–2.
43. The following references may be consulted for parallels between the accounts of Scotland in *Humphry Clinker* and *Present State* not quoted or referred to in the subsequent chapters: cf. *Works,* IV, 61, lines 20–5: *PS,* II, 115; *Works,* IV, 75, lines 8–18, 23–7: *PS,* II, 12, 13; *Works,* IV, 76, lines 12–17, 24–7: *PS,* II, 7, 113; *Works,* IV, 80, lines 13–20: *PS,* II, 18; *Works,* IV, 81, lines 1–7: *PS,* II, 14; *Works,* IV, 86, lines 7–12: *PS,* II, 124; *Works,* IV, 92, lines 11–14: *PS,* II, 18; *Works,* IV, 93, lines 5–29: *PS,* II, 19, 121, 112–13; *Works,* IV, 94, lines 16–18: *PS,* II, 124; *Works,* IV, 97, lines 19–23, p. 126, lines 17–19: *PS,* I, [404], [430]; *Works,* IV, 103, lines 5–14: *PS,* I, 436, 466; *Works,* IV, 114, lines 22–6: *PS,* II, 103–4; *Works,* IV, 115, lines 20–5: *PS,* II, 106–7; *Works,* IV, 133, line 24–p. 134, line 1: *PS,* II, 100; *Works,* IV, 140, line 29–p. 141, line 2: *PS,* II, 19; *Works,* IV, 148, lines 22–9: *PS,* II, 147.

VI

Imaginative Synthesis

WITHOUT such a previous preparation of materials, the section on Scotland in *Humphry Clinker*, I believe, could never have appeared in its present character. If, as Seccombe assumes,[1] Smollett had really been working primarily from notes taken in 1766, one might expect that the descriptions would bear great similarity in method and tone to those in Smollett's own *Travels*, which were to a large extent consciously compiled from notes and books. But such is not the case: the descriptions in *Humphry Clinker*, for the most part, rise to a different level: they flow forth lightly and smoothly through the mouths of fictitious characters; there is little cleavage between incident and description, between characterization and description; one never feels that Smollett is deliberately setting out to record facts from his notebooks; the materials seem to arise spontaneously.

In Smollett's *Travels*, however, there are sharp breaks between description and narrative. The accounts of Nice and Boulogne, and many passages descriptive of other places, are frequently so regularized and objectified that they could be transferred into a formal history with very little alteration. These parts of the *Travels*, admirable as they are in their exactitude and clarity, do not rise to the level of creative writing: they are, like *Present State*, the product of conscious compilation: the compiler is held down by his effort to present details which lie, not in his mind, but in his notebook and in the books of other authors.

Why, then, do not the descriptions of Scotland in *Humphry Clinker* assume this heavier character? The answer is found, I think, in the stock of materials on Scotland which had been fixed in Smollett's mind by the compilation of *Present State*, and in the further mnemonic fixation of later remarks through association with this description already prepared. Smollett had little need to take notes: because of *Present State* most of the materials were stored in his memory. Accordingly, in writing the section on Scotland in *Humphry Clinker*, he was not forced to halt the process of composition by consulting a journal or a printed source, or by laborious effort of memory. Hence, the tour through Scotland represents the integrated work of the creative imagination.

1. See above, p. 136.

Naturally, the materials thus prepared under the influence of *Present State* do not occur in continuous portions of *Humphry Clinker;* indeed they rarely occur in consecutive sentences. Smollett's labors of regularization had fixed the materials so firmly in his mind that they were fused with the totality of his experience. The distinct sections of *Present State,* in which Smollett had carefully grouped related facts, were therefore broken up, and the facts were distributed among different letters, in accordance with entirely different trains of association. Thus, by a pleasing variety, the novel maintains interest in facts which, by the regularity of their presentation, often become tedious in *Present State.* But these materials did not reappear in confusion: they were detached from the arbitrary order of *Present State* only to be placed in the new and higher order of the imagination.

The invigoration which results from this previous preparation is found at its best in Melford's description of Highland customs, where Smollett recalls an account of the family piper from the general section on inhabitants of the Hebrides in *Present State,* and an account of a funeral ceremony from the corresponding section on inhabitants of Scotland proper. The first account forms part of an amusing section on the household customs of Melford's Highland host, whose liberal education leads him to detest the bagpipe; yet despite his efforts, he cannot rid himself of this hereditary nuisance:

[*Present State:*] Another constant menial of the household is the musician, or bag-piper, whose business and privilege it is to wake the laird and his family in the morning with the sound of his instrument; to play for a certain length of time in the great hall, with a silken flag, or broad ribbon, affixed to his chanter-pipe; to walk in procession before his master to church, sounding the march, or pibroch, of the family; to entertain him and his guests at all festal meetings; . . . . Such is the power and influence of this simple minstrelsy over these people, that the piper, by varying his airs, can melt them into sorrow and despondence, and again rouse them to rage and revenge, and a total contempt of danger and of death.[2]

[*Humphry Clinker:*] His piper, for example, who is an hereditary officer of the household, will not part with the least particle of his privileges . . . a broad yellow ribbon, fixed to the chanter-pipe, is thrown over his shoulder, and trails along the ground, while he performs the function of his minstrelsy; and this, I suppose, is analogous to the pennon or flag which was formerly carried before every knight in battle— He plays before the laird every Sunday in his way to the kirk, which

2. *Pres. St.,* I, 434–5.

he circles three times, performing the family march, which implies defiance to all the enemies of the clan; and every morning he plays a full hour by the clock, in the great hall, marching backwards and forwards all the time, with a solemn pace, attended by the laird's kinsmen, who seem much delighted with the music— In this exercise, he indulges them with a variety of pibrachs or airs, suited to the different passions, which he would either excite or assuage.[3]

The impersonal, static catalogue of *Present State* has in *Humphry Clinker* been transformed into a series of vivid, dramatized scenes, related from the standpoint of the personal observer, Melford. The piper in the novel is introduced, not by a dry account of his duties, but by the description of an individual piper's appearance in action; here Smollett includes the details of regalia listed in the middle of the earlier account, but he vitalizes these by adding the exact description of how the ribbon is displayed, together with the personal conjecture of Melford. The account of the church-procession is then invigorated by more graphic details; and, finally, the morning serenade and the effect of the minstrelsy, distinctly separated in *Present State*, are merged into one vivid picture of the actual demonstration in the great hall.

Whether or not Smollett actually saw such a piper in action in 1766 is open to question; certainly his own account of his wretched state of health at the time[4] would lead one to doubt that he could have undertaken the arduous expedition to Inverary during which this incident allegedly occurred. However that may be, it is clear that Smollett was possessed of the essential elements for such an account before 1766, and without this tour could have produced the account in the novel simply by revising these elements in the light of his imagination.

After two pages on the bagpipe and other household matters Smollett produces his ludicrous account of the funeral attended by Melford:

Yesterday we were invited to the funeral of an old lady, the grandmother of a gentleman in this neighbourhood, and found ourselves in the midst of fifty people, who were regaled with a sumptuous feast, accompanied by the music of a dozen pipers. In short, this meeting had all the air of a grand festival; and the guests did such honour to the entertainment, that many of them could not stand when we were reminded of the business on which we had met. The company forthwith taking horse, rode in a very irregular cavalcade to the place of interment, a church, at the distance of two long miles from the castle. On our arrival, however, we found we had committed a small oversight, in

3. *Works*, IV, 106–7.   4. See *Letters*, p. 100.

leaving the corpse behind; so that we were obliged to wheel about, and met the old gentlewoman halfway, carried upon poles by the nearest relations of her family, and attended by the *coronach,* composed of a multitude of old hags, who tore their hair, beat their breasts, and howled most hideously. [At the grave, the orator, or *senachie,* pronounced the panegyric of the defunct, every period being confirmed by a yell of the *coronach.* The body was committed to the earth, the pipers playing a pibroch all the time; and all the company standing uncovered. The ceremony was closed with the discharge of pistols;] then we returned to the castle, resumed the bottle, and by midnight there was not a sober person in the family, the females excepted.[5]

The essential elements of this account, except the portion in brackets, had already appeared in *Present State* in a passage apparently taken from Burt's *Letters:*

. . . the corpse is carried on a bier, by the nearest relations, to the grave, where it is deposited, without any other ceremony than that of hat-lifting, when dust is committed to dust; the company return to the house of the defunct, and drown their sorrow in a deluge of drinking. . . . At Highland funerals, the company, both before and after the interment, are cheared with the musick of the bagpipe, which is garnished with long stripes of black crape, and the corpse is attended by professed mourners, who perform the *Coronach,* consisting of the most hideous yells of lamentation.[6]

Where did Smollett get the description of the elaborate service at the grave, as given in the above bracketed passage of the novel? Burt's *Letters* mention no such ceremony; moreover, that reliable historian, Dr. John Campbell, in his *Full and Particular Description of the Highlands of Scotland* (1752), declares that many of the funeral customs which Smollett describes in both *Present State* and *Humphry Clinker* were no longer practiced:

In former Times they used to have Pipers to accompany the Procession, playing all the way to the Grave, and mourning Women to make a Noise, and to enumerate the many Heroic Qualities, and warlike Deeds of the Deceased, but these Customs are entirely abrogated.[7]

Evidently Smollett had never really seen a funeral such as he describes, except, perhaps, in boyhood, before the customs disappeared. He seems to have formed an imaginative synthesis from Burt's account, written in 1730, and from materials found in other parts of *Present State.*

5. *Works,* IV, 108–9 (my brackets).
6. *Pres. St.,* II, 15–16. Cf. Burt, I, 228–32; II, 208–9.
7. Campbell, *Full and Particular Description,* p. 26.

The "discharge of pistols" was perhaps suggested by the account of weddings which immediately precedes the above quotation from *Present State:*

The weddings of the common people in Scotland are celebrated with the firing of guns and pistols. . . . The evening is generally concluded with drinking and debauchery. The practice is not much different at funerals: . . . .[8]

The part of the "orator, or *senachie,*" was perhaps suggested by a sentence which immediately precedes the above description of the bagpiper in *Present State:*

Every laird, or chief, entertains one or more of these shanachies, who, in old ballads, or extempore rhimes, recites the exploits of his patron's ancestors, in which he never fails to mingle extravagant flattery and fiction.[9]

Thus, in *Humphry Clinker* the imagination places in proximity these two accounts of the piper and the funeral, so widely separated in *Present State,* and, in the latter, coalesces scattered elements to produce one of the brightest passages of the novel.

In the preceding examples the superior vitality of *Humphry Clinker* arises largely from the dramatization of static details into vivid incidents; but in many other places the novel achieves superior vividness and fluidity largely by means of easy association of static materials, frequently colored by the personality of an observer.

A striking instance is found in Bramble's rhapsodic description of Loch Lomond, which represents the fusion of two distinct descriptions in *Present State:*

I have seen the Lago di Garda, Albano, De Vico, Bolsena, and Geneva, and, upon my honour, I prefer Lough-Lomond to them all; a preference which is certainly owing to the *verdant islands that seem to float upon its surface,* affording the most inchanting objects of repose to the excursive view . . . . the prospect terminates in *huge mountains covered with heath,* which being in the bloom, affords a very rich covering of purple. *Every thing here is romantic beyond imagination.* . . . What say you to a natural bason of pure water, near thirty miles long, and in some places seven miles broad, and in many above a hundred fathom deep, having *four and twenty habitable islands, some of them stocked with deer, and all of them covered with wood;*] [containing immense quantities of delicious *fish, salmon, pike, trout, perch, flounders, eels, and powans, the last a delicate kind of fresh-water herring peculiar to this lake;* and finally communicating with the sea, by sending off the Leven, through which all those species (except the powan) make their exit and entrance occasionally?[10]

The first part (down to the brackets) echoes an account of the lake in the section on Dumbartonshire in *Present State:*

But the greatest curiosity of this county is Loch-Lomond itself, a vast body of fresh water, supplied by subterraneous springs and rivulets, surrounded with *huge mountains,* extending five-and-twenty miles in length, and in some places five miles in breadth, incredibly deep in every part, interspersed with *four-and-twenty verdant isles, some of which are stocked with red deer, and inhabited. Nothing can be more wildly romantic* than this part of the country during the summer season, on the south-side of the lake: the high road runs in some places through natural woods, overhung on one hand by steep *mountains, covered with* flowery *heath;* and on the other opening in long vistas upon the lake, terminated by *green islands that seem to float upon the water.*[11]

The remainder of the passage in the novel corresponds to a description which occurs a page earlier in *Present State,* near the close of the account of Stirlingshire:

The rivers Clyde and Leven abound with excellent *salmon,* and those penetrate by the Leven as far as Loch-Lomond, which is replenished with a variety of other *fish, trout, pike, perch, flounders, and eels, exclusive of the powan, a species of the eel*[12] *peculiar to this lake,* in great esteem for its *delicate* flavour.[13]

A more complex example of such association is found in the following quotation from the novel, in which every part is expressly linked at the points marked by asterisks:

The university of Edinburgh is supplied with excellent professors in all the sciences; and the medical school, in particular, is famous all over Europe.—The students of this art have the best opportunity of learning it to perfection, in all its branches, as there are different courses for the *theory of medicine,* and the *practice of medicine;* for *anatomy, chemistry, botany,* and the *materia medica,* over and above those of *mathe-*

10. *Works,* IV, 119–20 (my italics and brackets).
11. *Pres. St.,* II, 94–5 (my italics).
12. The discrepancy here may result from a correction of the statement in *Complete System* which Smollett has evidently followed here: "It abounds with Fish, particularly one delicious Sort, called *Pollac,* of the Eel kind, that is peculiar to it." (I, 259.) Defoe says the same, but adds the alternative name, "Poans" (IV, 253).
13. *Pres. St.,* II, 93 (my italics). A similar fusion is found in Bramble's account of the peasantry of Scotland: cf. *Works,* IV, 153–4; *Pres. St.,* II, 11–12; I, 438–9.

matics and *experimental philosophy;* and all these are given by men of distinguished talents. *What renders this part of education still more complete, is the advantage of attending the infirmary, which is the best instituted charitable foundation that I ever knew. *Now we are talking of charities, here are several hospitals, exceedingly well endowed, and maintained under admirable regulations; and these are not only useful, but ornamental to the city. *Among these, I shall only mention the general work-house, in which all the poor, not otherwise provided for, are employed, according to their different abilities, with such judgment and effect, that they nearly maintain themselves by their labour, and *there is not a beggar to be seen within the precincts of this metropolis.* It was Glasgow that set the example of this establishment, about thirty years ago.[14]

All these institutions are described in the regular section on public structures of Edinburgh in *Present State.* The praise of the university with which Smollett opens the above passage bears some similarity to his earlier remarks on this institution, which, however, closed the section on structures in *Present State:*

. . . the institution is well supported by very able professors in divinity, philosophy, philology,[15] and especially in medicine, which is here taught in all its branches by men eminent for their learning and ability. It is accordingly crowded with students from all parts of the island, and may be justly deemed the best medical seminary in Europe.[16]

Half a page earlier, after a long description of Herriot's Hospital, Smollett had written:

Edinburgh contains divers other hospitals, a workhouse like that of Glasgow, a noble infirmary, including cells for lunatics, built and supported by voluntary contribution, ...[17]

In the novel the order of this list is changed by Smollett's link between the medical school and the infirmary.

In *Present State* Smollett passes over the workhouse at Edinburgh with the brief notice, "like that of Glasgow," because he has already described the workhouse at Glasgow in detail. In *Humphry Clinker,* however, the description of Edinburgh comes first; Smollett therefore gives at this point a description similar to that previously applied to the workhouse at Glasgow:

14. *Works,* IV, 91–2 (only the last italics and the asterisks are mine).
15. This list of professors comes from *Complete System,* I, 263.
16. *Pres. St.,* II, 119.
17. *Ibid.* The summary appears to be inspired by more detailed descriptions in *Complete System,* I, 264.

The institution is founded upon an excellent plan, conducted with great sagacity, and proves such an effectual provision for the poor, that *there is not a beggar to be seen within the precincts of Glasgow.*[18]

In the italicized clause the actual words of *Present State* are adapted to *Humphry Clinker* simply by substituting "this metropolis" for "Glasgow." This echo undoubtedly suggested to Smollett the addition of the sentence on Glasgow which follows in the novel.[19]

This smooth fusion of facts ultimately results in long sections of description which, though nearly as static as any part of *Present State,* possess the vitality of the creative imagination. Matthew Bramble's account of the Highlands, for instance, consists of seven pages[20] which are nearly void of fiction and incident and in which half the materials can be paralleled in *Present State;* yet the section is one of the most vigorous in the novel. The superiority of this account, as compared with *Present State,* lies almost entirely in the fluency with which it moves from general topography and climate to products, to inhabitants, and finally to economic suggestions, without any break in the train of imaginative association.

The link between products and inhabitants is particularly striking, for it echoes material from widely separated portions of *Present State.* In a general section in *Present State* on the animals of Shetland, Smollett mentions these facts, derived from *Complete System:*

. . . [Shetland horses]are never housed, either in winter or summer, and have no other provender than the grass they can nibble: when this fails, they visit the sea-shore regularly, every ebb, and feed upon seaware. The same shift is practiced by their black cattle and sheep, while the ground is covered with snow.[21]

18. *Pres. St.,* II, 106 (my italics).

19. At times such agglomeration takes the form of a simple list or summary: "The granaries of Scotland are the banks of the Tweed, the counties of East and Mid-Lothian, the Carse of Gowrie, in Perthshire, equal in fertility to any part of England, and some tracts in Aberdeenshire and Murray, where I am told the harvest is more early than in Northumberland, although they lie above two degrees farther north." (*Works,* IV, 114). Most of this information, I think, came from *Present State* and its sources: cf. *PS,* II, 43: *Complete System,* I, 266: Defoe, IV, 215; *PS,* II, 57: *Compl. Sys.,* I, [285] (mispr. 385); *PS,* II, 68: *Compl. Sys.,* I, 254; *PS,* II, 112, 128. See also the list of seats near the Clyde in *Humphry Clinker* (*Works,* IV, 154); all these seats, except Roseneath, are mentioned in *Present State.* Two occur in a section, almost identical with that in the novel, at the end of the account of Renfrewshire (*Pres. St.,* II, 100–1). Three others are mentioned in a regular section on seats of Lanarkshire (*Pres. St.,* II, 108–9; cf. *Compl. Sys.,* I, 276). The two remaining are found in *Pres. St.,* I, 508 (cf. Martin, *Descrip. of W. Is.,* p. 216), and II, 103 (cf. *Compl. Sys.,* I, 277).

20. *Works,* IV, 126–32.

21. *Pres. St.,* I, 408. Cf. *Complete System,* I, [283] (misprinted 383).

Eighty pages later he repeats these matters in a section on animals of Skye, taken from Martin:

. . . the black cattle are here, as in other part of this country, exposed to all the rigors of the severe winter, without any other provender than the tops of the heath and the alga marina; . . . . These animals distinguish the time of ebb, by a sure instinct, even when they are not in sight of the shore, whither they hasten in a string one after another.[22]

These two sections form the background for this passage in the novel, which closes a paragraph on topography, climate, and produce:

Those animals [black cattle] run wild all the winter, without any shelter or subsistence, but what they can find among the heath. When the snow lies so deep and hard, that they cannot penetrate to the roots of the grass, they make a diurnal progress, guided by a sure instinct, to the sea-side at low water, where they feed on the *alga marina*, and other plants that grow upon the beach.[23]

Smollett then opens a new paragraph in the novel with remarks which echo the opening of the section in *Present State* on "Trade and Manufacture" of the Hebrides; but he transforms them into a neat transition from products to the subsequent discussion of inhabitants:

[*Present State:*] The people of this country are generally reputed idle and lazy; but this laziness is probably owing to their want of employment, and the means of exercising their industry; for when they settle in other countries, they become remarkable for their diligence and oeconomy.[24]

[*Humphry Clinker:*] Perhaps this branch of husbandry [cattle-raising], which requires very little attendance and labour, is one of the principal causes of that idleness and want of industry, which distinguishes these mountaineers in their own country— When they come forth into the world, they become as diligent and alert as any people upon earth.[25]

On the next page of the novel, in the description of the Highlanders, one of Bramble's sentences represents an elision of distinct passages in *Present State*. In the general account of the Highlanders in the compilation Smollett ends the description of their clothing thus:

An Highlander, provided with a plaid, sets night and cold and storms at defiance. Wherever darkness overtakes him, whether in wood or

22. *Pres. St.*, I, 488. Cf. *Descrip. of W. Is.*, pp. 155–6.
23. *Works*, IV, 126–7.   24. *Pres. St.*, I, 441.   25. *Works*, IV, 127.

heath, or hut or den, he lays him down securely wrapped in his plaid, and sleeps as sound as if he were in a palace: nay, in the common course of travelling, he will not take the trouble to go half a mile out of his way, tho', by so doing, he is certain of finding a good bed and warm lodging.[26]

In the next sentence, without any associative link, he turns to a description of personal characteristics:

These people . . . are bold, resolute, and intrepid: and though naturally lazy, yet when their occasions require exertion, [remarkably active, and patient of hunger and fatigue.][27]

In Bramble's description Smollett combines the materials of the first quotation and the bracketed part of the second into one concise sentence:

They greatly excel the Lowlanders in all the exercises that require agility; they are incredibly abstemious, and patient of hunger and fatigue; so steeled against the weather, that in travelling, even when the ground is covered with snow, they never look for a house, or any other shelter but their plaid, in which they wrap themselves up, and go to sleep under the cope of heaven.[28]

By such associative connection Bramble's whole description of the Highlands achieves a fluency and vigor which all the careful arrangement of *Present State* cannot attain.[29]

The full effect of such associative rearrangements may be understood from the following annotated section of Bramble's description of Edinburgh:[30]

The palace of Holyrood house stands on the left, as you enter the Canongate— This is a street continued from hence to the gate called Nether Bow, which is now taken away; so that there is no interruption for a long mile, from the bottom to the top of the hill[31] on which the

26. *Pres. St.*, I, 433–4.   27. *Idem*, p. 434 (my brackets).
28. *Works*, IV, 128.
29. Further influence of *Present State* in this section may be found by consulting the following references: *Works*, IV, 126, lines 4–26: cf. *PS*, II, 46, I, [430]; *Works*, IV, 127, lines 25–7: cf. *PS*, II, 47; *Works*, IV, 129, line 28–p. 130, line 3: cf. *PS*, I, 436; *Works*, IV, 131, line 14–p. 132, line 20: cf. *PS*, II, 50, 51, 24, 23, I, 408–9, 419, 441.
30. *Works*, IV, 66–9.
31. Cf. *Pres. St.*, II, 113–14: "The High-Street of Edinburgh, counted the most spacious in Europe, stretches with an easy descent from the hither end of the Castle-Hill, a long mile in a direct line to the abbey or palace of the Holy-rood-House, which terminates this noble avenue: one half of this, however, belong to the suburbs called the Canon-gate, from a society of canons regular, who founded the

Castle stands in a most imperial situation[32]— Considering its fine pavement, its width, and the lofty houses on each side, this would be undoubtedly one of the noblest streets in Europe, if an ugly mass of mean buildings, called the Lucken-Booths, had not thrust itself, by what accident I know not, into the middle of the way, like Middle-Row in Holborn.[33] The city stands upon two hills, and the bottom between them; and, with all its defects, may very well pass for the capital of a moderate kingdom— It is full of people, and continually resounds with the noise of coaches and other carriages, for luxury as well as commerce. As far as I can perceive, here is no want of provisions— The beef and mutton are as delicate here as in Wales; the sea affords plenty of good fish; the bread is remarkably fine;[34] and the water is excellent, though I'm afraid not in sufficient quantity[35] to answer all the purposes of cleanliness and convenience; articles in which, it must be allowed, our fellow-subjects are a little defective[36]— The water is brought in leaden pipes from a mountain in the neighbourhood, to a cistern on the Castle-

abbey. The High-Street of Edinburgh, properly so called, extends no farther than the Netherbow port, ...*
[Footnote:] * "This gate is now removed, so that the street extends without interruption from the Castle-hill to the abbey."
Smollett apparently copied the description in the text of *Present State* from *Complete System*, I, 261: "It consists chiefly of one Street, but the noblest in the World; . . . [the street] is half a Mile easy Ascent from the *Netherbow* to the Castle, and about a Mile in Length from the Castle in the West to the Palace and Park of *Haly-* or *Holyrood-*House in the East, including *Cani-* or *Canon-Gate*, (so called from a Society of the *Canons*, who first founded the Abbey) which however is a distinct Corporation, and rather a Suburb than any part of the City."
The Netherbow Port was removed in 1764: see John Anderson, *A History of Edinburgh* (Edinburgh and London, 1856), p. 234. The correction probably represents Smollett's personal observation during his visit to the city in 1766.
32. Cf. *Pres. St.*, II, 113 (half a page before the above): "The situation of this citadel is altogether imperial, ..."
33. Cf. above, n. 31, and *Pres. St.*, II, 114–15: "The High-Street of Edinburgh is in all respects noble and magnificent, whether we consider the houses on each side built of ashler work, to the height of five and six stories; or the street itself extending to a great width, finely paved with smooth square stones, ..."
The qualification of the earlier praise is probably due to Smollett's reconsideration of the city in 1766. This passage in *Present State* may have been suggested by *Complete System*, I, 261: "This Street is exceedingly well paved with Stones, not half a Foot square, ... Their new Houses . . . are built of Stone; . . . and their Fronts . . . are generally of Free-Stone. They are very large, and so lofty, especially in the High Street, that five or six Stories is but an ordinary Height; . . . ."
34. Cf. *Pres. St.*, II, 122: "The markets of Edinburgh are well supplied with all kinds of butcher's meat, fish, poultry, game, greens, and fruit, at reasonable rates, and every species is sold in its own distinct markets. The bread is remarkably fine; . . . ."
This passage may have been suggested by *Complete System*, I, 262: "The Markets here are very well supplied with all Necessaries, and kept for most part in distinct Places walled in, for the particular Commodities that are there sold, ..."
35. See below, n. 38, b.
36. Cf. *Pres. St.*, II, 9: "If the truth must be owned, cleanliness is a virtue very rarely found in this part of the world."

hill, from whence it is distributed to public conduits in different parts
of the city[37]— From these it is carried in barrels, on the backs of male
and female porters, up two, three, four, five, six, seven, and eight pair
of stairs, for the use of particular families— Every story is a complete
house, occupied by a separate family; and the stair being common to
them all, is generally left in a very filthy condition; a man must tread
with great circumspection to get safe housed with unpolluted shoes—
Nothing can form a stronger contrast, than the difference betwixt the
outside and inside of the door; for the good-women of this metropolis
are remarkably nice in the ornaments and propriety of their apartments, as if they were resolved to transfer the imputation from the individual to the public. You are no stranger to their method of discharging
all their impurities from their windows,[38] at a certain hour of the night,
as the custom is in Spain, Portugal, and some parts of France and Italy—
A practice to which I can by no means be reconciled; for notwithstanding all the care that is taken by their scavengers to remove this nuisance
every morning by break of day, enough still remains to offend the eyes,
as well as other organs of those whom use has not hardened against all
delicacy of sensation.

The inhabitants seem insensible to these impressions, and are apt to
imagine the disgust that we avow is little better than affectation; but
they ought to have some compassion for strangers, who have not been
used to this kind of sufferance; and consider, whether it may not be
worth while to take some pains to vindicate themselves from the reproach that, on this account, they bear among their neighbours.[39] As

37. In the next sentence after the passage quoted in note 33, *Present State*, II,
115, continues: "At proper distances there are elegant conduits continually flowing
with delicious water, supplied from a reservoir on the Castle-hill, which is filled by
subterraneous leaden pipes brought from fountains at the distance of a mile to the
southward of the city."

38. Cf. *Pres. St.*, II, 115–16: "Every floor or story of this city is a separate tene-
ment, like those of the inns of court in London,[a] and the access to them is by a common staircase, ... [The sentence quoted in note 41 follows.] The nature of the
stair-cases, common to many different families, and free to the feet and filth of all
comers; the difficulty and expence of carrying a sufficient quantity [b] of water so
high upon the backs of porters; and the want of necessary-houses, contribute to
fix the imputation of nastiness on this otherwise magnificent city. The stairs are
dirty, dark, and dangerous; all the apartments, even of the best houses, though
nicely rubbed, and elegantly furnished, yet retain some smell of the convenience
with which every lodging-chamber must be provided: but the most disagreeable
consequence of this expedient is, the nocturnal discharge of those nauseous reservoirs."

    a. This appears to come from *Complete System*, I, 261: "Most of their Houses
       being parted into Tenements, they have as many Landlords as Stories, with-
       out Dependance on one another, like the Chambers at our Inns of Court."
    b. This remark is transferred in *Humphry Clinker* to the position marked by
       note 35 above, where it serves to introduce the general observation on lack
       of cleanliness, which, in turn, is really the topic sentence for the succeeding
       discussion of nasty habits.

39. Cf. *Pres. St.*, II, 116: "This ordure is cleared away very early in the morning by scavengers appointed for that purpose, except on Sundays, when those con-

to the surprising height of their houses,[40] it is absurd in many respects; but in one particular light I cannot view it without horror; that is, the dreadful situation of all the families above, in case the common stair case should be rendered impassable by a fire in the lower stories[41]— In order to prevent the shocking consequences that must attend such an accident, it would be a right measure to open doors of communication from one house to another, on every story, by which the people might fly from such a terrible visitation. In all parts of the world, we see the force of habit prevailing over all the dictates of convenience and sagacity— All the people of business at Edinburgh, and even the genteel company, may be seen standing in crowds every day, from one to two in the afternoon, in the open street, at a place where formerly stood a market-cross, which (by the bye) was a curious piece of Gothic architecture, still to be seen in lord Sommerville's garden in this neighbourhood— I say, the people stand in the open street from the force of custom, rather than move a few yards to an Exchange that stands empty on one side, or to the Parliament-close on the other,[42] which is a noble square, adorned with a fine equestrian statue of king Charles II[43]— The company thus assembled, are entertained with a variety of tunes, played upon a set of bells, fixed in a steeple hard by— As these bells are well-toned, and the musician, who has a salary from the city, for playing upon them with keys, is no bad performer, the en-

scientious cleansers, out of mere piety, rest from their labour, leaving the streets in a very nauseous condition.[a] The truth is, however strangers may be disgusted with these filthy customs, the natives of Edinburgh are, by use, become insensible to the annoyance; and when they perceive new comers giving marks of loathing and abhorrence, generally impute them to false delicacy and affectation. Their neighbours of England, it must be owned, have some reason to twit them in the teeth with these and other unsavoury practlces [sic]."
    a. This passage may have been suggested by Burt, I, 22: ". . . the main Street is cleaned by Scavengers every Morning early; except Sunday, which therefore is the most Uncleanly Day."
    40. Cf. *Pres. St.*, II, 115: ". . . they have been obliged to raise the houses to a surprizing heighth: . . . ."
    41. *Humphry Clinker* now brings in the passage omitted in note 38 above: "The great height of the houses is attended with numberless inconveniencies, and in cases of fire, renders the situation of the inhabitants very dreadful." (*Pres. St.*, II, 115.)
    Smollett thus avoids spoiling the continuity of his account of filth.
    42. Cf. *Pres. St.*, II, 118: "The market-cross, where all proclamations and public acts were read and published by sound of trumpet,[a] was a curious piece of architecture, but lately demolished, in order to disincumber the street: on the north side, opposite to the Parliament-Close, the citizens have completed a new exchange for the merchants on a very elegant plan; . . . ."
    a. This passage is taken nearly verbatim from *Complete System*, I, 262: ". . . the *Market-Cross*, where all their Proclamations and public Acts are read, and published by Heralds and Sound of Trumpet, ..."
    43. A page before the quotation in note 42 the following passage occurs in the midst of a detailed account of buildings: ". . . the Parliament-Close, which last is a noble quadrangle in the heart of the city, adorned with a fine equestrian statue of king Charles II." (*Pres. St.*, II, 117.)

tertainment is really agreeable, and very striking to the ears of a stranger.[44]

From the preceding annotation it is evident that the elements for most of this description had already appeared in *Present State*. None of the phraseology, however, can be said positively to come from a printed source of the compilation; and only a few parallels occur in portions of *Present State* which appear to represent revisions of a printed source. Thus, the importance of the previous work of compilation lies not so much in the new facts Smollett learned, as in the precipitation of personal knowledge and expression. A typical example of the process involved is found in note 42: the verbal parallel in *Present State* consists of the personal addition made to a clause taken almost verbatim from the *Complete System*. As usual, the fact in the source has evoked the personal memory.

The consequence of the previous precipitation of materials is the easy fluidity of the whole description. The facts stored up by the process of conscious regularization now fall into new associative order, more vivid, more vital than the arbitrary juxtapositions of the will. The description of Edinburgh in *Present State* is neat, but this arbitrary grouping results in many abrupt transitions which the smoother flow of memory usually avoids. Thus, in *Present State* Smollett first discusses the High-Street in its general extent,[45] then devotes a page to description of the other general sections of the city, and at length returns to describe the High-Street particularly.[46] In the next sentence he adds a description of the conduits on High-Street, linked with brief mention of the reservoirs and pipes into the city.[47] After this the account shifts to a

44. A dozen lines before the quotation in note 43 above, the following passage occurs in the midst of a description of Edinburgh cathedral: ". . . furnished with a set of well toned bells, on which all manner of tunes are played every day except Sundays, between the hours of eleven and twelve, as an entertainment to the merchants and men of business, who are then assembled at the cross or market-place, to transact their affairs." (*Pres. St.*, II, 117.)

Almost all the description of the cathedral in *Present State*, II, 116–17, is patently copied from *Complete System*, I, 262; the above quotation, however, shows some significant additions to and omissions from the source: "In the Steeple, there is a Set of Bells, which are not rung out, but all manner of Tunes are play'd on them by the Hand with Keys, like a Harpsicord; and this is performed every day, except Sundays and Holidays, from half an Hour after 11 to half an Hour after 12, by a Man who has a yearly Salary for it from the City."

The remarks on the musician, omitted from *Present State*, may have been remembered from this passage in the source. The different hours in *Present State* may come from Burt, I, 208. Smollett evidently gives the hours in *Humphry Clinker* from personal observation in 1766.

45. See n. 31.   46. See n. 33.   47. See n. 37.

discussion of the tall houses, the staircases, and the filthy habits of the residents. Then, immediately after a discussion of the "nocturnal discharges," *Present State* launches into a description of Edinburgh Cathedral and other public structures.

In *Humphry Clinker* Smollett's imagination first groups these two separated passages on the High-Street, to present the view of Bramble on entering the city. From this apt introduction Smollett proceeds to describe the general aspect of the city: its situation and business. The passage on provisions[48] is transferred to this place from a point near the end of the account in *Present State,* where it opens an orderly section on food and lodging, but abruptly follows a discussion of government and taxation. With food Smollett naturally connects water and then adds the associative link on uncleanliness which introduces the next page and a half. The sentence on transportation of water is neatly ordered by reversing the arrangement of *Present State* to pass from source, to cistern, to public conduits, and from here, in the next sentence, to the final destination "on the backs of . . . porters"—a detail not given until half a page later in *Present State.*[49] Having arrived upstairs with the water, Smollett naturally proceeds to describe the tenements themselves, the dirty stairs, and the dirty habit of tossing slops from the windows: the transition, easy in itself, is made even more fluent by the fact that the reader already knows there is not "sufficient quantity" of water "to answer all the purposes of cleanliness and convenience."

These sections on water and filth, so successfully merged in the novel, are in *Present State* separated by nearly half a page relating to the height of the houses. Smollett, having avoided such interruption, now groups into one sentence of the novel parts of two separated sentences from this section on height of houses.[50] The absurdity of incurring such a risk from fire then suggests to Smollett another absurdity: the practice of assembling in the open street. The shift here is really as sudden as any in *Present State;* but association through the common quality of absurdity closes the gap so successfully that it is scarcely noticed; whereas in *Present State* such changes result in a complete break of associative order. Finally, related details cluster about the new idea in the novel from scattered points in the description of public structures which incongruously follows the account of filth in *Present State.*

Thus, as I have said, the process of conscious regularization is, because of the intractable nature of its materials, almost untouched by imagination: accordingly, in *Present State,* Smollett's demand

48. See n. 34.   49. See n. 38.   50. See notes 40, 41.

for regularity tends toward the rigidity and dullness of a catalogue. In *Humphry Clinker,* however, the mind working from memory is free from restraint, and therefore can achieve the flexible, fluent, associative order of the free imagination.

VII

Incorporation of Present State *with* Character: Lismahago

AS I have intimated in the last chapter, fluent association of descriptive details is not the only advantage offered by the previous preparation of these materials on Scotland. Equally important is the fact that these details can be merged with the presentation of character in such a way that the vitality and consistency of the fiction is not impaired.

Thus, Smollett's account of Dumbarton and its castle, which covers a page and a half in *Present State*, is split into three sections in the novel; yet each section is inseparably associated with its context, and is appropriately assigned to the character who presents it. The first section forms part of Melford's account of the tour through the region near the Clyde:

> At length, we set out for the banks of Lough-Lomond, passing through the little borough of Dumbarton, or (as my uncle will have it) Dunbritton, where there is a castle, more curious than any thing of the kind I had ever seen— It is honoured with a particular description by the elegant Buchannan, as an *arx inexpugnabilis*,[1] and, indeed, it must have been impregnable by the antient manner of besieging. It is a rock of considerable extent, rising with a double top, in an angle formed by the confluence of two rivers, the Clyde and the Leven; perpendicular and inaccessible on all sides, except in one place where the entrance is fortified; and there is no rising-ground in the neighbourhood from whence it could be damaged by any kind of battery.[2]

1

In the following letter a sentence on the town is included among Bramble's comments on the ancient history of the region:

> Without all question, this was a Cumbrian kingdom: its capital was Dumbarton (a corruption of Dumbritton [*sic*]) which still exists as a royal borough, at the influx of the Clyde and Leven, ten miles below Glasgow.[3]

2

A page later another description of the castle occurs in Bramble's general account of the district:

1. The Latin is a false display of learning. Buchanan really refers to it as, "Haec arx, ut quae insuperabilis videretur, ..." (*Rerum Scoticarum Historia*, [Schouten ed., 1697], p. 675.)

2. *Works*, IV, 101.   3. *Idem*, p. 117.

The Clyde we left a little on our left-hand at Dunbritton, where it widens into an aestuary or frith, being augmented by the influx of the Leven. On this spot stands the castle formerly called Alcluyd,

3 washed by these two rivers on all sides, *except a narrow isthmus, which at every spring-tide is overflowed.* The whole is a great curiosity, from the quality and form of the rock, as well as from the nature of its situation.[4]

These three passages repeat portions of the following description in *Present State:*

2 { Dumbarton, the county-town, which bestows its name upon the shire, is a small inconsiderable royal borough, situated near the conflux of the Clyde and Leven; and at present remarkable for nothing

1 { but its castle, which has been described by the pens of Buchannan and Camden.[5] It is a steep rock, rising up in two points, and every where inaccessible except by a very narrow passage or entry, fortified with a strong wall and rampart. . . . The castle stands in the angle formed by the Clyde and Leven at their conflux, so that it is

3 { wholly surrounded with water, *except a narrow isthmus, which with every springtide is overflowed:* nor is there any hill or eminence

1 { within a long mile of this fortress. . . . The little town of Dumbarton, which stands in the neighbourhood of the castle, on the

2 { banks of the Leven, was of old a flourishing city, capital of the Cumbrian kingdom of the Britons, and for a considerable length of time under the immediate protection of the Roman stationary camp, maintained to defend the wall of Antoninus or Graeme's Dyke, which ends or begins at Kirkpatrick, within three miles of Dum-

3 { barton.[6] The ancient inhabitants called that place Alcluith, from the castle standing on the bank of the Cluith or Clyde: but the Scots

2 { and Picts gave it the name of Dunbrittan, or castle of the Britons, from which it was corrupted into Dumbarton.[7]

No doubt some of the above observations came from books, but in this case the description in *Present State* is so colored by personal memories that definite indebtedness to printed sources is

4. *Works*, IV, 118 (my italics).

5. *Complete System*, I, 259, cites descriptions by both Buchanan and Camden.

6. These facts, combined with other details copied from Gordon in *Present State*, II, 91–2, form the background for a general description of the Roman wall inserted four lines after quotation 2 above, as part of Bramble's dissertation on the ancient history of the region near the Clyde.

7. *Pres. St.*, II, 96–7 (my italics). Cf. *Complete System*, I, 259: " 'Twas by the Ancients called *Al-Cluyd*, which *Bede* interprets *Rock-Cluyd;* . . . . Succeeding Ages gave it the Name of *Dunbritton*, i.e. the *Britons Town* (and by a corrupt Transposition of the Letters, it came to be *Dunbarton*) because the *Britons* held it longer than any other Place against the *Scots, Picts*, and *Saxons:* . . . ."

For Smollett's personal interest in these details, see *Letters*, p. 36. Doubtless he learned some of this material while doing research for his *History of England*.

difficult to establish, except for the last few lines. The important fact, however, is that these materials were thus stored in Smollett's mind by his account in *Present State;* with the result that they could easily be transferred to the novel and adapted to the character of the correspondent. The modern description of the castle, with the military comment, is aptly given to young Melford; while the antiquarian details, as usual, are given to Bramble.

Attention to character is particularly evident in a passage which immediately precedes quotation 2 above; here Bramble's subsequent historical reflections are cleverly linked with his Welsh origin:

You must know I have a sort of national attachment to this part of Scotland— The great church dedicated to St. Mongah, the river Clyde, and other particulars that smack of our Welch language and customs, contribute to flatter me with the notion, that these people are the descendants of the Britons, who once possessed this country.[8]

This comparison with Wales is a frequent device throughout the novel: the same link with character is provided in a description which immediately follows Melford's account of Dumbarton (quotation 1 above):

From Dumbarton, the West Highlands appear in the form of huge, dusky mountains, piled one over another; but this prospect is not at all surprising to a native of Glamorgan—[9]

This is an adaptation of the description given in *Present State:*

Nothing can be more savage and horrendous to the eye of a stranger, than the appearance of the Highlands, composed of blue rocks and dusky mountains, heaped upon one another even above the clouds, ...[10]

Smollett's regard for congruity with character is equally evident in the echo of this description of Glasgow University in *Present State*—a description probably derived from Smollett's own experience at this institution:

. . . [the University] is well provided with able professors in the different branches of theology, mathematics, philosophy, and the languages. Every branch is taught by its own separate regent or professor, who, not contented with giving general lectures, attends assiduously to the business of his class, where he explains, sets tasks, and examines his pupils like any other school-master: . . . .[11]

8. *Works,* IV, 116–17.
10. *Pres. St.,* II, 2.
9. *Idem,* p. 101.
11. *Idem,* p. 105.

In *Humphry Clinker* Smollett pretends ignorance in order to adapt the account to Melford, who in his letter to a friend at Oxford declares his preference for the method of instruction at Glasgow over that at their own college, apparently because he "was tutor-sick at alma mater":[12]

Here is an university, with professors in all the different branches of science, liberally endowed, and judiciously chosen— It was vacation time when I passed, so that I could not entirely satisfy my curiosity; but their mode of education is certainly preferable to ours in some respects— The students are not left to the private instruction of tutors; but taught in public schools or classes, each science by its particular professor or regent.[13]

Even Winifred Jenkins's memorable remarks find their counterpart in *Present State:*

[*Humphry Clinker:*] . . . and at ten o'clock at night the whole cargo is flung out of a back windore that looks into some street or lane, and the maid calls *gardy loo* to the passengers, which signifies *Lord have mercy upon you!* and this is done every night in every house at Haddingborrough; so you may guess, Mary Jones, what a sweet savour comes from such a number of profuming pans; . . . .[14]

[*Present State:*] At ten of the clock every window is opened, and such a general deluge of these materials poured forth, that the whole air is impregnated with a most unsufferable odour, and the foot passenger in the most imminent danger of being overwhelmed with the most substantial part of the annoyance.

In former times, the dispersers of these benefits taught, in all probability, by their polite allies, the French, were accustomed to give warning, by calling aloud *gardez l'eau;* but now all that ceremony is laid aside, [and woe will be upon the head of that man,] who presumes to walk down the wynd at or about the hour of evacuation, without crying out *hold your hand* incessantly, until he finds himself fairly housed.[15]

In the novel Smollett has revived the discarded warning and apparently linked it with the bracketed passage, which seems to contain the germ of Winifred's eloquent translation. Here the similarity is certainly vague; yet the essential question remains: would the passage have appeared thus in the novel, if Smollett had not previously concentrated upon the corresponding description in *Present State?*

12. *Works*, IV, 86.   13. *Idem*, p. 100.   14. *Idem*, p. 71.
15. *Pres. St.*, II, 116 (my brackets). The last portion may have been suggested by Burt: " 'Being in my Retreat to pass through a long narrow *Wynde* or Alley, to go to my new Lodgings, a Guide was assigned me, who went before me to prevent my Disgrace, crying out all the Way, with a loud Voice, "Hud your Haunde." ' "
(I, 20.)

In a similar manner statements formulated for *Present State* are adapted to the paradoxical Lismahago. The long disquisition by "this original" on the merits of the Scottish language is introduced by a patent echo of *Present State:*

[*Humphry Clinker:*] He said, what we generally called the Scottish dialect was, in fact, true, genuine old English, with a mixture of some French terms and idioms, adopted in a long intercourse betwixt the French and Scotch nations; . . . .[16]

[*Present State:*] It may be unnecessary to observe, that the Lowlanders of Scotland speak an antient dialect of the English language, interlarded with many terms and idioms which they borrowed immediately from France, in a long course of correspondence with that kingdom: . . . .[17]

Similarly, Lismahago gives vent to Smollett's candid opinion of Scottish learning:

[*Humphry Clinker:*]My nephew remarking that the Scots in general were famous for their learning, he denied the imputation, and defied him to prove it from their works.—"The Scots (said he) have a slight tincture of letters, with which they make a parade among people who are more illiterate than themselves; but they may be said to float on the surface of science, and they have made very small advances in the useful arts."[18]

[*Present State:*] All the Scots are tinctured with learning, which, however superficial it may be, will always shine in some places and in certain companies; and they know full well how to turn this commodity to the best advantage.[19]

These are the only parallels with the previous description of Scotland which can be found in Lismahago's early polemics; but Smollett's introduction to the account of England in *Present State* provides a long parallel which leads the way to significant conclusions in regard to Smollett's inspiration and purpose in creating Lismahago:

[*Present State:*]	[*Humphry Clinker:*]
The constitution of England, though said to be as perfect as human wisdom could suggest, and human frailty permit, yet, neverthe[le]ss, contains in itself the seeds of its own dissolution. While individuals are corruptible, and the means of corruption so copi-	He [Lismahago] observed of the parliament, that the practice of buying boroughs, and canvassing for votes, was an avowed system of venality, already established on the ruins of principle, integrity, faith, and good order, in consequence of which the elected and

16. *Works*, IV, 35.
18. *Works*, IV, 41–2.

17. *Pres. St.*, II, 2–3.
19. *Pres. St.*, II, 10.

ously abound, it will always be in the power of an artful and ambitious prince to sap the foundations of English liberty. By means of the places and pensions in his gift, he will be able to procure a majority in parliament, devoted to his will. He has it in his power to model the army to his wishes. The parliament can protract its own date, consequently perpetuate itself. The commons can gradually increase the number of land forces, until the nation is saddled with a standing army devoted to the crown, sufficient to trample upon the constitution, and disposed to obey the most arbitrary commands of their sovereign. Then will the parliament become the slaves of the army they have reared. . . . Thus one branch of the legislature will always be able to influence the other two; and the crown being vested with the executive power, the command of the forces by sea and land, the prerogative of making treaties and alliances, of creating peers and bishops, to secure a majority in the upper house, and being reinforced by a venal house of commons, may easily acquire and establish an absolute dominion.

the elector, and, in short, the whole body of the people, were equally and universally contaminated and corrupted. He affirmed, that of a parliament thus constituted, the crown would always have influence enough to secure a great majority in its dependence, from the great number of posts, places, and pensions it had to bestow; that such a parliament would (as it had already done) lengthen the term of its sitting and authority, whenever the prince should think it for his interest to continue the representatives; for, without doubt, they had the same right to protract their authority *ad infinitum,* as they had to extend it from three to seven years.—With a parliament, therefore, dependent upon the crown, devoted to the prince, and supported by a standing army, garbled and modelled for the purpose, any king of England may, and probably some ambitious sovereign will, totally overthrow all the bulwarks of the constitution; for it is not to be supposed that a prince of a high spirit will tamely submit to be thwarted in all his measures, abused and insulted by a populace of unbridled ferocity, when he has it in his power to crush all opposition under his feet with the concurrence of the legislature.[20]

It is clear that Lismahago here is being used largely as a mouthpiece to express one of Smollett's political warnings. But, in accordance with the novel's dominant tone in regard to England, Lismahago's diatribe represents a deliberate departure from the judicious tone in which the warning was delivered in *Present State.* In the compilation Smollett introduces his general section on "Constitution, Government, Laws" with a lavish compliment:

20. *Pres. St.,* II, 165–6; *Works,* IV, 44–5.

The English constitution is a limited monarchy, and, with all its defects, may be considered as the best that ever was reduced to practice in any part of the world, whether we consider the dignity of the crown, or the happiness of the community.[21]

After four pages of objective explanation concerning the processes of government Smollett turns to the above analysis of faults, but further modifies this adverse criticism with praise of the vigilant spirit of the people, who, being "equally jealous, and well informed of their own privileges,"[22] would, he says, vigorously oppose any open attempt at such royal domination. In order to serve his satirical intention in the novel Smollett has removed all these compliments and placed the warning alone, more violently expressed, in the mouth of the truculent Lismahago; and, to increase the sting, he even provides an excuse for such arbitrary action of a prince, by denying his earlier compliment with vicious slurs on the disposition of the people.

The succeeding paragraph in the novel, devoted to juries, suggests that part of the purpose of such distortion is to provide a contrast with the virtues of Scottish government. In *Present State* Smollett had spoken proudly of the jury-system, without adding a word of detraction.[23] Lismahago, however, without the slightest compliment, launches into a diatribe against the English requirement of unanimous decisions, by which the jurors "must either starve in company, or one side must sacrifice their conscience to their convenience, and join in a verdict which they believe to be false."[24] After this denunciation, Lismahago takes care to point out that "This absurdity is avoided in Sweden,[25] where a bare majority is sufficient; and in Scotland, where two thirds[26] of the jury are required to concur in the verdict."[27] In this place the general contrast with Scottish government is not emphasized, but later, in Bramble's laudatory discussion of Scottish law, Smollett evokes the memory of this whole denunciatory section by referring once more to "the constitution of their jury, by which they certainly avoid the evil which I mentioned in my last from Lismahago's observation."[28] Thus Smollett, through both Bramble and Lismahago, gives vent to feelings and opinions which he has either suppressed or carefully modified in *Present State*.

21. *Pres. St.*, II, 161.
22. *Idem*, p. 166.
23. See *idem*, p. 164.
24. *Works*, IV, 46.
25. The comparison is probably inspired by the facts given in *Present State*, I, 230.
26. Smollett is in error: in *Present State*, II, 20, he correctly states that a Scottish jury decides by majority.
27. *Works*, IV, 46.
28. *Idem*, p. 91.

I have said that the development of Bramble's character is in large part motivated by Smollett's desire to denounce England and praise Scotland, the same motive, I believe, not only explains the essential peculiarities of Lismahago's character, but gives the fundamental reason for his appearance in the novel.

The proper rôle of Lismahago seems never to have been recognized. In Henley's edition he does not appear until page fifteen of the second (and final) volume of the novel. The interval from here to page thirty-one, where the section on Scotland begins, is entirely devoted to elucidation of his character and experiences. He soon emerges as one whose chief delight is controversy, one who "is so addicted to wrangling, that he will cavil at the clearest truths, and, in the pride of argumentation, attempt to reconcile contradictions."[29] With the reader thus prepared for polemics and paradox, the section on Scotland opens with controversial dialogues, which continue until page forty-eight, where Lismahago leaves the party "at a place half way betwixt Morpeth and Alnwick." Thus, of the first seventeen pages in the section on Scotland, ten are devoted to dissertations by Lismahago, of which the most important are his defence of the Scottish language (four pages in length)[30] and his attack on English commerce and government (three pages in length).[31] It therefore appears that the essential quality of Lismahago's character—his love for paradoxical argument—has been carefully developed in order to serve as a vehicle for the paradox which forms an essential part of Smollett's purpose in the novel as a whole: to decry the English and exalt the Scots. By praising the Scots in one of these long polemics and denouncing the English in the other, Lismahago serves as the axis upon which the emphasis of the novel shifts from satire to praise.

With this purpose served, Lismahago retires from the scene before the party reaches Scotland and does not return until more than a hundred pages later (p. 150), when the travellers meet him in Carlisle at the close of their tour through Scotland. Twenty-five pages later the section on Scotland is concluded with Lismahago's climactic defence of his homeland. Not one word on Scotland is given before Lismahago's initial appearance or after his final disquisition on the land.

It thus seems that, despite the humorous functions which Lismahago also serves, Smollett's aim in introducing him was primarily didactic, for he has deliberately discarded him throughout the actual tour of Scotland, apparently for two reasons: first, to avoid further grotesquerie which might unduly interrupt the descrip-

29. *Works*, IV, 19.   30. *Idem*, pp. 34–8.   31. *Idem*, pp. 44–6.

tion; and second, to allow the favorable account of Scotland, begun by Lismahago, to be carried on by South Britons whose approval of Scotland could not be discounted as prejudice. Then, when the truth of Scotland's excellence has been proved by accounts which arise from the uncoerced conversion of the visitors, Lismahago is brought back to resume his polemics, with both Bramble and the reader more willing to accept his paradoxical arguments.

Additional evidence of Smollett's primarily didactic purpose in creating Lismahago is found in the letter by Bramble which closes the section on Scotland with ten pages[32] chiefly occupied by Lismahago's peroratory defence of his native land. Nearly two pages of this letter repeat arguments already advanced by Smollett in the *Briton*, through the mouth of a fictitious character who is a prototype of Lismahago. In the *Briton* for January 15, 1763, Smollett gives a fictitious letter from one "Ben. Hempley," an English Scottophobe whose ire has been aroused by overhearing a "degenerate Englishman" defend the Scots by the very arguments later presented by Lismahago:

[*Humphry Clinker:*]	[*Briton:*]
"This was a very considerable and seasonable supply to a nation, whose people had been for many years decreasing in number, and whose lands and manufactures were actually suffering for want of hands. I need not remind you of the hackneyed maxim, that, to a nation in such circumstances, a supply of industrious people is a supply of wealth; nor repeat an observation, which is now received as an eternal truth, even among the English themselves, that the Scots who settle in South-Britain are remarkably sober, orderly, and industrious."	This pseudo English[man] affirmed, it was a maxim universally established, that an accession of people, was an addition of wealth to every country not already overstocked, provided those people brought health and industry along with them; that as population had been for many years decreasing in England, and the war occasioned an extraordinary expence of men, we were obliged to the Scotch for leaving their own country to settle among us; that all the world allowed them to be generally sensible, industrious and sober; . . . .
I allowed the truth of this remark, adding, that by their industry, oeconomy, and circumspection, many of them in England, as well as in her colonies, amassed	Nay, this advocate for the Scots, was transported to such a degree of zeal in their favour, as to insist, that granting they acquired fortunes in England, and conveyed their wealth to their own country,

32. *Works,* IV, 165–75.

large fortunes, with which they returned to their own country, and this was so much lost to South-Britain.—"Give me leave, sir, (said he) to assure you, that in your fact you are mistaken, and in your deduction, erroneous.—Not one in two hundred that leave Scotland ever returns to settle in his own country; and the few that do return, carry thither nothing that can possibly diminish the stock of South-Britain; for none of their treasure stagnates in Scotland—There is a continual circulation, like that of the blood in the human body, and England is the heart, to which all the streams which it distributes are refunded and returned: nay, in consequence of that luxury which our connexion with England hath greatly encouraged, if not introduced, all the produce of our lands, and all the profits of our trade, are engrossed by the natives of South Britain; for you will find that the exchange between the two kingdoms is always against Scotland; and that she retains neither gold nor silver sufficient for her own circulation.—The Scots, not content with their own manufactures and produce, which would very well answer all necessary occasions, seem to vie with each other in purchasing superfluities from England; such as broadcloth, velvets, stuffs, silks, lace, furs, jewels, furniture of all sorts, sugar, rum, tea, chocolate, and coffee; in a word, not only every mode of the most extravagant luxury, but even many articles of convenience, which they might find as good, and much cheaper in their own country."

that wealth contributed as much to the advantage of the nation in general, as if the circulation of it had been confined within the boundaries of South Britain. "The money (said he) which circulates in the remotest parts of Scotland, can no more stagnate there, than the blood which flows from the heart, can be detained in the extremities of the animal machine. It returns immediately in a thousand refluent streams to the center of trade, which every body knows must be the center of South Britain, in as much as the ballance of traffic, between the two united kingdoms, is always greatly in favour of England, from whence the Scots import all their luxuries, and many of the conveniencies of life. . . . Where, said he, does the whole Scotch nation purchase their tea and coffee, their porcelain, spices and other East Indian commodities; their silks, brocades, and gold and silver lace, their broad cloth, hats, toys and hardware; their houshold furniture, chairs, tables, mirrors, cabinets, bureaus, carpets, stoves and plate? Where, but in London, and other parts of South Britain? These were the vitals which this circulation continually revisited with a perpetual motion; . . . .[33]

33. *Works*, IV, 170–1; *Briton*, in *The Political Controversy: or, Weekly Magazine of Ministerial and Anti-ministerial Essays* (London, 1762–63), III, 31–2.

Hempley's report of these arguments is, of course, much less sympathetic than Bramble's; yet the general method of presentation is identical: in both cases Smollett's own arguments are presented by a character whose views are treated as paradoxical by the fictitious writer of the letter. Thus Smollett, by indirection, gains a hearing for views which the average Englishman would otherwise reject with scorn.

Furthermore, in the same letter of Bramble's, Smollett gains a hearing for information on Scotland which the average Englishman had evidently neglected in *Present State:* remarks totalling at least two pages echo the compilation. It is significant that the influence of *Present State* is most apparent in the opening portion, which sets the tone and theme of the letter. Bramble introduces the dialogue thus:

I congratulated him the other day on the present flourishing state of his country, observing that the Scots were now in a fair way to wipe off the national *reproach of poverty*, and expressing my satisfaction at the happy effects of the union, so conspicuous in the improvement of their agriculture, commerce, manufactures, and manners—[34]

Lismahago replies for a page with a denial of the imputation that poverty is a disgrace, and at last launches into an extended summary of Scottish national resources which is apparently derived from Smollett's earlier labors of compilation:

"But, granting that *poverty* were really matter of *reproach*, it cannot be justly imputed to Scotland. No country is poor that can supply its inhabitants with the necessaries of life, and even afford articles for exportation. Scotland is *rich in natural advantages:* it produces every species of provision in abundance, vast herds of cattle and flocks of sheep, with a great number of horses; prodigious quantities of wool and flax, with plenty of copse wood, and in some parts large forests of timber. The earth is still more rich below than above the surface. It yields inexhaustible stores of coal, freestone, marble, lead, iron, copper, and silver, with some gold. [The sea abounds with excellent fish, and salt to cure them for exportation;] and there are creeks and harbours round the whole kingdom, for the convenience and security of navigation."[35]

In two separate portions of *Present State* Smollett gives similar summaries for the identical purpose of emphasizing the riches of

34. *Works*, IV, 165 (my italics).
35. *Idem*, pp. 166–7 (my italics and brackets). The bracketed portion echoes this earlier statement in a section on the trade of Scotland (*Pres. St.*, II, 23): ". . . we shall only observe at present, that the improvement of the fishery is the more practicable, as plenty of salt may be had for curing them on every part of the coast."

Scotland. The first, evidently inspired by Martin,[36] occurs at the close of a general section on "Trade and Manufacture" of the Hebrides:

They are furnished with an infinite number of bays, creeks, and harbours, for the convenience of navigation: . . . . The sea affords myriads of fish for exportation: the lands might afford plenty of pasturage for black cattle, horses, and sheep, as well as plenteous harvests of corn, and other grain: woollen and linen manufactures might be prosecuted to great advantage, where labour is cheap and provisions are reasonable. The islands afford good stone and lime, and some parts of the opposite main land, timber for building: they have plenty of fuel, not only for the ordinary purposes of life, but also for salt-pans, which might be erected on different parts of the coast; . . . .[37]

The second summary occurs at the end of a similar general section on the "Strength, Manufacture, and Commerce" of Scotland proper:

In a word, this kingdom, though branded with the *reproach of poverty* and barrenness, might prove an inexhaustible source of wealth to the natives. It is almost surrounded with an open ocean, provided with a great number of excellent harbours, occupied by a race of hardy people, *rich in* many *natural advantages,* and every way adapted for commerce. [The inhabitants seem at length acquainted with their own interest: they understand the nature of commerce: they see the happy effects of industry: they take example by their southern neighbours and fellow-subjects, and pursue their steps with such emulation, as hath already opened a fair prospect of opulence and importance.][38]

In the last quotation the phrase "reproach of poverty" and the bracketed portion provide parallels with Bramble's introduction to the whole letter (quoted above), while the same phrase provides Lismahago with a transition to his general summary (quoted above). The list of resources in the novel seems clearly indebted to the above quotations from *Present State;* and other parallel details are found in various other parts of the two above-mentioned sections on trade and manufacture, as well as in two other general sections which list the products of Scotland and the Isles.[39]

36. This summary comes at the end of a page and a half which are patently copied from Martin's special section entitled: "A Brief Account of the Advantages the Isles afford by Sea and Land, and particularly for a Fishing Trade." (*Descrip. of W. Is.,* pp. 336–49.) The summary in *Present State* makes the identical recommendations found in Martin, pp. 341–3, but the account is too general to show specific indebtedness.

37. *Pres. St.,* I, 443.   38. *Idem,* II, 24–5 (my italics and brackets).

39. Cf. *idem,* I, 430–1, 441–4; II, 5–9, 22–5. For other resemblances to *Present State* in this part of the novel cf. *Works,* IV, 169, lines 10–17: *Pres. St.,*

It therefore appears that, in addition to other aims discussed above, Smollett has developed the eccentricities and arranged the entrances of Lismahago in order to provide a general frame for the particular description of the present state of Scotland. One should recall that in *Present State* the particular account of each country is preceded by an orderly introductory section which presents general comments on the characteristics of the country, its customs, produce, inhabitants, etc.; somewhat the same purposes appear in part to have motivated the composition of Lismahago's introductory and concluding polemics, which, as we have seen, echo such general sections in the accounts of England and Scotland in *Present State*. Although the materials in the particular account of Scotland are given at random in the novel, Smollett's tendency toward regularity could not be denied its expression in these orderly, formal disquisitions. But to include such sections, a formal speaker is necessary: Lismahago.

It is evident, then, that one must alter in great degree the traditional explanation of Lismahago's genesis in Smollett's personal acquaintance with Captain Robert Stobo. Indeed, after reading the *Memoirs* of Stobo,[40] and Kahrl's recent study of Stobo's career,[41] one can see little similarity between the characters, appearances, or lives of the two. Thus, for example, the *Memoirs* describes Stobo:

Setting aside the gentleness of his manner, there was something in his appearance very engaging; he was of the middle size, that is, about five feet nine and a half or near 10 inches high, of a dark brown complexion, a penetrating eye, an aquiline nose, round face, a good cheerful countenance, a very genteel person, rather slender than robust, and graceful in his whole deportment.[42]

Lismahago is of a "tall, meagre figure," "above six feet in height," with a face "at least, half a yard in length," distinguished by "a

---

II, 9–10; *Works*, IV, 172, lines 8–10: *Pres. St.*, II, 23. This defence of Scottish resources is not confined to Lismahago: Bramble devotes a page to a plea for encouragement of the fisheries, ending with the declaration: "Our people have a strange itch to colonize America, when the uncultivated parts of our own island might be settled to greater advantage." (*Works*, IV, 131–2.) This plea may have been influenced by a long prospectus for colonists in the Hebrides (*Pres. St.*, I, 442–3), which is clearly an elaboration of the similar prospectus given by Martin (*Descrip. of W. Is.*, pp. 336–9).

40. *Memoirs of Major Robert Stobo*, Pittsburgh, 1854 (reprint of original ed., London, 1800).

41. George M. Kahrl, "Captain Robert Stobo," *The Virginia Magazine of History and Biography*, XLIX (1941), 141–51, 254–68.

42. *Memoirs*, p. 22.

large hook-nose"; he is "very hard-favoured and forbidding" in countenance, and, until his astonishing metamorphosis by good fortune at the very end, he is "aukward, rude, and disputacious," "his whole appearance" denoting "dissatisfaction."[43]

Smollett himself, in a letter to Hume, describes Stobo as "modest and sensible";[44] and, as Kahrl observes, "There is no suggestion in the letter that he thought Stobo eccentric, conceited, vain, needy, or ambitious."[45] The list of books which Stobo used in prison suggests a range of reading comparable to Lismahago's; his acquaintance with Indian customs may be echoed in the novel;[46] he appears to have been tenacious and valiant; but such similarities are all so general that one cannot build much upon them. The chief similarities in their careers appear to be that both were Scots, both served in America during the Seven Years' War, both escaped from captivity in Canada and later returned to England. The particulars of these experiences vary radically. Stobo was a captain (or a major, in the colonial service), Lismahago a lieutenant. Stobo was given as hostage from Fort Necessity and sent to Fort Duquesne; Lismahago was taken on the battlefield at Ticonderoga. Stobo was imprisoned at Quebec, Lismahago at Montreal. Stobo escaped by boat down the St. Lawrence to Louisburg, whence he came back to Quebec with Wolfe, and later accompanied Amherst in the Lake Champlain expedition; he then returned to Virginia, where he had settled, and rewards were there heaped upon him: in 1760 he went to England on furlough with full pay. In the same year he returned to America for further military service, but in 1768 came back with his regiment to England, where he met Smollett, and died in 1770, as senior captain of his regiment. Lismahago escaped overland, spent several years with the Miamis, who captured him, and after his return to civilization sold out upon half-pay. Certainly the similarities are slight.

If Stobo did provide some general suggestions for Lismahago's background, these have been developed under other forces. His mental qualities, as I have said, appear to have been determined primarily by Smollett's purposes in regard to England and Scotland; as for the details of his adventures, they appear to have been derived largely from a "History of Canada" which appeared serially in the *British Magazine,* January, 1760–March, 1763. The greatest influence of this history is found in the following account of the tortures inflicted upon Lismahago and his companion in escape, Ensign Murphy:

43. *Works,* IV, 15, 16, 19, 33. 44. *Letters,* p. 103.
45. Kahrl, *op. cit.,* p. 266. 46. See Kahrl, *op. cit.,* pp. 143–4, 147.

The intention of these Indians was to give one of them as an adopted son to a venerable sachem, who had lost his own in the course of the war, and to sacrifice the other according to the custom of the country. Murphy, as being the younger and handsomer of the two, was designed to fill the place of the deceased, not only as the son of the sachem, but as the spouse of a beautiful squaw, to whom his predecessor had been betrothed; but in passing through the different whigwhams or villages of the Miamis, poor Murphy was so mangled by the women and children, who have the privilege of torturing all prisoners in their passage, that, by the time they arrived at the place of the sachem's residence, he was rendered altogether unfit for the purposes of marriage: it was determined therefore, in the assembly of the warriors, that ensign Murphy should be brought to the stake, and that the lady should be given to lieutenant Lismahago, who had likewise received his share of torments, though they had not produced emasculation.—A joint of one finger had been cut, or rather sawed off with a rusty knife; one of his great toes was crushed into a mash betwixt two stones; . . . .

The Indians themselves allowed that Murphy died with great heroism, singing, as his death song, the *Drimmendoo,* in concert with Mr. Lismahago, who was present at the solemnity. After the warriors and the matrons had made a hearty meal upon the muscular flesh which they pared from the victim, and had applied a great variety of tortures, which he bore without flinching, an old lady, with a sharp knife, scooped out one of his eyes, and put a burning coal in the socket. The pain of this operation was so exquisite that he could not help bellowing, upon which the audience raised a shout of exultation, and one of the warriors stealing behind him, gave him the *coup de grace* with a hatchet.[47]

The intended replacement of a relative by a captive, the tortures sustained, and Lismahago's bride, the gifted Squinkinacoosta, all find their counterparts in this story of an Indian taken captive by the Hurons:

. . . in one of the skirmishes that ensued, an Iroquois of some distinction was taken prisoner; and, by the council of the elders, destined to replace the nephew of a Huron chief, who had been slain in the engagement. . . . But before it was determined that his life should be saved, he had been tortured, according to custom. One hand had been crushed between two stones, and one finger torn off: they had likewise chopped off two fingers of the other hand; . . . . This cruel treatment he had received in the march; for, as soon as he entered the first village of the Hurons, he was treated with great ceremony and magnificence, . . . and even complimented with a young woman to live with him as his wife.

47. *Works,* IV, 23–5.

The Indian, however, like Murphy, has been so mutilated that he is not acceptable as a substitute, and is instead condemned to death:

. . . they began to exercise the most excruciating tortures on this poor wretch, who bore them without flinching, ... He calmly exhorted them to persevere; sung his death song; . . . . they at last put a period to his sufferings, by striking his head off with a hatchet.[48]

All these details, apparently adapted from memory, are fused with other materials from widely scattered portions of the same history. The tortures endured by captives en route from village to village are mentioned in several passages of the history;[49] while the details of Murphy's death are expanded by the addition of materials found in the following passage, from which Smollett has transferred the italicized part almost verbatim:

The fathers Brebeuf and Lallemant, being here taken in the exercise of their offices, were put to death with torments, the description of which is horrible to human nature. The former, possessed of great fortitude, and transported with joy at the prospect of martyrdom, continued to preach with a loud and resolute voice, while they tortured him on a scaffold, with the most excruciating torments . . . . then they *pulled out one of his* [Lallemant's] *eyes, and thrust a burning coal into the socket.* Their exultation over this miserable sacrifice was altogether extraordinary, because he severely felt the tortures they inflicted, and from time to time uttered such dismal shrieks, as would have filled any other of the human species, but those Indians, with horror and remorse.[50]

This passage also bears strong resemblance to the account of the death of the two French missionaries who, during Lismahago's stay among the Miamis, were "condemned to the stake, where they died singing *Salve regina,* in a rapture of joy, for the crown of martyrdom which they had thus obtained."[51] The compiler of the "History of Canada" in the *British Magazine* also treats contemptuously the Catholic missionaries: they are generally presented as fanatics and bigots who worked "with all the fury of enthusiasm,"

48. *British Magazine,* I, 352–3.
49. See for example *idem,* p. 538: "At length they arrived at one of the villages of the Iroquois, where they were set upon by the women and children, who mangled them in such a manner, that there was not a spot on their bodies free of scar or wound, ..." Also *idem,* II, 184: "Next day the two prisoners being stripped naked, were led from village to village, and buffeted by the women and children."
50. *Idem,* p. 154.
51. *Works,* IV, 30; see pp. 29–30 for the whole incident.

and who "thirsted after the crown of martyrdom,"[52] just as did the missionaries in *Humphry Clinker.*

Moreover, both the history and the novel use the same general method of irony to satirize the pretensions of these missionaries. In *Humphry Clinker* Smollett says:

. . . when they talked of mysteries and revelations, which they could neither explain nor authenticate, and called in the evidence of miracles which they believed upon hearsay; . . . the Indians were shocked at the impiety of their presumption.—They were examined by the assembly of the sachems, who desired them to prove the divinity of their mission by some miracle.—They answered, that it was not in their power.—"If you were really sent by Heaven for our conversion, (said one of the sachems) you would certainly have some supernatural endowments, at least you would have the gift of tongues, in order to explain your doctrine to the different nations among which you are employed; but you are so ignorant of our language, that you cannot express yourselves even on the most trifling subjects."[53]

Accordingly, the Indians in the novel "were convinced of their being cheats, and even suspected them of being spies."[54] Similarly, the *British Magazine* declares that the Indians held "an established opinion, that those missionaries acted as spies, under the cloak of propagating the Gospel";[55] and shortly afterward adds the following ironical comments:

. . . the Indians could not help being astonished, when they saw that heaven did not protect the lives of its own immediate servants [converted Indians], in the very article of preaching the gospel; [they asked] why an All-wise, and All-powerful Being, who created man, and influenced every emotion of the human heart, had not revealed himself in such a manner to the poor savages, as would have effectually secured their eternal salvation; . . . . Such was the reasoning of ignorant savages, unacquainted with the philosophy of the Christian religion.[56]

There can be little doubt, then, that these two portions of Lismahago's narrative are inspired by this "History of Canada" in the *British Magazine.* Indeed, some of the correspondences are so close that it seems impossible Smollett could have remembered everything simply from a casual reading; yet, from the way in

52. *British Magazine,* I, 351; see also *idem,* pp. [315–17] (misprinted 131–3), esp. [316]: "Every fanatic brother thought himself happy in being sent upon the Indian mission, and in treading the dangerous path that leads to the crown of martyrdom."
53. *Works,* IV, 29–30.
54. *Idem,* p. 30.
55. *British Magazine,* II, 83; see also *idem,* I, 414.
56. *Idem,* II, 153.

which details are fused and transformed, it seems improbable that Smollett looked up these materials for the specific purpose of composing these parts of *Humphry Clinker*. One is tempted to assign either the compilation or the editorship of this history to Smollett himself. The style is similar to that of the *Compendium* and the *Complete History of England;* it appeared at the time (1760–63) when we know Smollett was working on the magazine as editor and contributor; the history breaks off, unfinished, in March, 1763, with the words, "To be continued": about this time Smollett's health became so bad that he was forced to give up all such work, and shortly after (June, 1763), he left for the Continent. At least one may attribute his careful reading of the history to his personal interest in the magazine.

Thus, in a variety of ways, the character, opinions, and adventures of Lismahago find their origins in the hack work which Smollett had been performing during his long "fallow period." The *British Magazine,* the *Briton,* and *The Present State of All Nations* combined to produce essential parts of his narrative and polemics; the national partiality intensified in Smollett by his struggles with the *Briton* undoubtedly helped to motivate the creation of this Scot whose every paradox "savoured strong of a partiality for his own country";[57] the practice of writing general introductions for accounts in *Present State* may have helped to determine the form and position of Lismahago's polemics; and the descriptions of Scotland and England in *Present State,* helping to induce the dual tone of the novel, naturally played a part in the evolution of a character who accentuates this dual tone.

Smollett, of course, had other motives which were important in creating the total effect of Lismahago: the desire to provide a suitable "original" as mate for Tabby, the love of the ludicrous incidents in which such a grotesque figure could participate; but these motives, I believe, were secondary: instruction, not amusement, was for Smollett the primary function of Lismahago in the novel.

57. *Works,* iv, 38.

VIII

The Style of Smollett's Later Works

OF SMOLLETT'S later creative period Thomas Seccombe has shrewdly remarked:

In the 'Travels' and 'Humphrey Clinker,' which bear a close relationship in point of style the one to the other, whilst retaining all his old causticity of phrase, Smollett shows increased judgment and concentrative power together with the perfection of clear and idiomatic expression.[1]

This, I think, exactly describes the difference one finds when comparing Smollett's treatment of similar materials in his earlier and later works. Let me illustrate with two long but significant quotations, the first from *Peregrine Pickle*, the second from the *Travels*:

It being low water when they arrived on the French coast, the vessel could not enter the harbour, and they were obliged to bring to, and wait for a boat, which in less than half an hour came along-side from the shore. Mr. Jolter now came upon deck, and snuffing up the French air with symptoms of infinite satisfaction, asked of the boatmen, with the friendly appellation of *Mes enfans,* what they must have for transporting them and their baggage to the pier. But how was he disconcerted, when those polite, candid, reasonable watermen, demanded a Louis d'or for that service! Peregrine, with a sarcastic sneer, observed, that he already began to perceive the justice of his encomiums on the French; and the disappointed governor could say nothing in his own vindication, but that they were debauched by their intercourse with the inhabitants of Dover. His pupil, however, was so much offended at their extortion, that he absolutely refused to employ them, even when they abated one half in their demand, and swore he would stay on board till the packet should be able to enter the harbour, rather than encourage such imposition. . . .

The skipper, very much mortified at this peremptory reply, which was not over and above agreeable to Mr. Jolter, dismissed the boat, notwithstanding the solicitations and condescension of the watermen, who promised to submit to the generosity of their employer; and running a little farther in-shore, came to an anchor, and waited till there was water enough to float them over the bar. Then they stood in to the harbour, and our gentleman, with his attendants and baggage, were landed on the pier by the sailors, whom he liberally rewarded for their trouble.

1. *Cornhill Magazine,* n.s., XI (1901), 210.

He was immediately plied by a great number of porters, who, like so many hungry wolves, laid hold on his luggage, and began to carry it off piece-meal, without his order or direction. Incensed at this officious insolence, he commanded them to desist, with many oaths and opprobrious terms that his anger suggested; and perceiving that one of them did not seem to pay any regard to what he said, but marched off with his burthen, he snatched a cudgel out of his lacquey's hand, and overtaking the fellow in a twinkling, brought him to the ground with one blow. He was instantly surrounded by the whole congregation of this *canaille*, who resented the injury which their brother had sustained, and would have taken immediate satisfaction of the aggressor, had not Pipes, seeing his master involved, brought the whole crew to his assistance, and exerted himself so manfully, that the enemy were obliged to retreat with many marks of defeat, and menaces of interesting the commandant in their quarrel.[2]

About five years ago, in my passage from Flushing to Dover, the master of the packet-boat brought to all of a sudden off the South Foreland, although the wind was as favourable as it could blow. He was immediately boarded by a custom-house boat, the officer of which appeared to be his friend. He then gave the passengers to understand, that as it was low water, the ship could not go into the harbour; but that the boat would carry them ashore with their baggage.

The custom-house officer demanded a guinea for this service, and the bargain was made. Before we quitted the ship, we were obliged to gratify the cabin-boy for his attendance, and to give drink-money to the sailors. The boat was run aground on the open beach; but we could not get ashore without the assistance of three or four fellows, who insisted upon being paid for their trouble. Every parcel and bundle, as it was landed, was snatched up by a separate porter; one ran away with a hat-box, another with a wig-box, a third with a couple of shirts tied up in a handkerchief, and two were employed in carrying a small portmanteau that did not weigh forty pounds. All our things were hurried to the custom house to be searched, and the searcher was paid for disordering our cloaths: from thence they were removed to the inn, where the porters demanded half a crown each for their labour. It was in vain to expostulate; they surrounded the house like a pack of hungry hounds, and raised such a clamour, that we were fain to comply.[3]

It is evident that any difference in style between these two passages is not absolute: the passage from the novel, particularly the first two paragraphs, is generally precise and clear, and several sen-

2. *Peregrine Pickle* (first ed., 1751), II, 6–8. (*Works*, V, 224–6, of course, gives the passage as revised for the second ed., 1758. The changes are slight, except for some significant simplification in the first sentence of the second paragraph above.)
3. *Works*, XI, 5.

tences are quite as simple and direct as any in the other quotation. But the closing sentences from the novel are involved and turgid: they are inflated with neo-classical diction and complicated by dependent clauses; the same qualities are found in lesser degree in some of the earlier sentences. In the second passage all this pomp and complexity disappears, as if a film had been removed: the expression becomes consistently simple, idiomatic, and direct.

What is the cause of this change? Apparently it is in part due to a difference in Smollett's attitude toward fact and fiction. In the passage from the *Travels* he is interested only in setting down the truth in the fewest possible words: in the fictional form he feels called upon to expand; and it is noteworthy that the passage in the novel becomes most elaborate as Smollett turns to the fight at the end which is evidently not, like the earlier part, based on the facts of travel.[4] Throughout Smollett's earlier novels his style is frequently thus expansive; he makes little effort to maintain economy and concentration, and frequently prefers to write loosely constructed and deliberately digressive sentences. Such a style is often extremely effective: ironical overtones are achieved by inclusion of ridiculously digressive materials, or by use of a purposely inflated style which forms a ludicrous contrast with the triviality of the matter.

A digressive passage, typical of this earlier style, is found in Roderick Random's account of the divided leadership to which Smollett attributes the failure of the expedition against Carthagena:

. . . I may venture to affirm, that by this time, the Daemon of discord with her sooty wings, had breathed her influence upon our counsels; and it might be said of these great men, (I hope they will pardon the comparison) as of Caesar and Pompey, the one could not brook a superior, and the other was impatient of an equal: So that between the pride of one, and insolence of another, the enterprize miscarried, according to the proverb, "Between two stools the backside falls to the ground."—Not that I would be thought to liken any publick concern to that opprobrious part of the human body, although I might with truth assert, if I durst use such a vulgar idiom, that the nation did hang an a—se at its disappointment on this occasion; neither would I presume to compare the capacity of our heroic leaders to any such wooden convenience as a joint-stool or a close-stool; but only signify by this simile, the mistake the people committed in trusting to the union of two instruments that were never joined.[5]

4. Smollett's experiences in his voyage to Boulogne, related in his *Travels* (*Works*, xi, 7–8), together with the above account of conditions at Dover, proves that this account of impositions is largely based on fact.
5. *Works*, i, 269.

Compare this with Smollett's later treatment of the same discord in the "Account of the Expedition against Carthagene" included in his *Compendium of Voyages:*

Instead of conferring personally, and co-operating with vigour and cordiality, they began to hold separate councils, draw up acrimonious remonstrances, and send irritating messages to each other; and while each of them piqued himself upon doing barely as much as would screen him from the censure of a court-martial, neither seemed displeased at the neglect of his colleague; but, on the contrary, both were in appearance glad of the miscarriage of the expedition, in hope of seeing one another stigmatized with infamy and disgrace. In a word, the admiral was a man of weak understanding, strong prejudices, boundless arrogance, and over-boiling passions; and the general, tho' he had some parts, was wholly defective in point of experience, confidence, and resolution.[6]

Clearly, in the passage from *Roderick Random*, Smollett is striving for ingenious irony; he is not attempting to give a precise historical account of these quarrels; accordingly, he allows his thoughts to ramble and expand in whatever direction will produce the most ludicrous effects. But in the *Compendium*, in accordance with his historical purpose, the style becomes precise and regular; each sentence is blocked out into tight phrases, producing three of those enumerative structures which I have already discussed in Part I, Chapter IV.

Thus a change in purpose naturally produces a change in style: and this change from diffuse wit to precise information was no mere transient, superficial shift in Smollett's career. During the years after 1753 he was constantly concerned with the compilation of history, as well as with other tasks of Grub Street which gave him practice in marshalling facts. In the course of these labors he inevitably developed a more concentrated, precise, straightforward style. As he composed his final novel this style remained with him, not only in the historical parts of *Humphry Clinker,* but in its narration of fictional incidents.

It is, I think, primarily this change which is rather indistinctly felt by George Saintsbury in these remarks upon *Humphry Clinker:*

. . . throughout the book one is constantly surprised by the evidence that Smollett, when he chose, was perfectly competent to attend to those minutiae of the craftsman which, in his earlier work, he has so constantly and, to some extent, so unfortunately neglected. Perhaps the letter-form helped him; it is at anyrate certain that such an episode

6. *Comp.,* v, 334.

as that in which Quin makes his appearance is presented with an infinitely better grace, as well as more naturally, than the numerous similar episodes in all the other books.[7]

True, but I do not think that this change should be attributed merely to "the letter-form": the epistolary novel, as Richardson has abundantly proved, can be turgid and expansively "elegant." Why did Smollett write his letters in this neater, suppler fashion? Primarily, I think, because of his long labors of historical compilation and other hack work.

The truth of this explanation, as well as the exact nature of the change which Saintsbury describes, may be seen in the following contrast between two narrations of a fight: one, in *Count Fathom;* and the second, in *Humphry Clinker*—the famous battle of females at the Bath tea-party, which occurs in the section on Quin specifically cited by Saintsbury:

The German enraged at this comparison, was quite abandoned by his patience and discretion: he called the knight an English clown, and swearing he was the most untoward beast of a whole nation of mules, snatched up one of the candlesticks which he launched at him with such force and violence, that it sung through the air, and winging its flight into the anti-chamber, encountered the skull of his own valet, who with immediate prostration received the message of his master.

The knight, that he might not be behind hand with the Westphalian, in point of courtesy, returned the compliment with the remaining chandelier, which also missed its mark, and smiting a large mirrour that was fixed behind them, emitted such a crash as one might expect to hear if a mine were sprung beneath a manufacture of glass. Both lights being thus extinguished, a furious combat ensued in the dark; the Italian scampered off with infinite agility, and as he went down stairs, desired that nobody would interpose, because it was an affair of honour, which could not be made up. The ladies consulted their safety in flight; count Fathom slily retired to one corner of the room, while the abbé having upon him the terrors of the commissaire, endeavoured to appease and part the combatants, and in the attempt, sustained a random blow upon his nose, which sent him howling into the other chamber, where finding his band besmeared with his own blood, he began to caper about the apartment, in a transport of rage and vexation.

Mean while, the old gentlewoman being alarmed with the noise of the battle, and apprehensive that it would end in murder, to the danger and discredit of herself and family, immediately mustered up her myrmidons, of whom she always retained a formidable band, and putting

7. Introduction to *Humphry Clinker,* in Smollett's *Works* (Navarre Society ed.), XI, xi.

herself at their head, lighted them to the scene of uproar: Ferdinand, who had hitherto observed a strict neutrality, no sooner perceived them approach, than he leaped in between the disputants, that he might be found acting in the character of a peace-maker; and indeed, by this time, victory had declared for the baronet, who had treated his antagonist with a cross-buttock, which laid him almost breathless on the floor.[8]

The tea-drinking passed as usual; and the company having risen from the tables, were sauntring in groupes, in expectation of the signal for attack, when the bell beginning to ring, they flew with eagerness to the desert, and the whole place was instantly in commotion. There was nothing but justling, scrambling, pulling, snatching, struggling, scolding, and screaming. The nosegays were torn from one another's hands and bosoms; the glasses and china went to wreck; the tables and floor were strewed with comfits. Some cried; some swore; and the tropes and figures of Billingsgate were used without reserve in all their native zest and flavour; nor were those flowers of rhetoric unattended with significant gesticulation. Some snapped their fingers; some forked them out; some clapped their hands, and some their back-sides; at length, they fairly proceeded to pulling caps, and every thing seemed to presage a general battle; when Holder ordered his horns to sound a charge, with a view to animate the combatants, and inflame the contest; but this manoeuvre produced an effect quite contrary to what he expected. It was a note of reproach that roused them to an immediate sense of their disgraceful situation. They were ashamed of their absurd deportment, and suddenly desisted. They gathered up their caps, ruffles, and handkerchiefs; and great part of them retired in silent mortification.[9]

The complexity of the sentences in *Count Fathom* here contrasts with the simplicity and directness of those in *Humphry Clinker,* particularly with the precision and economy achieved by enumerative parallelism. The earlier passage is leisurely, expansive, and discursive; but the later passage is swift, concentrated, and perfectly proportioned. The later passage has nothing of the epistolary in it: such carefully moulded composition could hardly be expected in a letter. In other parts of *Humphry Clinker* Smollett does sometimes attempt the informality of the familiar letter, and in these places, of course, the simplicity is due to the epistolary form: but such an explanation surely does not account for the generally precise and succinct style of the novel.

The influence of Smollett's labors in Grub Street is, I think, even more clearly shown in the contrast between the description of Mrs.

8. *Works,* VIII, 150–1.   9. *Idem,* III, 80–1.

Grizzle in *Peregrine Pickle* and the description of her counterpart in *Humphry Clinker*, Tabby Bramble:

In this resolution he was comforted and encouraged by his only sister Mrs. Grizzle, who had managed his family, since the death of his father, and was now in the thirtieth year of her maidenhood, with a fortune of five thousand pounds, and a large stock of oeconomy and devotion. These qualifications, one would think, might have been the means of abridging the term of her celibacy, as she never expressed any aversion for wedlock; but, it seems, she was too delicate in her choice, to find a mate to her inclination in the city: for I cannot suppose that she remained so long unsollicited; tho' the charms of her person were not altogether enchanting, nor her manner over and above agreeable. Exclusive of a very wan (not to call it a sallow) complexion, which perhaps was the effect of her virginity and mortification, she had a cast in her eyes that was not at all engaging, and such an extent of mouth, as no art or affectation could contract into any proportionable dimension: then her piety was rather peevish than resigned, and did not in the least diminish a certain stateliness in her demeanour and conversation, that delighted in communicating the importance and honour of her family, which, by the bye, was not to be traced two generations back, by all the power of heraldry or tradition.[10]

I have already told you, that Mrs. Tabitha Bramble is a maiden of forty-five. In her person, she is tall, raw-boned, aukwar[d], flat-chested, and stooping; her complexion is sallow and freckled; her eyes are not grey, but greenish, like those of a cat, and generally inflamed; her hair is of a sandy, or rather dusty hue; her forehead low; her nose long, sharp, and, towards the extremity, always red in cool weather; her lips skinny, her mouth extensive, her teeth straggling and loose, of various colours and conformation; and her long neck shrivelled into a thousand wrinkles— In her temper, she is proud, stiff, vain, imperious, prying, malicious, greedy, and uncharitable. In all likelihood, her natural austerity has been soured by disappointment in love; for her long celibacy is by no means owing to her dislike of matrimony: on the contrary, she has left no stone unturned to avoid the reproachful epithet of old maid.[11]

Here, as in the passages on Carthagena, we find a change toward particularity and directness, accompanied by increased precision, order, and concentration of style, and by an increase in enumerations. One can, of course, find in the earlier novels descriptive passages which are much closer in style to this account of Tabby than is this account of Mrs. Grizzle. But in thus comparing these two passages, one does not, I think, misrepresent the general differ-

10. *Works*, v, 3. 11. *Idem*, iii, 94.

ences in style found in Smollett's final novel. Naturally, the style of *Humphry Clinker* is not completely different from that of the earlier novels: Smollett's innate tendency toward precision and succinctness sometimes produces passages in the earlier works which can hardly be differentiated from the passages which I have chosen as representing the distinctive qualities of Smollett's later style. Similarly, in *Humphry Clinker,* Smollett frequently employs the ironical periphrasis used so often in the earlier novels. This change in style, like the change in subject-matter, is not sudden and complete, but gradual and partial.

One can already begin to feel the trend of the later style in *Sir Launcelot Greaves,* which is remarkably simpler in its presentation of incidents. The *Travels,* dealing so largely with historical facts, displays this simple, concise style in its barest form. The style of the *Adventures of an Atom* is inevitably less simple than that of the two preceding works, since it is so often deliberately inflated for satirical purposes; but even here the effect of Smollett's previous hack work is found, I believe, in the streams of enumerations which dominate the style of the work.

Indeed, the direction of the change in Smollett's style is fairly illustrated by the remarkable increase in enumerations shown in the above quotations from later works. *Sir Launcelot Greaves,* in proportion to its size, shows an increase of about eighty-five per cent in number of enumerations, when compared with *Peregrine Pickle* and *Count Fathom. Humphry Clinker,* proportionately, shows an increase over *Greaves* of about twelve per cent in number of enumerations, or almost double the number found in the two earlier novels. Moreover, in *Pickle, Fathom,* and *Greaves,* less than a third of these enumerations extend to more than three elements; whereas in *Clinker* nearly two-fifths consist of four or more elements. In the *Travels* and the *Atom,* which are so largely concerned with historical matter, the number of enumerations is much greater than in any of the novels; in the *Atom* these structures really become a vice. As I have said in Part I, Chapter IV, these enumerations are the result of a desire to set down details with a maximum of economy, order, precision, and emphasis. In themselves frequent enumerations exert a great effect upon the style of a work; but they form only one specific indication of the stylistic traits which distinguish Smollett's later career.

Part of this increase in enumerations naturally is due to the change in subject-matter frequently mentioned throughout this study. In static description and exposition of historical facts the tendency to make lists is inevitably greater than in narrative; but this increase does not depend entirely upon the subject-matter. As the above quotations show, enumerations also permeate narrative portions of the later works; indeed, one may say that the style developed in treating static facts has been transferred to narration.

Specific correlation between the style of *Humphry Clinker* and Smollett's works of compilation is found by reading in Smollett's *Present State*, which was apparently completed very shortly before he began work on his last novel; perhaps parts of the two works may even have been composed at the same time. Even in passages dealing with diverse materials, one can feel the same methodical style emerging:

[*Present State:*] The country [Ayrshire] is generally level, pleasant, and fertile, well watered with streams and rivers, plentifully supplied with fish; yielding abundance of freestone, limestone, coal, and peat for fuel; producing large harvests of corn, a great number of sheep, horses, and black cattle; shaded and adorned with woods and plantations, belonging to the seats of noblemen and gentlemen, of which there is a great number in this county. The people are rigid presbyterians, numerous, industrious, and wealthy, exercising themselves in the various employments of farming, fishing, wool-combing, and the linen manufacture.[12]

[*Humphry Clinker:*] He [Dennison] is blessed with a consort, whose disposition is suited to his own in all respects; tender, generous, and benevolent— She, moreover, possesses an uncommon share of understanding, fortitude, and discretion, and is admirably qualified to be his companion, confidant, counsellor, and coadjutrix. . . .
These objections did not deter Mr. Dennison, because they were chiefly founded on the supposition, that he would be obliged to lead a life of extravagance and dissipation, which he and his consort equally detested, despised, and determined to avoid— The objects he had in view, were health of body, peace of mind, and the private satisfaction of domestic quiet, unallayed by actual want, and uninterrupted by the fears of indigence— He was very moderate in his estimate of the necessaries, and even of the comforts of life— He required nothing but wholesome air, pure water, agreeable exercise, plain diet, convenient lodging, and decent apparel.[13]

But it is not necessary to depend upon such general similarities to *Present State:* the parallel passages in the preceding chapters fully show how the style of *Present State* permeates the description of Scotland in *Humphry Clinker*. Indeed, in some cases, the novel is even more regular than the compilation:

12. *Pres. St.,* II, 134.   13. *Works,* IV, 243–5.

[*Present State:*] The commonalty of Scotland are mostly raw-boned, hard-featured, lean, lank, and muscular. In size they are rather smaller than their neighbours of South-Britain: . . . . They are clothed after the English fashion, with this difference, that the peasants, instead of hats, wear flat blue caps, which they call bonnets; besides, their apparel is neither so good nor so clean as that worn by the people of the same rank on the south side of the Tweed.[14]

[*Humphry Clinker:*] If I had never been in Wales, I should have been more struck with the manifest difference in appearance betwixt the peasants and commonalty on different sides of the Tweed. The boors of Northumberland are lusty fellows, fresh complexioned, cleanly, and well cloathed; but the labourers in Scotland are generally lank, lean, hard-featured, sallow, soiled, and shabby, and their little pinched blue caps have a beggarly effect.[15]

The antithesis, imperfectly expressed in *Present State*, is regularized in the novel: first, the contrast is set in a topic sentence; then it is emphasized by adding a descriptive enumeration for the English to parallel that already given for the Scots; lastly, the regularity achieved by the original enumeration in *Present State* is increased by addition of another element, and by use of three more alliterative words.

The same style extends to parts of the novel which represent development of short passages in *Present State:*

[*Present State:*] The surprizing attachment of the clans to their respective chieftains was not only founded upon the nature of their tenures, . . . but likewise flowed from inclination, inculcated from father to son, and cherished from their tender years by exhortation and example.[16]

[*Humphry Clinker:*] The connection between the clans and their chiefs is, without all doubt, *patriarchal*. It is founded on hereditary regard and affection, cherished through a long succession of ages. The clan consider the chief as their father, they bear his name, they believe themselves descended from his family, and they obey him as their lord, with all the ardour of filial love and veneration; while he, on his part, exerts a paternal authority, commanding, chastising, rewarding, protecting, and maintaining them as his own children.[17]

In passages such as this in the novel, Smollett appears simply to be writing a revision or continuation of the description of Scotland in *Present State*, couched in the same concise and regular expression.

14. *Pres. St.*, II, 11.   15. *Works*, IV, 60.
16. *Pres. St.*, I, 436.   17. *Works*, IV, 129–30.

This style, of course, pervades the description of England in *Humphry Clinker*. Note, for example, the impressionable Lydia's accounts of Ranelagh and Vauxhall:

Ranelagh looks like the inchanted palace of a genie, adorned with the most exquisite performances of painting, carving, and gilding, enlightened with a thousand golden lamps, that emulate the noon-day sun; crowded with the great, the rich, the gay, the happy, and the fair; glittering with cloth of gold and silver, lace, embroidery, and precious stones.[18]

. . . I was dazzled and confounded with the variety of beauties that rushed all at once upon my eye. Image to yourself, my dear Letty, a spacious garden, part laid out in delightful walks, bounded with high hedges and trees, and paved with gravel; part exhibiting a wonderful assemblage of the most picturesque and striking objects, pavilions, lodges, groves, grottoes, lawns, temples, and cascades; porticoes, colonades, and rotundos; adorned with pillars, statues, and painting: the whole illuminated with an infinite number of lamps, disposed in different figures of suns, stars, and constellations; . . . .[19]

The lists here used to convey a sense of girlish wonder and enthusiasm are not a bit longer than many enumerations which Smollett evolved in *Present State* to describe the various beauties of a landscape.[20]

Similarly, in places where Smollett retracts the compliments which he has made to England in *Present State*, his denials are couched in precise, regular prose. In two of the best letters in the entire novel—Matthew Bramble's vitriolic letters on life in London[21]—the energy and humor of the descriptions depends in large part on their regularity, as particularly manifested in a great number of enumerations:

The different departments of life are jumbled together— The hod-carrier, the low mechanic, the tapster, the publican, the shop-keeper, the pettifogger, the citizen, and courtier, *all tread upon the kibes of one another:* actuated by the demons of profligacy and licentiousness, they are seen every where, rambling, riding, rolling, rushing, justling,

18. *Works*, III, 147–8; this bears some similarity to the account of Ranelagh in *Pres. St.*, III, 216.

19. *Works*, III, 149; this bears some similarity to the account of Vauxhall in *Pres. St.*, III, 230.

20. "[Perthshire] extends above seventy miles in length, and near sixty at its greatest breadth, exhibiting a variety of Highlands and Lowlands; mountains, hills, dales, and straths, diversified with pasture-grounds, corn-fields and meadows, rivers, lakes, forests, woods, plantations, inclosures, towns, villages, and a great number of elegant seats, beautifully situated, belonging to noblemen and gentlemen." (*Pres. St.*, II, 51.)

21. *Works*, III, 138–45, 190–200.

mixing, bouncing, cracking, and crashing in one vile ferment of stupidity and corruption— [22]

Another such list, with more variety, occurs in the letter which Bramble significantly calls his "catalogue of London dainties";[23] for, the whole letter is a description in the catalogue-style of *Present State*, enlivened by satire, but composed fundamentally of the same methodical expression. This example catalogues the ingredients of London milk:

. . . but the milk itself should not pass unanalysed, the produce of faded cabbage-leaves and sour draff, lowered with hot water, frothed with bruised snails, carried through the streets in open pails, exposed to foul rinsings, discharged from doors and windows, spittle, snot, and tobacco-quids from foot-passengers, over-flowings from mud-carts, spatterings from coach-wheels, dirt and trash chucked into it by roguish boys for the joke's-sake, the spewings of infants, who have slabbered in the tin-measure, ...[24]

In many other cases the enumerations consist of more than such voluble accumulations: in the account of Bath, for example, we find complex parallelism which Johnson himself could not surpass:

Instead of that peace, tranquility and ease, so necessary to those who labour under bad health, weak nerves, and irregular spirits; here we have nothing but noise, tumult, and hurry; with the fatigue and slavery of maintaining a ceremonial, more stiff, formal, and oppressive, than the etiquette of a German elector.[25]

Even the ejaculations of Sir Thomas Bullford over his practical joke on Lismahago consist of little more than an amazing series of enumerations:

"Matt, (cried he) crown me with oak, or ivy, or laurel, or parsley, or what you will, and acknowledge this to be a *coup de maitre* in the way of waggery—ha, ha, ha!—Such a *camisicata, scagliata, beffata!—O, che roba!*—O, what a subject!—O, what *caricatura!*—O, for a Rosa, a Rembrandt, a Schalken!—Zooks, I'll give a hundred guineas to have it painted!—what a fine descent from the cross, or ascent to the gallows! —what lights and shadows!—what a groupe below!—what expression above!—what an aspect!—did you mind the aspect?—ha, ha, ha!— and the limbs, and the muscles—every toe denoted terror!—ha, ha, ha!—then the blanket!—O, what *costume!* St. Andrew! St. Lazarus! St. Barrabas!—ha, ha, ha!" . . . "Ay, and such a joke! (cried our landlord) such a farce! such a *denouement!* such a *catastrophe!*"[26]

22. *Works*, III, 141.   23. *Idem*, p. 198.   24. *Idem*, pp. 197–8.
25. *Idem*, p. 49.   26. *Idem*, IV, 208–9.

These examples should be sufficient to indicate the succinctness, precision, and ease which Smollett achieves throughout *Humphry Clinker* by increased frequency and length of enumerations. And this increase in enumerations, one must remember, forms only the most striking manifestation of a change in style which pervades nearly every paragraph of the novel.

The superiority generally found in *Humphry Clinker,* over the novels of Smollett's earlier period, must therefore, I think, be attributed in large part to a style so neat that the reader is carried along swiftly and easily, with none of the retardation which results from the frequently diffuse and turgid style of the earlier novels. Certainly Smollett's mood has also changed: he is mellower, more genial; and this change, too, is in part responsible for the superior enjoyment which so many readers have found in Smollett's last novel. But I suspect that much of this comment on Smollett's "change of mood" is in reality based on his change of style. Saintsbury, for instance, suggests that "the ease, the geniality, the unforced and varied merriment" of *Humphry Clinker* are the result of "a sojourn in the Land of Beulah before he crossed the river."[27] Now one cannot deny that the imminence of death and the nostalgia of exile mollified Smollett's harshness; and an author's mood and style cannot, of course, be actually separated: a gentler mood may produce a simpler style. On the other hand, a neater style may give a total effect of ease and naturalness, without any real change in the author's outlook. Moreover, a relaxation of Smollett's astringent temper could hardly be expected to result in preciseness and economy of style: rather, one might expect to find increased looseness and rambling. However much one may attribute to mood, there can be no doubt that the style of *Humphry Clinker* is primarily a method of expression gradually developed throughout seventeen years of grinding labor toward the advancement of knowledge.

Thus, ironically, these labors of Grub Street, disastrous to Smollett's body and frequently repugnant to his literary ideals, were in large part responsible for both the subject-matter and the style of the final novel which has won for him his highest reputation as a literary artist.

27. Introduction to *Humphry Clinker,* in Smollett's *Works* (Navarre Society ed.), XI, ix.

APPENDIX I

A Compendium of Voyages

Contents and Sources

(For references to Barclay, Campbell, Churchill, and Purchas, see "Bibliographical Note," p. xi)

1. "The First Voyage of Columbus." (I, [1]–39.)
   "The Second Voyage of Columbus." (I, [40]–69.)
   "The Third Voyage of Columbus." (I, [70]–90.)
   "The Fourth Voyage of Columbus." (I, [91]–129.)
   Source:
   a. *The History of the Life and Actions of Adm. Christopher Columbus,* . . . . *Written by his own Son D. Ferdinand Columbus,* Churchill, II, [479]–604.
2. "The Voyage of Vasco de Gama." (I, [130]–57.)
   Principal source:
   a. *The History of the Portuguese, During the Reign of Emmanuel:* . . . . *Written originally in Latin By Jerome Osorio, Bishop of Sylves. Now first translated into English By James Gibbs* (2 vols., London, 1752), I, 35–6, 46–83.
   Supplementary source: Churchill, I, xxi.
3. "The Voyage of Pedro Alvarez de Cabral." (I, [158]–77.)
   Source: same as item 2, a. (See Osorio, I, 84–5, 96–121.)
4. "The Conquest of Mexico, by Hernando Cortes." (I, [179]–286; II, [1]–181.)
   Source:
   a. *The History of the Conquest of Mexico by the Spaniards. . . . Translated into English from the Original Spanish of Don Antonio de Solis, . . . By Thomas Townsend, Esq; . . . . The whole Translation Revised and Corrected By Nathanael Hooke, Esq.,* 2 vols., London, 1738.[1]
5. "The Discovery and Conquest of Peru, by Francis Pizarro." (II, [183]–261.)
   Sources:
   a. "The Conquest of Peru," Barclay, pp. 105–48.
   b. "The History of the Discovery and Conquest of the Empire of Peru by Francis Pizarro, together with the Discovery of Chili, and the Conquest of that Country also," Campbell, II, 143–62.
6. "The Voyages of the several first Adventurers, particularly of

[1]. This is the edition which I have used; Smollett may have used the reprint issued in 1753.

Ferdinand de Soto, for the Discovery of Florida, 1539." (II, [263]–88; III, [1]–36.)
Principal sources:
   a. "The Discovery of Florida," Barclay, pp. 162–79.
   b. "A Relation of Alvaro Nunez," Purchas, XVII, 437–521.
   c. "Ferdinando de Soto his Voyage to Florida and Discoverie of the Regions in that Continent," Purchas, XVII, 525–[550]; XVIII, 1–51. Also the Preface "To the Reader," *idem,* XVII, 521–5.
Supplementary source: Campbell, II, 56–9.
7. "The Voyage of Fernandes Magalianes, commonly called Magellan." (III, [37]–63.)
Source:
   a. "Of Fernandus Magalianes," Purchas, II, 84–119.
8. "The First Voyage of Sir Francis Drake." (III, [65]–83.)
   "The Second Voyage of Sir Francis Drake." (III, [84]–119.)
Principal source:
   a. *The English Hero: or, Sir Francis Drake Reviv'd,* by Nathaniel Crouch, thirteenth ed., London, 1739.[2]
Supplementary sources:
   b. "The Voyage of Sir Francis Drake round the Globe," Campbell, I, 14–22.
   c. "The first Voyages made to divers parts of America by Englishmen," Purchas, XVI, 106–35. (See esp. pp. 108–9 and 113–33, the latter of which sections bears the subtitle: "A briefe Historie of Sir Francis Drakes Voyages.")
   d. "The second Circum-Navigation of the Earth: Or the renowned Voyage of Sir Francis Drake," Purchas, II, 119–49.
9. "The Life and Various Voyages of Sir Walter Raleigh, and of several Adventurers under his Direction." (III, [121]–80.)
Principal source:
   a. *The Life of Sir Walter Ralegh. By William Oldys, Gent.,* prefixed to vol. I of the eleventh edition of Raleigh's *History of the World,* 2 vols., London, 1736.[3]
Supplementary sources:
   b. *The Naval History of England,* . . . . *By Thomas Lediard, Gent.,* London, 1735. (See pp. 201–5, 215–16, 221–2, 225–7, 275–7, 293–5.)
   c. Campbell, II, 202–3, 213–16.
10. "The Voyage of Sir Thomas Rowe to India, sent by King James I. in Quality of Ambassador to the Great Mogul." (III, [181]–249.)
Principal source:
   a. *The Journal of Sir Thomas Roe,* Churchill, I, 617–58. Fol-

---

2. This is the edition which I have used; Smollett could have used the fourteenth edition, 1750, which I have not been able to examine; but I have seen a copy of the sixteenth edition, 1762; it is merely a reprint.

3. Smollett may have used the separate edition of this Life, London, 1740.

lowed by an appendix of letters and notes, pp. 658–67.

Supplementary sources:

b. Purchas, IV, 430–67; an appendix of letters and notes following "Observations collected out of the Journall of Sir Thomas Roe."

c. "A Letter of Mr. Thomas Coryat," Purchas, IV, 469–76. (See pp. 475–6.)

11. "The Voyage of Captain John Monk. To which are prefixed, Some curious Memoirs, relating to Old and New Greenland." (III, [251]–85.)

Source:

a. An Account Of a most Dangerous Voyage Performed by the Famous Captain John Monck, In the Years 1619 and 1620. . . . With a Description of the Old and New Greenland, ... Translated from the High-Dutch Original, Churchill, I, 419–44.

12. "A brief Narrative of the wonderful Preservation of Eight Men, who were left behind by their Ship's Company in the Year 1630, on the Coast of Greenland." (IV, [1]–13.)

Source:

a. God's Power and Providence, Shewed in the Miraculous Preservation and Deliverance of Eight English-Men, Left by Mischance in Greenland, Anno 1630. . . . Faithfully reported by Edward Pellham, one of the eight Men aforesaid, Churchill, IV, [743]–55.

13. "Journal kept by seven Sailors, who wintered in the Isle of St. Maurice in Greenland, where they died anno 1634." (IV, [14]–21.)

Source: see item 14, a.

14. "A short Journal kept by seven Sailors, who were left to winter at Spitzbergen, anno 1634, and died there in the Year 1635." (IV, [22]–5.)

Source:

a. Two Journals: The First Kept by seven Sailers in the Isle of St. Maurice in Greenland, In the years 1633, 1634; Who pass'd the Winter, and all died in the said Island. The Second Kept by seven other Sailers, who in the years 1633 and 1634, wintered at Spitzbergen; . . . Done out of Low-Dutch, Churchill, II, [347]–60. (First journal, pp. 349–58; second journal, pp. 359–60.)

15. "A short Account of a Shipwreck near Spitzbergen, in the Year 1646." (IV, [26]–7.)

Source:

a. "A True and Short Account of Forty Two-Persons [sic] Who perished by Shipwreck near Spitzbergen, In the year 1646," Churchill, II, 361–2.

16. "A Description of the Country and Inhabitants of Iceland." (IV, [28]–41.)
    Source:
    a. "An Account of Iseland, sent to Monsieur de la Mothe de Vayer," by Isaac de La Peyrère, Churchill, II, 363–75.

17. "The dangerous Voyage of Captain Thomas James, employed to discover the North-west Passage." (IV, [42]–78.)
    Source:
    a. *Captain Thomas James's Strange and Dangerous Voyage In his intended Discovery of the North-West Passage into the South Sea, In the years 1631 and 1632*, Churchill, II, [407]–53.

18. "The Voyages and Adventures of Mr. John Nieuhoff, in the East-Indies, and several Other Parts of the World." (IV, [79]–299.)
    Source:
    a. *Voyages and Travels into Brasil and the East-Indies. . . . By Mr. John Nieuhoff. . . . Translated from the Dutch Original*, Churchill, II, 1–305.

19. "Baldaeus's Account of the Coast of Malabar and Coromandel." (V, [1]–49.)
    Principal source:
    a. *A True and Exact Description of the Most Celebrated East-India Coasts of Malabar and Coromandel; As also of the Isle of Ceylon: . . . . By Philip Baldaeus, Minister of the Word of God in Ceylon. Translated from the High Dutch*, Churchill, III, [509]–732.
    Supplementary source: Campbell (see above, p. 38).

20. "A Description of the Island of Ceylon, with a short Review of the Disputes therein between the Portuguese and the Dutch. Extracted from the Account of Philip Baldaeus." (V, [50]–130.)
    Principal source: same as item 19, a.
    Supplementary source: Campbell (see above, p. 38).

21. "A Voyage to the North of Europe, containing an Account of the Sea-Coasts and Mines of Norway and the Laplands, Siberia, Borandia, Iceland, Zembla, and other Countries, interspersed with curious Remarks: to which are added, some authentic Memoirs, relating to the ancient Manners and Customs of the Russians. Extracted from the Observations of a Gentleman, employed by the North-Sea Company at Copenhagen, to make Discoveries." (V, [131]–243.)
    Principal source:
    a. "A Voyage to the North, ... Extracted from the Journal of a Gentleman employed by the North-Sea Company at Copenhagen; and from the Memoirs of a French Gentleman, who, after serving many Years in the Armies of Russia, was at last banished into Siberia," Campbell, II, [457]–92.

Supplementary source:

    b. *A New Geographical and Historical Grammar,* by Thomas Salmon (third ed., London, 1754), pp. 192, 194–5.[4]

22. "The Voyage of Mr. Lionel Wafer to the Isthmus of America." (v, [244]–312.)

    Source:

    a. *A New Voyage and Description of the Isthmus of America. . . . By Lionel Wafer,* third ed., London, 1729. In *A Collection of Voyages* (chiefly Dampier's), published by Knapton (4 vols., London, 1729), III, [261]–398.[5]

23. "An Account of the Expedition against Carthagene, in the West Indies, besieged by the English in the Year 1741." (v, [313]–42.)

    Principal source:

    a. *A Journal of the Expedition to Carthagena,* London, 1744.

    Supplementary sources:

    b. *Original Papers Relating to the Expedition to Carthagena,* London, 1744.[6]

    c. *The Adventures of Roderick Random* (London, 1748), Chapters XXVIII–XXXIV.

24. "A Voyage round the World by Captain William Dampier." (VI, [1]–122.)

    Principal source:

    a. *A New Voyage round the World. . . . By Capt. William Dampier,* seventh ed., London, 1729. Forms vol. 1 of Knapton's *Collection* (see item 22, a, above).

    Supplementary source: Campbell, I, 85.

25. "A Voyage round the World by Dr. John Francis Gemelli, undertaken in the Year 1693." (VI, [123]–339; VII, [1]–143.)

    Source:

    a. *A Voyage round the World, by Dr. John Francis Gemelli Careri. . . . Written Originally in Italian, Translated into English,* Churchill, IV, [1]–568.

26. "A Voyage round the World, begun in the Year 1708, by two Bristol Ships called the Duke and Duchess, Captain Woodes Rogers." (VII, [144]–278.)

    Principal source:

    a. *A Cruising Voyage round the World: . . . . By Captain Woodes Rogers,* second ed., London, 1726.[7]

4. I assume that Smollett used the latest edition.

5. This was probably the edition most easily available, although it is possible that Smollett used one of the separate editions. The same comment applies to the account of Dampier (item 24, a). Since both these were in the collected edition, it is improbable that Smollett sought out separate editions of each.

6. The same materials were also available in a pamphlet entitled *Authentic Papers Relating to the Expedition against Carthagena* (London, 1744); but since the above pamphlet is more comprehensive and apparently official, I assume that Smollett used this better source.

7. Smollett could have used the first edition (London, 1712), or another "second edition" (London, 1718).

Supplementary sources:
b. *An Account of A Voyage from Spain to Paraquaria; Perform'd by the Reverend Fathers Anthony Sepp and Anthony Behme, ... Translated from the High Dutch Original,* Churchill, v, 669–95.
c. Campbell, II, 209–12.

27. "An Account of the Voyage round the World, made in the Years 1740, 41, 42, 43, and 44, by George, now Lord Anson." (VII, [279]–366.)
Source:
a. *A Voyage round the World, In the Years MDCCXL, I, II, III, IV. by George Anson, Esq; . . . Compiled From Papers and other Materials of the Right Honourable George Lord Anson, and published under his Direction. By Richard Walter, M.A.,* London, 1748.[8]

Index to Appendix I

8. Smollett could have used any one of eight editions published by 1756.

APPENDIX II

The Sources of the Description of Scotland in The Present State of All Nations

Burt, Captain Edward, *Letters from a Gentleman in the North of Scotland to His Friend in London*, 2 vols., London, 1754. (In this study I refer to the reprint published in Edinburgh in 1876.)

Camden, William, *Britannia: or a Chorographical Description of Great Britain and Ireland, Together with the Adjacent Islands. Written in Latin By William Camden, . . . And Translated into English, with Additions and Improvements. The Second Edition. Revised, Digested, and Published, with large Additions, By Edmund Gibson*, 2 vols., London, 1722.[1]

A Complete System of Geography, 2 vols., London, 1744–47.

Defoe, Daniel (and Richardson, Samuel), *A Tour Thro' the Whole Island of Great Britain, Divided into Circuits or Journeys*, fifth ed., 4 vols., London, 1753.

Gordon, Alexander, *Itinerarium Septentrionale: or, A Journey Thro' most of the Counties of Scotland, And Those in the North of England*, London, 1726.

Martin, Martin, *A Late Voyage to St. Kilda, The Remotest of all the Hebrides, or Western Isles of Scotland. With A History of the Island, Natural, Moral, and Topographical*, London, 1698.[2] Also, *A Description of the Western Islands of Scotland*, London, 1703.[3]

Wallace, James, *An Account of the Islands of Orkney*, London, 1700.

1. Smollett could have used the third edition of 1753.
2. Smollett could have used the fourth edition of 1753.
3. Smollett could have used the second edition of 1716.

INDEX

SMOLLETT'S works have been listed separately, by title, except for works of translation or editing, which appear under the name of the original author, where possible. Sources of Smollett's works have been listed separately, by author, where possible, otherwise by name of the most important place or person concerned. Accounts in the Compendium of Voyages *(Comp.) have been listed separately, by name of traveller, where possible, otherwise by name of the most important place or person concerned. All fictitious characters are listed separately, by last name, where possible. Under the entries for Smollett's* Travels, *Adventures of an Atom,* and Humphry Clinker, *I have arranged special lists of topics which will enable the reader to find references to or discussions of particular passages in these works. The Preface and Appendices are not indexed here. For full references to contents and sources of the* Compendium, *see the special index to Appendix I, p. 200.*

ADDISON, JOSEPH, *Remarks on Italy,* 86; *Spectator,* 91

Adventures of an Atom, 15, 90–103, 130; date of publication of, 90 n. 1; editions of, 90; form of, summarized, 90; influence of Smollett's hack work on, summarized, 103; models for conception of atom in, 91–4; organization of, similar to *Univ. Hist.,* 96–7; parodies style of Oriental Tale, 101–2; product of new inspiration, 124; style of, 188

Oriental setting of: amount of detail, 102–3; based upon *Univ. Hist.,* 94–101; compared with other Oriental settings, 96; germinated in *Critical Review,* 94–6; integration of details with satire, 96–100; models for, 92–4; superficial use of details, 100–2; virtues of, summarized, 103

Oriental setting of, details discussed or referred to: Ami, 102; Bonzas, 99 n. 38; Bupo, 97–8, 100–1; Cambadoxi, 101 n. 44; Chew, 100–1; China, 96, 102; Copan, 101 n. 44; Corea, 96; Cuboy, 97–8, 102; Dairo, 97–9, 102; Day, 99 n. 38; Fakkubasi, 97–8; Fatsissio, 101 n. 44; Fatzman, 99; Fide-tada, 101 n. 44; Fo, 99 n. 38; Foggien, 97, 97 n. 27; Frenoxena, 99 n. 38; Fune, 99 n. 38; Gotto-Mio, 101 n. 44; Jacko, 100–1; Jodo, 102; Jodo-gava, 102; Kio, 98, 100–1; Koan,

101 n. 44; Kobot, 98, 100–1; Kowkin, 101 n. 44; Kugava, 102; Matsuri, 101 n. 44; Meaco, 99 n. 38, 102; Meckaddo, 100–1; Menoki, 100; Moxa, 100; Nem-buds-ju, 99 n. 38; Niphon, 96; Osaca, 102; Quambacundono, 101 n. 44; Quanbuku, 99 n. 38; Senkei, 100–1; Sey-seo-gun, 99 n. 38; Shi-wang-ti, 100–1; Soo-Son-Sinno, 101 n. 44; Syko, 99 n. 38; Tartary, 96; Taycho, 98–9, 102; Tensio-dai-sin, 100–1; Whey-vang, 100–1; Xicoco, 96; Ximo, 96; Yesso, 102

Alembert, Jean Le Rond D', *Encyclopédie,* 4–5

Almagro, Diego de, account of in *Comp.,* 50–1

Alvarado, Pedro de, account of in *Comp.,* 51

Amazon, river, account of in *Comp.,* 37, 45

Anderson, John, *History of Edinburgh,* 156 n. 31

Anderson, John P., *Bibliography of Smollett's works,* 104

Anderson, Dr. Robert, *Life of Smollett,* 104

Anne, Queen of England, satirized in *Atom,* 99 n. 38

Annual Register, 8 n. 40

Anson, George Anson, Lord, account of by Barrow, 19; account of in *Comp.,*